Intervention with children

Intervention with children

Edited by

Rajinder M. Gupta
Peter Coxhead

ROUTLEDGE
London and New York

First published 1990
by Routledge
11 New Fetter Lane, London EC4P 4EE

Simultaneously published in the USA and Canada
by Routledge
a division of Routledge, Chapman and Hall, Inc,
29 West 35th Street, New York, NY 10001

Typeset by Pat and Anne Murphy, Highcliffe-on-Sea, Dorset
Printed and bound in Great Britain by Mackays of Chatham PLC, Kent

British Library Cataloguing in Publication Data

Intervention with children.
1. Maladjusted children. Education
I. Gupta, Rajinder M. *1939–* II. Coxhead, Peter
371.94

Library of Congress Cataloging in Publication Data

Intervention with children / edited by Rajinder M. Gupta, Peter Coxhead.
p. cm.
1. Behavior disorders in children—Treatment. I. Gupta, Rajinder. M., 1939– . II. Coxhead, Peter.
[DNLM: 1. Child Behavior Disorders—therapy. 2. Education, Special. 3. Learning Disorders—therapy. LC 4801 I61]
RJ506.B44I57 1989
618.92′891—dc20
DNLM/DLC
for Library of Congress 89-10162
CIP

ISBN 0-415-00790-9 (hbk)
ISBN 0-415-00791-7 (pbk)

Contents

Contributors

Ms Carol Aubrey, Lecturer in Education, University College, Cardiff.

Dr Hazel B. Baker, Consultant Child Psychiatrist, Manor Hospital, Walsall.

Dr Nigel Blagg, Senior Educational Psychologist, ALPS Development Unit, Bridgewater.

Dr Peter Coxhead, Lecturer, University of Aston, Birmingham.

Dr. Gilbert R. Gredler, Professor of Psychology, University of South Carolina, Columbia, USA.

Dr Rajinder M. Gupta, Educational Psychologist, Psychological Service (North), Birmingham.

Dr I. A. Hyman, Director, Department of School Psychology, Temple University, Philadelphia, USA.

Dr David J. Leach, Senior Lecturer in Psychology, Murdoch University, Murdoch, Western Australia.

Dr T. R. Miles, Professor Emeritus of Psychology, University College of North Wales, Bangor.

Elaine Miles, Course Adviser on Teacher Training, Dyslexia Unit, University College of North Wales, Bangor.

Dr L. Mountain, Professor of Education, The University of Houston, Houston, USA.

Mr John Presland, Principal Educational Psychologist, Wiltshire County Council, Trowbridge, Wilts.

Dr Ken Reid, Reader and Head of In-Service Teacher Education, West Glamorgan Institute of Higher Education, Swansea.

Mr Philip White, Senior Educational Psychologist, Wiltshire County Council, Trowbridge, Wilts.

Introduction

Rajinder M. Gupta and Peter Coxhead

The major goal of this book is to bring together, in one source, information on some practical and effective strategies for interventions with children. Reports on studies of such strategies are often available only in learned journals, and thus are not readily accessible to many of those who most need their results, particularly the vital evidence of effectiveness. A secondary goal of the book is to act as a source of ideas and a model of good practice for those who may currently be developing their own intervention strategies, or may wish to do so in the future.

Some definitions are in order. 'Intervention strategies' are teaching and management approaches which are designed to bring about changes in children in circumstances where 'normal' classroom practices are failing. They may be intended to modify deviant behaviours, to ensure school attendance, or to improve the reading level of retarded readers; the needs to be met and the situations where intervention is useful are virtually endless. Intervention often (but not always) involves three parties: consultants, consultees, and subjects. By consultants or interveners, we mean such professionals as local education authority advisers, advisory teachers, social workers, researchers, psychiatrists, psychologists, and so on, who are often asked to intervene or offer advice in cases where normal practice has failed. The recipient of such advice is described here as a consultee or practitioner; a typical consultee might be a teacher, a nursery nurse, or a parent. The subjects of the intervention are the children whose behaviour or abilities it is desired to change. This book is primarily intended for consultants, whether practising or in training, although others will undoubtedly find much of value.

In all cases, intervention strategies are based on the assumption that they offer more effective alternatives for promoting normal growth, development, and competence (at least for some children), than the practices they replace. This assumption requires careful examination in each case, since little useful purpose would be served by replacing existing and familiar practices with new and unfamiliar ones which have failed to demonstrate their superiority. On the other hand, there is every justification for replacing or modifying a prevalent but less effective practice, if the result is a more successful outcome.

The consultant needs to have a much more critical and objective view of the strengths and weaknesses of current practices than the practitioner or consultee, so as to be able to decide which of the available intervention strategies is likely to succeed in a given situation. It is vital that the consultant avoids dogmatism. No particular strategy is going to be a panacea for all educational ills, and any strategy needs to be justified by evidence of its success. Unfortunately many consultants seem to find it difficult to avoid being 'blinkered' and favouring one approach over others without critically evaluating their respective merits. This point has been made very aptly by Gredler (see Chapter 9, p. 179).

> A recent review of American textbooks in special education observed that a number of authors will eloquently defend a particular remediation technique yet fail to offer [any] empirical evidence of its real superiority over other techniques. . . . The field of special education and school psychology is ill served by the presence of what can be described as the 'doctrinaires' — educators and psychologists who so emphasize one approach or remediation method that they neglect to discuss data which indicate that some children may fail to progress with the use of their preferred technique.
>
> Professional personnel frequently underestimate the degree to which the remediation field is subject to fads. An approach used by many educators for a number of years falls out of favour; an educator emphasizes the value of a different method, and if such a method receives monetary support from a private foundation, government support, or media emphasis, then these different methods come into favour and so the cycle of acceptance and rejection continues.

At the worst, professionals who become 'followers' of a particular strategy or style of working can become unjustifiably critical, intolerant, and even hostile towards anyone who does not share their belief system. Apart from the harm done to children, who may suffer inappropriate and ineffective interventions, such attitudes stifle innovation. Our strongly held belief is that although true professionalism does not preclude specialization, it requires the consultant to engage in an open-minded consideration of a range of possible approaches, and to make determined efforts to evaluate their effectiveness. In this volume, therefore, we have intentionally sought to show varied approaches to particular problems; for example, although we have strong sympathies for broadly behavioural approaches, we have not in any way excluded others. It is hoped that this approach will also have an appeal to a wide audience (depending on their training and background).

However effective an intervention strategy may have been shown to be in general, it cannot work in a particular situation unless it is implemented, and this requires both the consultant and the strategy to have credibility in the eyes of the consultee. The lack of credibility of the consultant can often be a serious problem. The old joke — 'Those who can, do; those who can't, teach; those who can't do either, teach teachers' — is well known, and most of us know from personal experience that it does reflect a certain feeling among those at the 'chalk-face' that lecturers, advisers, psychologists, and so on, are inexperienced and out of touch with the stark realities of the practitioner's life. Similarly the intervention strategy itself must have credibility. No matter how useful an approach may be, if it happens to lack face validity to consultees and practitioners, it is far less likely to be accepted and thus implemented. A good example is behaviour modification. Although its usefulness in various settings has, in our view, been well documented, there are question marks over its acceptance by many practitioners, and even where the technique is proving effectice, many teachers tend not to acknowledge its usefulness. As Rosenfield (1985: 153) puts it:

> Behavioural consultants encounter teachers who refuse to continue using behavioural techniques, saying that they were not really helping the child even though the child's behaviour had changed in the expected direction.

Where such credibility gaps exist, it is unlikely that a suggested new intervention approach will be accepted, no matter how effective it may be.

The need for intervention strategies is great, and the range available is large, but the space available in a book is restricted, so that considerable selection is inevitable in the choice of problem areas to be dealt with. We have chosen to focus mainly on interventions concerned with behavioural problems of varying degrees of severity; however, learning problems have not been totally neglected.

The first two chapters 'set the scene' to some extent. In Chapter 1 David Leach discusses an intervention strategy which involves both the school and the home, and which may well be equally effective in changing children's classroom behaviour and their academic performance. The author has tried these reinforcement programmes in Australia for the last six years or so and has found them practical, low cost, and effective. In Chapter 2 Rajinder Gupta and Peter Coxhead describe a modified behaviour modification strategy which, although developed independently, has strong similarities with Leach's approach.

In Chapter 3 Carol Aubrey explores the concept of the 'consultant' (as defined above) in managing interventions. Concentrating on teachers (as consultees) rather than on children may be a more efficient use of the consultant's time, since the consultee may gain insights and increased skills which can be generalized to other situations. Alternatively, teachers' knowledge and skills can be increased through training courses, such as that outlined and evaluated by John Presland and Philip White in Chapter 4.

Chapters 5 to 8 concentrate on one particular behavioural problem, namely non-attendance. Ken Reid, in Chapter 5, outlines some of the educational issues and suggests some practical approaches. In Chapter 6 Irwin Hyman tackles the problem of 'class-cutting'. He believes that many practitioners are reluctant to accept theory and instead recommends and expounds a 'bag of tricks' approach. Chapters 7 and 8 look at strategies for dealing with school phobia. Hazel Baker emphasizes the need for a 'wholistic' approach, aimed at removing the underlying neurotic condition as well as getting the child back at school. Nigel Blagg's intervention strategy is more strongly rooted in behavioural principles, reminding his readers of the value of employing a range of behaviourally based techniques, both from the classical and the operant conditioning paradigms.

The last three chapters provide a brief introduction to intervention in cases of learning difficulties. In Chapter 9 Gilbert Gredler reviews and evaluates a range of intervention strategies, from a research as well as a practical perspective. He makes specific recommendations for organizing and implementing remedial programmes. Elaine Miles and Timothy Miles in Chapter 10 argue that a small minority of poor readers and spellers — whether labelled dyslexics or not — have specific learning difficulties and thus require carefully structured interventions. As teaching such children is not easy, the choice of an intervention strategy cannot be left to the vagaries of current fashion, but must address the children's particular problems. Finally, Lee Mountain in Chapter 11 shows some of the detailed techniques which can be used to help remedial readers. It is fitting that the book should end with such direct, practical advice, since above all else, interventions should offer realistic and effective methods of improving children's lives.

Reference

Rosenfield, S. (1985) 'Teacher acceptance of behavioural principles: an issue of values', *TESE* 8, 3: 153–8.

Chapter one

Home-based reinforcement for changing children's school behaviour

David J. Leach

As a result of over twenty years of research, applied behavioural psychologists working in educational settings have a wide range of demonstrably effective procedures to call on in order to reduce disruptive classroom behaviour, increase appropriate behaviour, and accelerate learning. The availability of a pool of effective procedures, however, does not infer that any one procedure may be selected at random and applied with equal success to any other in the resolution of a referred problem. This is particularly true in open settings such as schools and homes where psychologists often work as consultants, advising others (especially teachers and parents) on the implementation of intervention programmes for child behaviour change. When others are to carry out the behavioural intervention, they must understand the recommended procedure and then carry it out to its conclusion before it can begin to be successful. A mis-applied or non-applied intervention plan, however carefully designed, is simply no intervention at all and is unlikely to be of value. Indeed, a programme that has failed to be implemented as intended could lead to negative effects, such as a reduction in the perceived utility of consultant advice or generally less satisfactory collaborative problem-solving efforts in the future. Consultee acceptance, co-operation, and persistence then are of paramount importance when choosing between alternative interventions which involve others as mediators or deliverers of the programme; successful interventions are likely to be those which are matched not only to desired target behaviours but also to the direct change agents themselves.

There has been much speculation as to what consultant practices are likely to lead to successful consultee-delivered programmes. For example, in an account of effective parent-training practices (Leach 1986), some general principles for intervention design were described. Amongst these, consultants were advised to choose

1 effective, pre-tested, pre-packaged procedures that are demonstrably the most suitable for the problem presented,
2 procedures which were minimally intrusive and maximally consonant with the people involved,
3 procedures that were readily understood and which required the least amount of training,
4 procedures that could be integrated in the mediator's general life so as to be maintained for a sufficient time to reach the goals of the intervention.

It was also suggested that a collaborative, collegial style of consultation might involve consultees to a greater extent than a unidirectional, 'expert' style. Similar 'rules of thumb' have been described for improving the effectiveness of consultations with teachers. They have been useful reminders that full account needs to be taken of the mediator's perspective in plans for intervention if mediator commitment and compliance is to be maximized.

More collaborative interchanges, carefully matched programmes, and fewer unthinking applications of behavioural packages may seem obvious ways to increase consultee satisfaction and commitment. However, until fairly recently, there has been little research to support or disconfirm these views. Fortunately this is now changing. Reimers *et al.* (1987), for example, reviewed twenty studies completed since 1980 which have addressed aspects of the mediator acceptance and compliance problem. In brief, they found that several factors related to consultees' ratings of an intervention's acceptability. These were

1 the severity of the problem behaviour,
2 the time needed to implement a procedure,
3 the procedure's perceived effectiveness,
4 the type of treatment recommended (i.e. those designed to increase appropriate behaviour vs. those designed to decrease inappropriate behaviour,
5 the extent to which the proposed intervention plan was understandable.

In general, they found that higher ratings of acceptability were more likely the greater the severity of the problem, and the less the time required to implement the intervention procedures. The same was true for effective, well-understood and positive (as opposed to reductive) interventions. Reimers *et al.* end their review with a useful model which highlights some relationships between these variables. This is reproduced in Figure 1.1.

Witt (1986) summarized research which has examined factors related to teacher satisfaction with behavioural interventions. He pointed out that effectiveness of treatments is not as important as perceived effectiveness, and that treatments which appeal to teachers' values and common sense appear to be adopted widely despite the absence of published data to support them (see also Somerville and Leach, forthcoming). Other factors related to satisfaction have been identified as preferences for low time, personnel and material costs, lack of ecological intrusiveness, and use of pragmatic descriptions rather than behavioural jargon. Quite clearly, as Happe (1983: 33) nicely put it: 'The plan that requires the consultee to become a timer-setting, data-taking, token-counting, head-patting octopus has a very low probability of implementation and maintenance'.

On the whole, simulation research of the type described by Reimers *et al.* and Witt provides support for the collaborative, mini-max approach to planning behavioural interventions (see Leach, forthcoming) where consultant and consultee share equally the referred problem, and the procedures required for its resolution, and strive for the best match between intervention, the consultee, and the consultee's setting as an approach which may increase consultee acceptability and maintenance of effort. Support for this approach also comes from studies employing such an approach in school settings (Medway 1979; Tunnecliffe *et al.* 1986). More to the point, it is the implementation of home-based reinforcement programmes for children's behaviour in school that exemplifies the approach in action to a nicety.

Home-based reinforcement (H-BR) programmes

In the school context, H-BR programmes are essentially frequent, teacher-completed ratings of children's behaviour in class which are

Figure 1.1 The possible relationship between mediator understanding, acceptability and compliance and the effectiveness of behavioural programmes.

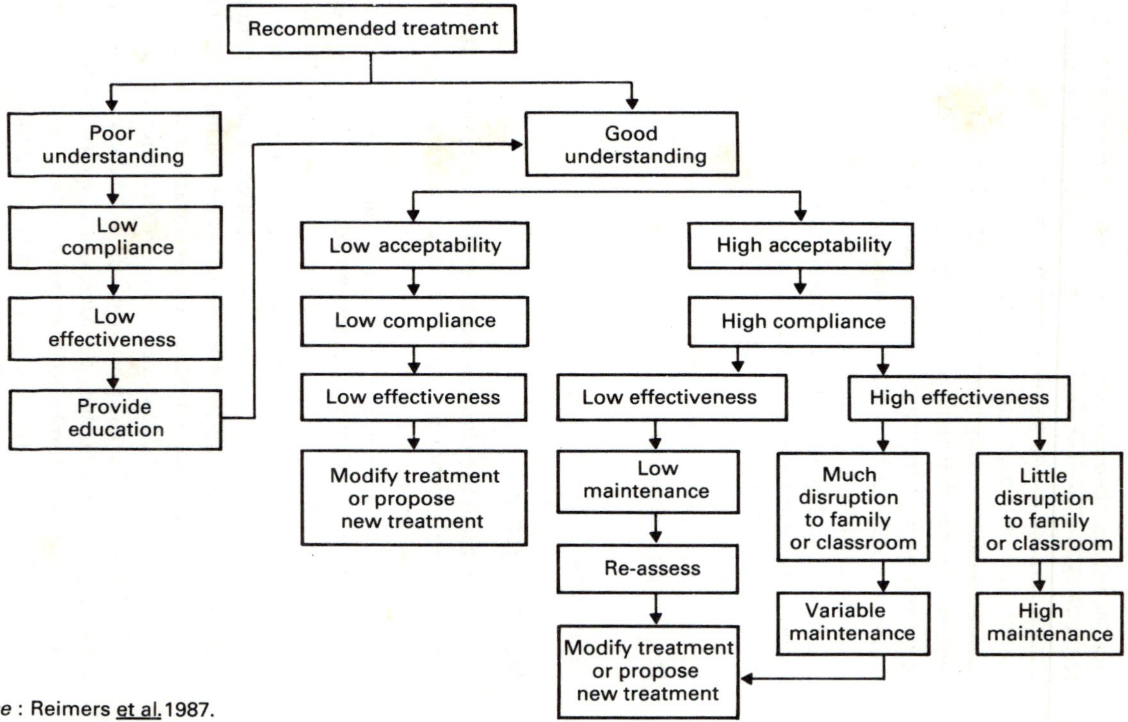

Source : Reimers et al. 1987.

subsequently paired with parent-controlled differential reinforcement at home. A growing number of experimental studies have shown them to be effective and cost-efficient in a variety of educational settings (including regular and special, kindergarten, primary and secondary schools), and across a variety of pupil behaviours (such as attention-to-task, task completion, reading and homework). It is not the intention here to describe this research. Most of the studies have been included already in comprehensive reviews such as those by Atkeson and Forehand (1979) and Barth (1979). Suffice it to say that well-run H-BR programmes have been found to be robust, non-intrusive, flexible interventions which capitalize on the strengths of both teachers and parents. It is largely because of their relative simplicity and minimal disruption to existing routines, that they are readily adapted to the collaborative, behavioural problem-solving model of consultative practice sketched out earlier. It is also likely that their interest for practitioners lies not so much in the novelty of their behavioural components, as through this potential for more effective consultative practice with teachers and parents.

Establishing a H-BR programme

Student selection

Invariably there are children who, for various reasons, are identified by school personnel as 'problem students'. They may often not attend class or they arrive late. They may be children whose behaviour is socially inappropriate or disruptive, who fail to attend to instruction or complete assignments, or who for various reasons fall behind others in their academic performance. H-BR programmes can be targeted at changing any one or more of these kinds of behaviours. They can also be applied to single students or large groups; they can involve one or many teachers; they can be conducted within one school or across a number of schools.

The choice of suitable students for a programme is determined in some degree by the motivation of their teachers and parents to effect behavioural change. The size and scope of the intervention will depend on the number of referred problems that the consultant has to deal with and the number of teachers and parents wishing to participate. In Gilroy's (1982) intervention, for example, a total of twenty-four students, ranging in age from 6 to 12 years, were drawn from ten regular classrooms in two primary schools. Given a teacher willing and able to record ratings of students on a regular basis, and a parent willing and able to give and withhold reinforcement contingent upon the ratings, then most common in-class problems may be targeted for change.

The teacher

The teacher's main responsibilities in a H-BR programme can be summarized as follows:

1 To specify between five and ten pro-social and pro-learning behaviours that, where possible, are incompatible with each student's identified 'problem' behaviours (e.g. is on time for class; brings appropriate supplies to lesson; talks in class at appropriate times; attends to classwork; completes assignments set).
2 To write the behaviour on cards for each student.
3 To give the cards to the students with a full explanation of their content.
4 To mark each student's card when it is presented after a pre-arranged period indicating, in an unbiased and objective manner, whether or not each listed behaviour has been observed during that period.
5 To return the cards at the end of the pre-arranged period to the students concerned and give social reinforcement for each positive behaviour recorded.
6 To check each card from the previous day for a parent's signature (to prove that it has been seen at home) and to retain the cards in a folder.
7 (Optional) To record the total number of positive ratings earned by a student each day and plot the results on a graph.

The consultant's role is to facilitate the completion of these tasks by working collaboratively with the teacher. Sometimes teachers will define behaviours clearly and draw up the cards with little guidance other than that from a how-to-do-it manual or a brief interview. If this is not sufficient, the consultant might observe students to help define the problem behaviours more precisely or demonstrate how a card should be designed. Either way, the consultee's understanding of all the tasks in the programme needs to be checked before it is begun. A three-day trial run is also advisable before the cards are given out to students to iron out operational difficulties.

The main problems to arise at this stage are likely to be the listing of too many behaviours that overlap one another (e.g. 'Is on-task' and 'Pays attention to teacher') and negative behaviours (e.g. 'Will not sit down at desk when asked'). On the whole, behaviours should be discrete and stated positively. It is also advisable to target a few key academic behaviours, such as 'completion of work set', rather than a larger number of subordinate behaviours, such as 'listens to teacher's instructions' or 'begins work when requested'. The reason for this is that as a student's behaviour becomes more task-related, then less time can be spent on any off-task or disruptive behaviour and hence, by definition, 'task completion' subsumes behaviours that prevent it (Witt *et al.* 1983). When academic behaviours like task completion are targeted, however, the consultant must check with the teacher that the children are not lacking the prerequisite skills or knowledge to complete the tasks successfully. No amount of reinforcing contingencies will change a student's academic behaviour if the tasks set are too difficult. An appropriate student–task match for instruction would be where a student, working with 80–90 per cent attention to task, is able to complete about 90 per cent of the task correctly (Gickling and Armstrong 1978). A task is too difficult if, with 80–90 per cent attention to task, a student can complete only 60 per cent correctly.

The report card

A typical example of a completed report card is given in Figure 1.2. In the example, a teacher is asked to record whether or not each targeted behaviour occurred throughout the whole of a lesson by a simple 'yes' or 'no'. Also in the example it will be noted that, instead of a dichotomous 'tasks completed' check, there is a rating from 0 (no tasks completed) to 4 (all tasks completed). This is an additional feature that can provide some room to improve for children who are very poor performers. Other conventions may be used, but consideration of more informative reports should be

Figure 1.2 An example of a daily report card

Name: Time Period: From — To —

Week: Date:

Subject: Time received: Time returned:

Behaviours	*Monday* Yes/No	*Tuesday* Yes/No	*Wednesday* Yes/No	*Thursday* Yes/No	*Friday* Yes/No
* Brought necessary materials to lesson					
* Was on-task over two-thirds of the time during seat-work					
* Talked only when appropriate for lesson					
* Was on-task over two-thirds of the time in oral work					
* Interacted with other pupils according to classroom rules					
* Amount of work set completed					

0 = 0%
1 = 25%
2 = 50%
3 = 75%
4 = 100%

Teacher's signature: ____________________

Parent's signature: ____________________

balanced carefully against the increase in demands being made of the teacher.

Report cards should be marked immediately after a prearranged period, whether this be a lesson, a morning or afternoon session, or a whole school day, and returned to the students. The choice of the time period for rating behaviour depends on the setting (primary or secondary) and on the severity of the problem behaviours (the more severe, the shorter the time interval). On the whole, cards should be given back to students at the end of the rated periods. Sluyter and Hawkins (1972) provide evidence that the return of the card to the students at the end of a day may promote generalization of good behaviour outside the rated sessions. This suggests that a delay in returning cards could be built into the programme as the intervention progresses. Likewise, fewer periods need to be rated once appropriate behaviours have been well established. This 'fade-out' phase of the H-BR programme is described in a later section.

Report cards are open to student abuse and wear and tear. Some practical ground rules for teachers are needed to prevent this. A sample list is as follows:

1 Provide cards made of cardboard which are small enough to go into a wallet or pocket.
2 Use ink to mark cards.
3 Initial and date all cards and initial all changes or corrections.
4 Draw a line through behaviours that do not pertain to a particular day's activities.
5 Mark 'No' for all behaviours if a student has to receive major disciplinary action during a session (e.g. being sent out of a classroom or reported to the principal).
6 Provide a new card and mark 'No' for all behaviours if a student has lost or mutilated a card.
7 Subtract one point from the total earned if a student fails to present a card at the beginning of a period or fails to collect it after marking.
8 Mark 'N/A' for all behaviours if a student is absent from a session or if a period is cancelled for any reason.

Once the teacher has drawn up the cards and has tested the marking procedure, the consultant can shift attention to the tasks of the parents.

The parent

The parent's main responsibilities are as follows:

1 To agree on a list of five to ten positive consequences, in collaboration with the student, which are under his/her full control. Five to seven positive consequences should be privileges which can be readily arranged on a daily basis, such as a small amount of pocket money, a period watching television, or a favourite food. Three to five should be special privileges which can be arranged more suitably on a weekly or less frequent interval. Special events might be having a friend to stay, a choice of outings, going out with mother or father, or bonus pocket money.
2 To assign points to each short-term and long-term consequence listed. In general, daily consequences are assigned fewer points than longer-term consequences. One point can be earned by the student for each positive behavioural rating made by the teacher on the report card. Points earned are recorded each day in a points book. This acts as a 'bank-book' of points from which payments are to be made for the listed privileges. The points given for each privilege should be such that a perfect score on the report card on each day of the week enables the student to exchange the points for at least one privilege per day *and* one longer-term special privilege. A 'nil' score on any day should lead to no points being earned and, in some cases, could lead to a loss of 50 per cent of the points earned up to that time in the points book. The range of points obtained between these extremes should enable related proportions of the privileges being earned. For example, 50 per cent of the available positive ratings over a week should earn points to the value of half one daily privilege and half one longer-term special privilege.
3 To put the list of privileges and their cost in points in a prominent position that can be seen by parents and student.
4 To ask the student each day to see the report card and to check it at an agreed time as soon as possible after the student arrives home from school.
5 To record the points earned by the student in the points book.
6 To make socially reinforcing comments to the student about any of the behaviours marked positively by the teacher.

7 To ask the student whether an exchange of points for listed privileges is desired.
8 To provide any privilege or consequence requested by the student from the list, *whatever other circumstances prevail*, provided that there are enough accumulated points to pay for them.
9 To deduct points 'spent' from the points book.
10 To sign the report card in ink and return it to the student.

The consultant's role is again to facilitate the completion of these tasks in a collaborative effort with the parents. The consultant must check that the parents understand all that is required of them, that they feel able to provide the privileges listed and that they can operate the points system. Some interventions (Lahey *et al.* 1977) have used the minimal instruction procedure of explaining the tasks to parents by letter only with some success. However, a 'letter only' instruction is probably best suited for 'praise only' parental rewards. A points and privileges system, such as the one described, will require a conference of two or three hours with the consultant and parents to be properly arranged. Although this expenditure of time might be daunting with one set of parents, it reduces considerably when a group of parents meet in a conference together. It is also likely to lead to greater maintenance of parental involvement in the long term (Karraker 1972).

During the parent conference, the consultant must be prepared to teach, by demonstration, any aspect of the procedure of which parents seem unsure. Some parents will need more teaching than others and may need to be seen on a number of occasions. Others will need only the briefest of interviews.

Once instructed in the procedural aspects, the relationship of the consultant to the parents returns to one of equals. They must be encouraged to think through the programme and to examine whether it can become consonant with their home demands, constraints, and routines. It is essential to let them have the final say in determining the details of the programme and how it can be tailored to their satisfaction. If the family can assimilate the programme, in an ecological sense, it is less likely that it will be rejected before it has run its course.

The main problems to arise at this stage are usually related to the choice of suitable privileges. In order to be fully effective, the positive consequences should not be objects, actions, and events that the student has ready access to during other times of the week, nor which parents cannot control. Instead they must be consequences that can be earned only through the report-card system. They must be consequences that the parents can and will provide without argument. Thus an amount of time watching television is a good choice if the child can be prevented from watching television at other times, but is a poor choice if the child can turn on a television set or can listen in when the rest of the family are watching. Likewise a small amount of pocket money is a good choice if it is the only way a child can earn money, but is a poor choice if the child has unconditional access to amounts of money throughout the week. Finally, parents must accept that none of the listed privileges is to be given if a child fails to bring home a card, whatever reasons are given for its loss.

The student

The student's main responsibilities are as follows:

1 To receive a report card, signed and dated each day from the teacher at the end of a designated teaching period and, if more than one teacher is involved, to deliver it to the next teacher for marking.
2 To deliver the report card to his/her parents for their signature at the end of each school day.
3 To return the signed card to the teacher at the beginning of the next teaching period.
4 To read and understand all the behaviours listed on the card so as to be able to give positive and negative examples of each when asked.
5 To help his/her parents draw up lists of privileges if asked.
6 To understand, so as to be able to explain fully, all details of the points system and how privileges can be earned.
7 To understand, so as to be able to explain fully, the costs involved for losing, destroying, or altering a card.

The kind of involvement of children in a H-BR programme depends on their age and development. The responsibilities listed above are more appropriate for school-aged children aged 8 years plus than for children in the pre-school and early school years. Younger children will need to have their report cards put into their school bag by the teacher and taken out by their parents. The marks on their card might be 'happy' and 'sad' faces rather than ticks (✓) and crosses (x). Reinforcers need to be similarly age-relevant. Older children and young adults, on the other hand, can be expected to take full responsibility for carrying their card and delivering it to teachers and parents. They should also be included in planning the intervention at all its stages as much as possible. In some cases, it may be worth formalizing their agreement to carry out their responsibilities in the form of a signed contract.

Monitoring, review, and evaluation

Monitoring for programme integrity, review of progress and evaluation of its cost-effectiveness are not only essential aspects of the behavioural consultant's role as a scientist practitioner, but also necessary to enhance the likelihood of the programme's success. First, consultants should arrange to check that the programme is being implemented as planned by telephone contact, periodic conferences, direct observation, or by the use of trained observers. Second, they need to ensure adequate data collection and collation for formative and summative evaluation.

Ideally both these tasks are required. However, it is worth noting that only one-third of successful published H-BR interventions have reported using observers in the classroom to assess, for example, the validity of teachers' ratings, and none has directly monitored treatment implementation in the home (Atkeson and Forehand 1979). While these experimental studies are not necessarily models of ideal practice, they do suggest that, *at least initially*, if consultants are pressed for time, they might concentrate on collecting formative and summative data rather than spend time on direct observation of consultees' compliance to the programme plan. Telephone contact or brief conferences during each phase of the intervention seem to be equally effective checks on programme integrity. As a safeguard, it is advisable to encourage committees to contact the consultant immediately problems arise.

Direct observation of student behaviour change is the most satisfactory method of formative and summative evaluation. Measures might be taken as specific behaviours, academic output and accuracy, or academic engaged time. However, a daily data base for programme evaluation can be obtained from the report cards themselves (for example, the number of positive ratings earned or percentage of rules followed by a student per day).

Ratings or behaviours might be plotted on a graph to examine trends in the data over different phases of the intervention. These might be the pre-intervention or 'base-line' period, when the cards are completed by the teacher but not given to the students; the intervention phase, when the H-BR programme is conducted; the 'fade-out' phase (described later) when the cards are gradually withdrawn; and the follow-up phase, when cards are again completed for a few days but not returned to the students. Recording, plotting on a graph and interpreting time-series data are well described by Hersen and Barlow (1976), Kratochwill (1978), Gelfand and Hartmann (1984), and Barlow *et al.* (1984). The feedback from daily measures of target behaviour will indicate whether or not the programme is on its way to reaching its set goals. All aspects of the programme will need to be checked thoroughly and, if necessary, modified if the desired behaviour change is not occurring. The consultant should examine the data with the consultees and provide regular feedback to them as it progresses.

Other aspects of the programme's conduct requiring attention include setting a date for a formal review of the programme, establishing a criterion, such as 'ten consecutive days when positive ratings are 90% and over', before introducing plans for withdrawing the cards, and planning for generalization of the behaviours on its completion.

'Fading-out' the cards and maintaining gains

The ultimate goal of any worthwhile behaviour-change programme is for desired behavioural gains to be maintained under similar conditions to those existing prior to the intervention and to generalize to other settings. Thus instituting a procedure which will effectively 'fade-out' the contrived aspects of the intervention (i.e. the cards, the points, and the specially arranged consequences) and planning for long-term maintenance of behaviours are an essential next stage.

The kind of fade-out procedure chosen may not be so important as the fact that such a procedure is employed. Gilroy (1982), for example, compared the effectiveness of three types of fading procedures — pupil self-rating, social reinforcement, and semi-weekly reports. In the self-rating group, students were instructed how to rate themselves and complete their card at the beginning of the fade-out period. They then took home a reduced report card which stated their 'adjusted points total' based on their self-ratings and teacher ratings. To arrive at an adjusted points total, student ratings were compared with teacher ratings at the end of term and the student lost a point for every discrepancy between the two ratings. Home reinforcement was made contingent on the adjusted points total. In the social reinforcement group, a letter was sent home asking parents to enquire about their children's school performance every day and to praise specific behaviour in reports which had 80 per cent of behaviours rated positively. In this condition, teachers too were encouraged to provide social reinforcement for positive ratings when reports were returned to students. In the third group, the students took home report cards only twice a week (Tuesdays and Fridays). The Tuesday card stated an average of points earned over Monday and Tuesday, and the Friday card averaged points for the rest of the week. The parents were asked to multiply the average points by the number of days to achieve parity with previous point exchange arrangements. Gilroy found that all three fade-out strategies were equally effective in maintaining positive classroom behaviours, and all were superior to a control group from which cards were suddenly withdrawn without the provision of any back-up procedure.

Schumaker *et al.* (1977) describe a more finely graded fade-out strategy which might be necessary when dealing with more resistant behaviour problems. They move students gradually to a stricter criterion of points to be earned to gain daily privileges whilst reducing the frequency of cards to take home. Beginning at 60 per cent of positive ratings on the daily card, the criterion is shifted to 75 per cent and then 90 per cent. The student then carries a shortened version of the card, which has fewer, more general rating categories and which requires 80 per cent of positive ratings to earn points. Following fifteen consecutive days of at least 80 per cent of positive ratings, the student is allowed to move to a twice-weekly card. Three weeks on this card at 80 per cent criterion allows a move to a weekly card. However, if there are two consecutive days below 80 per cent, the student returns to the daily card and the process is repeated.

Finally, regular quarterly and half-yearly reports become the basis of the reinforcement system.

A major problem with Schumaker *et al.*'s fade-out procedure is its complexity and its resultant increase in consultant (and consultee) time over the simpler procedures described earlier. It is also unclear from research whether or not such a finely grained procedure significantly improves maintenance of target behaviours and in which circumstances it is particularly useful.

One other fade-out procedure is worth considering. Saudargas *et al.* (1977) investigated the comparative effectiveness of fixed-time and variable-time report cards on the academic performance of third graders. Students under the fixed-time schedule received at the end of each week take-home reports on the quantity and quality of work completed during the week. Students under the variable-time schedule were chosen randomly each day to receive a report card. It was found that academic output and number of correct assignments was significantly higher under the variable-time schedule. Although long-term maintenance was not measured, it could be predicted from a theoretical point of view that the variable schedule would be superior as the students would be less able to predict reinforcement and thereby the situation would more closely approximate the 'natural' conditions they face in classrooms.

The cost-benefits of H-BR programmes

H-BR programmes are often described as cost-efficient because they involve relatively little consultant and consultee time for the size of behavioural gains made. Gilroy (1982) found that she spent twenty-eight minutes per student per week in establishing, maintaining, and completing her programme, which involved twenty-four students in two schools over twelve weeks. The two teachers involved averaged an increase of only five and a half minutes of their time per student per week. The time-cost resulted in an average of 30 per cent improvement in rule-following behaviour in the classrooms during the intervention period and an average of 21 per cent improvement during a two-month post-intervention period; 95 per cent of the parents rated the programme a success. Interestingly in the single-case study by Leach and Ralph (1986), an average of seventy-six minutes per week consultant time over the fifteen weeks' intervention was needed. Although more evidence is required, group-administered H-BR programmes seem to be more cost-efficient than single-case interventions. Unfortunately far too few comparative analyses of consultant practices have been reported to ascertain the relative superiority of H-BR programmes over other methods of changing school learning and behaviour.

A potential cost-saving feature of H-BR programmes was investigated by Leach and Byrne (1986). They examined whether the beneficial effects of a programme delivered to a proportion of disruptive students in a secondary school classroom 'spilled over' to other, equally disruptive students in the same class who did not receive the programme. Their results were equivocable. In one class (A) of twenty-eight students, the five 'target' students showed a rapid increase in 'rule-following' from 31.4 per cent during the base-line period, to 91 per cent during the programme. The five 'control' students also increased their 'rule-following' from 25.2 to 38.9 per cent immediately and then gradually to 50 per cent later in the intervention period, showing clear signs of a positive spill-over effect that was being mediated by events in the classroom itself. Measures of the amount of work completed by these students showed a similar trend. In the second class (B) however, spill-over effects were not apparent. The target students again showed a rapid increase in rule-following (from 41.8 to 85.9 per cent) and work completed (from 24.6 to 71.7 per cent) after the introduction of the programme, but the control students' behaviour and work output remained, at best, unchanged, and even showed signs of deterioration as the intervention proceeded.

Clearly it is important to identify what factors are operative in certain classrooms but not in others in order to plan for spill-over effects and so make significant savings in the time-costs of consultants and teachers. Although no measures were made of possible mediating factors in Leach and Byrne's study, a number of informal observations were made that could be considered further. In particular, it was noted that the increase in rule-following and attention to work by the target group in class (A) might have acted as an 'establishing stimulus' (Michael 1982) that prompted the teacher's use of more effective class management strategies, which in turn gradually increased the positive behaviours of all class members (including the control students) and helped to maintain those of the target group at a high level. This assumed that the teacher of class (A) already had effective skills and strategies to draw on but that he needed the impetus of some relief from disruptive behaviours in order to apply them. Cognitively, too, he might have perceived the class more favourably after the introduction of the programme thus enabling him to use more positive reinforcement. It was suggested that the teacher in class (B), however, although receiving a similar 'enabling stimulus' in a reduction of disruptive behaviour by a section of the class, might not have had appropriate management skills to draw on and thus was unable to gain control of the class. They hypothesize further that this teacher's lack of knowledge, or his inability to apply effective management strategies, led to his continuing to reinforce disruptive behaviour in the class as a whole. This would have had the effect of increasing the disruption by control students and having a counter influence on the H-BR programme received by target students.

In the light of recent research that indicates apparently much less potent 'enabling stimuli' can prompt teachers to generate effective classroom management strategies for themselves (Leach and Dolan 1985), their explanation appears parsimonious. If correct, it has important implications for 'spill-over' effects in H-BR programmes in the future. For example, it points to the consideration of a two-stage intervention process whereby the minimal approach is tried first and then, using spill-over data as a guide, a more intrusive one (in this case some in-service training for teacher (B)) follows when necessary.

Some studies have suggested that H-BR programmes can act to supersede the deleterious effects of teacher behaviour, such as contingent attention for inappropriate pupil behaviour (Clark 1972; Todd *et al.* 1976). The results of Leach and Byrne's study suggest that this may be true only in the short term. In the longer term it is more likely that, *unless the teacher's behaviour towards the students also changes during the programme*, its beneficial effects will not be maintained. Goodall (1985) found her H-BR programme changed the students' behaviour *first*, giving the teachers an opportunity to change their behaviour towards the class as a whole and to maintain and generalize the more positive student behaviours which emerged.

H-BR programmes in retrospect

H-BR programmes are robust, flexible, and effective intervention strategies which are suitable for a wide range of typical classroom learning and behaviour difficulties. Several conditions are essential for their success:

1 the teacher's ability to differentiate between appropriate and inappropriate behaviours,
2 the availability of relevant reinforcers in the home,
3 the teacher's compliance with the rules for administering the report card,
4 the parent's compliance with the rules for delivering contingent reinforcement.

The programmes utilize the strengths of parents for child behaviour change in that parents control varied and powerful reinforcers for children in the home. They utilize the strengths of teachers in that teachers are in the best position to observe and provide information on what is happening in the classroom. They are particularly useful in the problematic setting of secondary schools where in-class reinforcement opportunities are sometimes severely limited, where students have many teachers during the day, where student peer-groups are a powerful, controlling influence, and where home–school communication can be intermittent and ill defined.

H-BR programmes require minimal training of teachers, parents, and consultants. They are readily understood and are not overly demanding of time and energy. They can be integrated with traditional consultee roles and practices without undue disruption to routines and existing behaviour management techniques. They lend themselves to a collaborative, problem-solving style where teachers, parents, consultants, and, if possible, the students themselves share responsibilities for designing and carrying out all stages of the intervention plan. In short, they exemplify minimal procedures that can have maximal, significant effects.

There is evidence to suggest that the above conditions are likely to optimize mediator or consultee compliance with behavioural intervention plans (Hughes and Falk 1981; Yeaton and Sechrest 1981; Witt 1986; Reimers *et al.* 1987). As compliance to treatment plans is such a critical factor in determining the success of behavioural interventions, any programme that is high on acceptability, effectiveness, and compliance is to be welcomed. In the final analysis, however, H-BR programmes are likely to bring about significant change only in the short term. The relatively quick reduction in disruptive behaviours or increase in academic output, that is common to many programmes, will simply 'buy time' during which consultants and teachers must develop alternative in-class behaviour management and instructional strategies which will then become longer-term features of the classroom environment. It is highly unlikely that H-BR programmes will bring about long-term changes alone. If the opportunity to change managerial and instructional practices is not taken, for all their practical usefulness they will become yet another one-off, washed-out behavioural programme that, rather unrealistically, promised far more than it delivered.

References

Atkeson, B. M. and Forehand, R. (1979) 'Home-based reinforcement programmes designed to modify classroom behaviour: a review and methodological evaluation', *Psychological Bulletin* 6: 1298–308.

Barlow, D. H., Hayes, S. C., and Nelson, R. O. (1984) *The Scientist-Practitioner: Research and Accountability in Clinical and Educational Settings*, New York: Pergamon.

Barth, R. (1979) 'Home-based reinforcement of school behaviour: a review and analysis', *Review of Educational Research* 3: 436–58.

Clark, H. B. (1972) 'A programme of delayed consequences for the management of class attendance and disruptive behaviour of 124 special education children', in G. Semb, D. R. Green, R. P. Hawkins, J. Michael, E. L. Phillips, J. A. Sherman, H. Sloan, and D. R. Thomas (eds) *Behaviour Analysis and Education*, Lawrence, Kan: University of Kansas.

Gelfand, D. M. and Hartmann, D. P. (1984) *Child Behaviour Analysis and Therapy*, New York: Pergamon.

Gickling, E. E. and Armstrong, R. L. (1978) 'Levels of instructional difficulty as related to on-task behaviour, task completion and comprehension', *Journal of Learning Disabilities* 11: 32–9.

Gilroy, S. (1982) 'An investigation of home-based reinforcement programmes for managing children's classroom behaviour and factors that affect the maintenance of behaviour changes', unpublished thesis, Murdoch University, Perth, Western Australia.

Goodall, K. (1985) 'Home-based reinforcement: an examination of how rule-following behaviour influences changes to untargeted child and teacher behaviour under conditions where experimental contingencies are and are not operating', unpublished thesis, Murdoch University, Perth, Western Australia.

Happe, D. (1983) 'Behavioural intervention: it doesn't do any good in your briefcase', in J. Grimes (ed.) *Psychological Consultation*, Des Moines, Iowa State Department of Education.

Hersen, M. and Barlow, D. H. (1976) *Single-Case Experimental Designs: Strategies for Studying Behaviour Change*, New York: Pergamon.

Hughes, J. and Falk, R. (1981) 'Resistance, reactance, and consultation', *Journal of School Psychology* 19: 130–42.

Karraker, R. (1972) 'Increasing academic performance through home-managed contingency programmes', *Journal of School Psychology* 10: 173–9.

Kratochwill, T. R. (ed.) (1978) *Single Subject Research: Strategies for Evaluating Change*, New York: Academic Press.

Lahey, B. B., Gendrich, J. G., Gendrich, S. I., Schnelle, J. F., Gant, D. S. and McNees, M. P. (1977) 'An evaluation of daily report cards with minimal teacher and parent contacts as an efficient method of classroom intervention', *Behaviour Modification* 1: 381–94.

Leach, D. J. (1986) 'Working with parents as direct intervention agents', *Australian Educational and Developmental Psychologist* 3: 1–5.

——— (forthcoming) 'Increasing the use and maintenance of behaviour-based practices in schools: an example of a general problem for applied psychologists?' *Australian Psychologist*.

Leach, D. J. and Byrne, M. K. (1986) 'Some "spill-over" effects of a home-based reinforcement programme in a secondary school', *Educational Psychology* 6: 265–76.

Leach, D. J. and Dolan, N. (1985) 'Helping teachers increase student academic engagement rates: the evaluation of a minimal feedback procedure', *Behaviour Modification* 9: 55–71.

Leach, D. J. and Ralph, A. (1986) 'Home–school reinforcement: a case study', *Behaviour Change* 3: 58–62.

Medway, F. J. (1979) 'How effective is school consultation? A review of recent literature', *Journal of School Psychology* 17: 275–82.

Michael, J. (1982) 'Distinguishing between discriminative and motivational functions of stimuli', *Journal of Applied Behaviour Analysis* 3: 149–55.

Reimers, T. M., Wacker, D. P., and Koeppl, G. (1987) 'Acceptability of behavioural interventions: a review of the literature', *School Psychology Review* 16: 212–27.

Saudargas, R. W., Madsen, C. H., and Scott, J. W. (1977) 'Differential effects of fixed- and variable-time feedback on production rates of elementary school children', *Journal of Applied Behaviour Analysis* 10: 449, 464.

Schumaker, J. B., Hovell, M. F., and Sherman, J. A. (1977) *Managing Behaviour: A Home-Based School Achievement System: Manual for Using Daily Report Cards and Home Privileges in Improving Conduct and Academic Performance of Problem Students*, Lawrence, Kan: H & H Enterprises.

Sluyter, C. and Hawkins, R. (1972) 'Delayed reinforcement of classroom behaviour by parents', *Journal of Learning Disabilities* 5: 16–24.

Somerville, D. E. and Leach, D. J. (forthcoming) 'Direct or indirect instruction? An evaluation of three types of intervention programme for assisting students with specific reading difficulties', *Educational Research*.

Todd, D. D., Scott, R. B., Bostow, D. E., and Alexander, S. B. (1976) 'Modification of the excessive inappropriate classroom behaviour of two elementary school students using home-based contingencies and daily report card procedures', *Journal of Applied Behaviour Analysis* 9: 106.

Tunnecliffe, M. F., Leach, D. J., and Tunnecliffe, L. P. (1986) 'Relative efficacy of using behavioural consultation as an approach to teacher stress management', *Journal of School Psychology* 24: 123–31.

Witt, J. C. (1986) 'Teachers' resistance to the use of school-based interventions', *Journal of School Psychology* 24: 37–44.

Witt, J. C., Hannafin, M. J., and Martens, B. K. (1983) 'Home-based reinforcement: behavioural co-variation between academic performance and inappropriate behaviour', *Journal of School Psychology* 21: 337–48.

Yeaton, W. H. and Sechrest, L. (1981) 'Critical dimensions in the choice and maintenance of successful treatments: strength, integrity and effectiveness', *Journal of Consulting and Clinical Psychology* 49: 156–67.

Chapter two

An adapted behavioural approach to the treatment of behavioural problems

Rajinder M. Gupta and Peter Coxhead

Introduction

The literature concerning the efficacy of behaviour modification is voluminous and its growth does not seem to be abating; indeed more than a decade ago, Winnett and Winkler (1972) even questioned the merit of conducting further research in this field. Over the years, besides innumerable journal articles, a number of books have appeared (e.g. Ullman and Krasner 1965; Becker 1971; Fargo *et al.* 1970) which document research evidence supporting behaviour modification as an effective technique in modifying undesirable patterns of behaviour in a wide range of settings. Some of its adherents even suggest that the technique can be applied 'to almost any setting' (Tharp and Wetzel 1969: 4). O'Leary and O'Leary (1977: 16) state: 'Laboratories investigating the application of behavioural principles to children's problems now exist in almost every state'. They report a wide range of problem areas (e.g. enuresis, delinquency, childhood autism, childhood schizophrenia, various phobias, and so on) where behaviour modification has been successfully and beneficially applied.

Notwithstanding behaviour modification's impressive track record, a considerable number of workers in the field have claimed that the traditional behaviour modification paradigm is not only impractical, but also often unacceptable to many teachers.[1] The basis for this claim is briefly reviewed below, following which an 'adapted' model is described and illustrated.[2]

Brief review of the literature

Chazan and Laing (1985) consider that many teachers feel somewhat 'uneasy' with the jargon of behaviour modification, or, as Reppucci and Saunders (1974; cited in Rosenfield 1985) put it, the language of behaviour modification can be the source of a clash between the values of 'behavioural consultants' and those of teachers. Chazan and Laing add further that it is sometimes difficult for teachers to ignore undesirable patterns of behaviour and to achieve the consistency of response required in busy classrooms. Personal experience of 'delivering' behaviour modification to teachers also lends support to the belief that teachers express — and genuinely experience — difficulty in collecting the base-line data. Teachers have rightly argued that it is not realistic for them to concentrate simultaneously on teaching, watching the class, and collecting data on the target child. In the case of children where the manifestation of the problem is quite acute and its occurrence quite frequent, teachers can hardly wait for days to collect the base-line data (cf Rosenfield 1985).

In situations where the child's behavioural difficulties (and/or the teacher's mismanagement) have made the teacher's life 'miserable' over a period of time, the teacher, possibly unwittingly, becomes somewhat prejudiced and less tolerant towards the child. In circumstances such as these, when the teacher is asked to reinforce the child with approval or praise or some other suitable reward, either the teacher shows disagreement with the principle of reinforcement, or fails to reinforce desirable patterns of behaviour systematically, or fails to ignore — where possible — undesirable patterns of behaviour (cf Chazan and Laing 1985; Hyman and Lally 1982; Rosenfield 1985). Gutkin and Curtis (1982) cite Lambert's (1976) conclusion that elementary-school teachers find it difficult to state children's behavioural difficulties in concrete observable terms. Rosenfield (1985) draws attention to yet another important but often underestimated point, where she says that the principles underlying behaviour modification may appear quite simple to 'behavioural consultants' but fairly involved to teachers. The authors too, on numerous occasions, have experienced this in their advocacy of behaviour modification to teachers and head-teachers. Hyman and Lally (1982) consider that teachers show resistance to the systematic use of such reinforcers as teacher praise and attention and the demand that most 'operant programmes' make on teacher time and effort. Elliot *et al.* (1984) also regard teachers' lack of an adequate amount of time as one of the contributory factors in their showing resistance to accepting the traditional behaviour modification paradigm. Other factors which lead to teacher resistance according to Elliot *et al.* (1984) are shortage of material resources and additional staff, and the lack of an adequate knowledge of behaviour modification techniques (Rosenfield 1985). A further, although less frequently encountered, cause of teacher resistance is that they have objections on the grounds of ethics or value differences (Rosenfield 1985). These feelings may be so strong as to override any defence based on the existence of professional codes e.g. the codes of conduct of the American Psychological Association (1973) or of the British Psychological Society (1985).

In the applied setting, the acceptance of behaviour modification has also come under attack for its failure to deal with the question of generalizability, its poor reliability, and its unsatisfactory experimental design (Hyman and Lally 1982), as well as for its lack of 'social validation' (Kazdin 1980).

According to Meador and Ollendick (1984), outside the clinical setting it is difficult to manipulate external contingencies and in the absence of this, treatment changes are transient and dissipating. Meichenbaum (1977) considers that if behaviour modification is applied in its strict sense, it overrates the role of antecedents and consequences, but undervalues the client's own perception and evaluation of his problem. While not denying the importance of environmental factors, Meichenbaum does not view them as being of critical importance. He argues that 'what the client says to himself about these events influences his behaviour' (1977: 8). Kratochwill and Someren (1985), based on their experience of 'practice and training', describe a number of factors which impinge on the successful outcome of the application of behaviour modification. Some of the factors which are discussed in detail in their paper are: 'the lack of standardization of consultation, lack of specific training of consultants, little or no consultee (teacher) training, problems surrounding target behaviour identification, and external constraints to consultation' (1985: 225). Tharp and Wetzel (1969) drawing on their experience of using behaviour modification in 'natural settings' conclude as follows:

> In the natural environment, however, things do not work out with such simplicity. Adequate reinforcers are not always available, either for the target or mediators. Logistical problems are sometimes insurmountable. Indeed, few cases did not include at least one form of these resistances, and most resisted in several ways. . . . The point made here is that these resistances cannot be assumed unique to any case. They represent technical difficulties which must be faced by anyone who chooses to attempt behaviour modification in the natural environment. Thus some resistances help us to perceive the limitations on the advisability of behaviour modification in the natural environment.
>
> (Tharp and Wetzel 1969: 126–7)

A recent survey carried out by the authors found that there was not even one practising educational psychologist in a sample of seventy-eight who always recommended the traditional version of behaviour modification (for a somewhat similar study carried out in the USA see Shapiro and Lentz 1985). This would suggest that there is almost no use of the unmodified traditional model — at least in the applied setting. Another finding from this survey was that 91 per cent of the respondents thought that behaviour modification 'has the potential for adaptation and still remain effective'. It is findings such as these and the other studies reviewed above which provide some justification for our attempts at developing an adapted version of behaviour modification which our experience and evidence show is effective, efficient, and acceptable to a vast majority of teachers.

The adapted model

Assuming that in general behaviour modification methods are efficacious, but that the strict traditional model[3] is not wholly satisfactory, what alternatives are there? The personal experience of one of us (Gupta) has, over a number of years, gradually led to the position of being able to present a distinct 'adapted' model. All the changes to the traditional model have been made gradually and in the light of experience and of feedback received from teachers during implementation. Over the years, the 'finished product' has been tried on about twenty children, mostly from secondary schools, with such problems as petty thieving, truancy, lack of motivation to work, lack of co-operation in children's homes, complete disregard of school rules, assault on a member of staff, vicious attacks on other children, and lack of self-control. On the basis of information gleaned from school records, from discussion with teachers, and from assessment where considered necessary, all the children 'treated' with this model were of low average to average ability. In a few cases, their achievement in the basic subjects was quite commensurate with their chronological ages, while in others, there was a substantial discrepancy.

The model has three key stages, which are described in some detail below, together with their rationale and, where possible, some supportive evidence from the literature. The assumption made is that the person applying the model is an educational psychologist, who has been approached by a school about the problems of an individual child. With appropriate changes, the model can be transferred to different settings and used by other professionals (e.g. clinical psychologists, social workers, or teachers with appropriate training).

First stage: achieving appropriate co-operation

It is critically important to ensure that the school (the referrer) is willing to offer full co-operation. This will entail making plain the demands which are likely to be made, which may include being less negative, making realistic academic demands where the child has learning difficulties, recognizing and rewarding any signs of improvement in the child's behaviour, and giving feedback to the parents when the child shows any signs of improvement. For example, in order to achieve the latter, the head-teacher might be asked to send simple notes to parents, such as 'Johnny has not attacked anybody today and we are extremely pleased with his behaviour'. Feedback of this kind can be quite important in certain cases and can accelerate improvement in the child's behaviour, but makes demands on the school which go beyond 'normal routine'; those involved must be aware of this from the start. Since schools are the original referrers, they are normally very co-operative, but in one case a head-teacher did not send brief notes to the child's parents at regular intervals as was originally promised; although he claimed not to be opposed to doing so, he did not actually do it, despite repeated reminders.

An integral part of enlisting the school's support and co-operation is to agree to see the child, the staff, and the parents, when and if necessary. If for any reason the school is less than keen on extending full co-operation, it is best not to follow this approach, but to pursue alternative means to solve the problem.

Teachers must be alerted to the fact that any reward or praise should not be tinged with subtle negative or sarcastic comments. Presland (1974) puts it quite aptly: 'When giving praise, beware of making it into a lecture; the reward element of "well done" often disappears if it is followed by "why can't you always do it that way?" '. In addition, teachers should also be made aware that in no case should they delay the reward. Sometimes they tend to think that they should let a child be good for a week or a fortnight before they show any signs of acknowledging his good behaviour. They seem to fear that if they reward their desired patterns as soon as there is any evidence, the child might regress to his old behaviour.

Parents are usually supportive, but this cannot be taken for granted: in one case, the father was extremely aggressive and sabotaged efforts to help his 14-year-old son who was otherwise making excellent progress. It is important to secure parental co-operation and to explain to them what is being done. They need to be advised that when their child brings home a letter about his improved behaviour in school, they should try to make a 'fuss' about it, and reinforce it. The concept of reinforcement will generally need explaining at some considerable length.

Second stage: developing a relationship with the child

The next stage is to see the child. It may seem unnecessary to justify seeing the child as a stage in itself, but the value of 'seeing the child' is not universally agreed. Some of the literature seems to take a rather cynical view. For instance, Tharp and Wetzel state:

> In the psychotherapy model, the professional specialist interacts with the patient. Various strategies have been invented to purify this dyadic interaction, and it is the aim of psychoanalysis to re-create in this dyadic arena all of those behavioural and emotional proclivities which constitute the 'mental illness'. The therapeutic dyad — doctor and patient — derives from medical

> organization, and is comfortably consistent with the consulting room pattern by which disease is treated.
>
> (Tharp and Wetzel 1969: 46–7)

The present authors do not share these views regarding 'seeing the child'. Seeing and talking with the child has some major benefits. Perhaps the most important is being able to see the child's version of the problem and his motivation to change, which are quite critical factors in bringing about any change in behaviour. More information can be gained about the antecedents and consequences of the problem. Being closely involved with the child enables the psychologist to see what makes this child 'tick' (i.e. to learn more about human behaviour), and this process helps in professional development.

Other benefits of agreeing to see the child concern the school. The psychologist is no longer perceived as someone who comes, gives a bit of 'impractical' advice or 'theory', and disappears without actually seeing the child. It is vital that teachers have faith in the psychologist's advice. Without the necessary credibility, the teacher is less likely to implement any advice offered (see also Rosenfield 1985). Seeing the child helps in other ways too. The fact that the psychologist has agreed to interview the child assures the much-harassed teacher that positive steps are being taken to remedy the problem. He may not feel as hopeless about the situation as he did before and, with some of the pressure taken off, he can perhaps deal with the situation in a more rational way, and is less likely to become impatient or irritable each time the child mildly or seriously deviates from acceptable forms of behaviour.

The first step in actually seeing the child is to ensure that the reason for interviewing him is carefully explained. Extreme caution is required in the way that this is handled. The child must not get the impression that the psychologist is simply partisan with the referrer. The impression that he should get is that the psychologist is willing to listen and accept his version of the problem as well. To achieve this goal the following procedure has often been adopted.

After the psychologist has been introduced to the child and left in a room with him, the conversation is initiated by asking if he knows why he is being seen. The answer often ranges from 'don't know' to an exact delineation of the problem. In cases where the child does not know (or professes not to know) the reason for being seen, this is explained in a careful and sensitive way, ensuring all along that he does not get the impression that he is being accused or criticized. At this stage, much broader terms should be used than those in which the child has been described by his teacher, as these could be hurtful or embarrassing. It is important to ask if what is said about him is 'fair' or correct in his view. If he regards it as unfair or incorrect, he should be encouraged to present his own version. At this time, the child's version is not questioned, challenged, or doubted.

Having thus allayed the child's anxiety as to why he is being seen, an attempt should be made to avoid any further discussion of sensitive issues. The main aim during the first meeting with the child is to build a warm, trusting relationship with him. The fostering of such a relationship is very important as it is at the heart of helping the child to modify his behaviour. Since this occupies a very central position, it is strongly recommended that one should not proceed further unless it is absolutely certain that the child feels that he has managed to establish a trusting relationship with the psychologist. In this context the authors take a very similar position to Rogers (1961; see also Axline 1964). In the words of Rogers, the relationship with the child should not be:

> as a scientist to an object of study, not as a physician expecting to diagnose and cure, but as a person to a person. It would seem that the therapist feels this client to be a person of unconditional self-worth, of value no matter what his condition, his behaviour or his feelings. It would mean that the therapist is genuine, not hiding behind a defensive façade, but meeting the client with the feelings the therapist is experiencing . . . and that he can convey something of his empathetic understanding to the client . . . [and that the therapist can provide] a climate which will permit the client the utmost freedom to be himself.
>
> (Rogers 1961: 185)

The time taken to establish such a relationship can vary from child to child. With one child, only one session may be necessary, while with another, more than one session may be required. In most cases, it does not seem to require more than one session.

Various strategies can be employed to achieve the required goal. During the warm-up phase of the interview, one could talk about the child's favourite hobbies or interests. Alternatively, or in addition, one could also ask the child about the things that he likes or dislikes, or that make him feel sad, angry and so on — both at school and at home. Two points worthy of note are that it is important to show a genuine interest when the child starts talking about his areas of interest, and that it is best not to touch on any sensitive or delicate issue at this stage.

The Mooney Problem Check-List (Mooney 1950) is a useful tool in helping the child to talk, in a non-threatening way, about the difficulties he is experiencing or perceives. The reader familiar with this check-list will know that it has 210 statements such as: 'Don't like school', 'Being jealous', or 'Too few nice clothes'. The directions for use are simple: 'Read the list slowly, and as you come to a problem which troubles you, draw a line under it'. At the end of the 210 statements, there are three open-ended questions. The check-list has been found to be non-threatening; the child feels less self-conscious and less reluctant to talk about himself. Once the check-list is completed, the problems underlined can be discussed at some length. As well as these strategies, tangible rewards can also be used. These may include sweets, chocolate, or some similar items. These strategies, designed to secure a trusting relationship with the child, are of course given only for illustrative purposes and are not prescriptive. What is being strongly advocated here is the forging of a trusting relationship which is considered to be a *sine qua non* in the paradigm that is being presented here.

Third stage: changing behaviours

Following the development of a trusting relationship, one can begin to discuss with the child the problems at school and his motivation to change. This motivation is an indirect index of his 'commitment to change'. In recent years, behaviourists have begun to appreciate the value of the client's commitment to change himself (e.g. Kanfer and Karoly 1972; cited in Davison and Neale 1974). Davison and Neale add that 'Even the most powerful change procedure will have limited effect on a person who is not resolved to use it' (1974: 501). Children who have been interviewed, following the procedure described above, have almost all shown ample keenness to change, and have displayed unhappiness and dissatisfaction with the status quo. With children who have a number of problems — which is almost invariably the case — a list of them should be drawn up. It is a useful strategy to discuss with the child whether he agrees with all the problems that the school claims he is presenting. Experience shows that a large majority of the children tend to 'own up' to the problems they present and offer explanations where they disagree (these can then be discussed with the school). In this way, the child's point of view is presented to the school and hopefully the mismatch between the teachers' and the child's perceptions is clarified.

Once all the problems have been listed, they should be put into order. The criterion used for ordering is the child's own perception of his difficulty level and his ability/motivation to change. Rarely should the child's judgement be influenced or questioned. Invariably the child is encouraged to decide which problem from the list should be tackled first. The reasoning here is that a child is more likely to persevere with and solve a problem which is reasonably manageable, than one which is intractable. If he is successful this will reinforce and motivate him to tackle with the next most difficult problem. It is useful to discuss with the child whether the target behaviour that he has agreed to modify is not too difficult to manage. This is important as little useful purpose would be served in asking the child to undertake a task in which he is likely to fail. Needless to say, failure to accomplish the goal would demotivate the child, and would reduce teachers' belief in the approach as well as their motivation to play an active role in the modification of the child's behaviour.

In addition it is also worthwhile to discuss with the child the strategies he is likely to employ to deal with the problem. For example, how would a child who has established a reputation as being a fighter/attacker, stop himself in a situation where he would previously have acted aggressively? If he did not stop himself, would he not be seen as a 'sissy'? One strategy offered by a child himself was that even if he were provoked he would ignore his provokers — and he was able to do so. It has already been indicated that involvement of the child in any behavioural change programme is the first stage towards securing his commitment to change, failing which any change is highly unlikely (Davison and Neale 1974). It is for this reason that at every stage of this programme so much emphasis has been placed on the child's involvement. Having thus discussed and mutually agreed on the behaviour which should be the target of change, the agreement can be formalized. One possibility is to write down what has been agreed between the child and the psychologist in some simple form such as:

I will try not to hit anybody.

Signed: (child) and (psychologist)
Dated:

A copy of this contract is given to the child and a copy is kept by the psychologist. It is worth pointing out that the operative word is 'try'; if the child fails to achieve what he originally set out to achieve, but has genuinely tried, he can still be rewarded for trying. Also, at this stage the child is deliberately not being asked to make a life-long commitment; it is effectively only for a week, when he will be seen again by the psychologist and the situation carefully reviewed. If necessary, amendments or adjustments can then be made in the contract. As soon as the child agrees to enter into a contract and undertakes to change, much verbal praise should be given as well as a small reward.

Prior to ending this session, two questions are worth checking with the child. First, would he like to be seen again? In the authors' experience, only one child has ever not shown keenness to be seen again. The next appointment is arranged for the following week at a time when he is not likely to miss his favourite lesson or activity. Second, the child's permission should be sought for the psychologist to report to his teachers on what has been agreed. This is to ensure that if teachers do observe any change in his behaviour they make positive comments. If the child agrees — and often he does — then it is brought to the attention of his teachers that he has agreed to do so-and-so, and that any observable change in the agreed behaviour should be rewarded. In addition, the school is also asked, provided the child has maintained his progress, to write a brief note at the end of the week to his parents expressing their approval and pleasure at what the child has been able to achieve. (As has been mentioned earlier, the note, which is meant to be reinforcing and positive, should not have negative or sarcastic undertones.)

The underlying rationale behind all this is the authors' concurrence with the theoretical stand-point that it is important to restore the positive regard of 'significant others' towards the child. The absence of such a regard can both distort his self-concept and cause severe difficulties in his adjustment (Rogers 1951). Cooley (1902) and Mead (1934) believe that the genesis of our self-perception lies in the views taken towards us by significant others in our social environment. Through a process of inferring the attitudes of others towards us, we eventually incorporate what we feel to be their views into our self-perception. The effect and the significance of other's perception on one's behaviour can be clearly witnessed in the following story (cited in Purkey 1970). Henry Carson was of average academic ability, but was diffident of himself and his abilities. Through sheer coincidence, a mouse accidentally triggered the apparatus while his data on a test were being scored. In consequence, he obtained a far higher score on a college entrance examination and exceeded everyone's expectations. When Henry Carson's brilliant performance became known to 'significant others', it resulted in their revising their opinions about him. As a result, the story goes, Henry Carson ended up as one of the best known men of his generation.

Sceptics could easily argue — and quite legitimately claim — that the Henry Carson story was just a freak and that the conception of self could not play such a vital role in academic performance. Although the story can easily be dismissed, the experimental evidence that has accumulated over the years of a significant correlation between positive self-concept and school achievement cannot be disregarded so readily (for details see Caplin 1966; Purkey 1968; Thomas 1973; Gergen 1971). This rationale does not appear to be inconsistent with the behaviourist approach towards behavioural change.

When the child is seen again, this time little time and effort are required to build rapport, as this has already been accomplished in previous sessions. One of the major goals of this stage is to check with the child as to how well he succeeded with his contract or the agreed task. It is worth asking the child if it was difficult to achieve what he had set out to accomplish. The child should then be asked if he genuinely tried not to indulge in the behaviours which he used to indulge in, and whether the teachers took note of it and made appropriate comments.

More often than not, children have a good 'go' at adhering to the contract. Thus they are rewarded if they have been successful, or have really tried but have encountered factors which have hindered their being fully successful. There can be times when the child may not have been successful. Under these circumstances, it is important to discuss with him the possible reasons which may have contributed to his failure. He should not get the impression from this discussion that he is being criticized for not being successful. Notwithstanding his failure, if he is willing to try again, the child is usually asked to have another 'go'. Conjointly with the child, a record of his success or failure is kept. The type of format shown has been found simple but useful.

Target Behaviour: (e.g. not hitting)

Date	*Successful*	*Partly successful*	*Not successful but tried*	*Not successful but tried hard*	*Not successful and only tried half-heartedly*	*Neither successful nor tried*
12/10 to 19/10						
19/10 to 26/10						

The child's full agreement is sought when keeping this type of record. The child should be promised that he will be seen the following week (or other appropriate period), when his progress will be reviewed.

Following this, the teachers concerned should be seen with a view to determining their responses to the child's behaviour and their observations of it. Several things need to be ascertained. First, have teachers noticed any improvements in the target behaviour? If so, have they remembered to reinforce it? Sometimes, as noted above, teachers tend to fear — though erroneously — that if they reward the child's desirable behaviours too soon he may revert to his old patterns of behaviour again. Unfortunately they tend to associate rewards — again mistakenly — with being 'soft', and feel they should not be given unless the child has demonstrated 'good' behaviour over a period of time. Second, have teachers managed to ignore those undesirable behaviours which it is possible to ignore?

Though apparently simple, it is surprising how long it takes teachers before they fully grasp the concept of ignoring undesirable behaviours and rewarding desirable ones (cf. Rosenfield 1985).

By the time the child has been seen two or three times on the lines described above, he often begins to show some improvements in his behaviour. It is important to reiterate here the importance of ensuring that all of those involved with the child are aware of what is happening the moment he begins to demonstrate any signs of improvement. Equally important is that those involved with the child do not become complacent over rewarding his desirable patterns of behaviour, irrespective of whatever procedure they have adopted. Once this stage has been reached (i.e. the child has started to show some noticeable improvements in his behaviour), then what remains to be done is essentially to carry on pursuing the procedure outlined above until the undesirable patterns of behaviours have been modified.

It is important to mention that one should not attempt to modify all unacceptable behaviours at the same time; nor should it be expected that all would change at once. However there is sometimes some positive 'spill-over' effect on other undesirable behaviours which have not been a target for modification. Once the behaviour begins to improve, and there is some consistency, the child can be seen fortnightly instead of weekly, and then once a month, and so on. When all the parties concerned, including the child himself, confirm that he no longer exhibits his old patterns of behaviour, seeing the child ceases, but before this happens, the psychologist should explain to the child that there is little further need for him to be seen since the reason for it does not exist any longer. However, it is not a bad idea to assure the child — and indeed all those who are involved with him — that should the psychologist's help be needed at any future date, they should not hesitate to contact him. What then remains to be done is to phone the school once in a while (say once in three months) to ensure that the desirable patterns of behaviour are still being maintained, and that the school has not started to ignore the child totally.

To summarize, after ensuring the referrer's co-operation and building rapport with the child, the key factor is to continue to see the child on a regular basis until the unwanted behaviours have been modified. Seeing the child entails discussing with him as to how he is getting on with what has been agreed between him and the psychologist. This may necessitate bringing about some changes in the contract; making a note on his contract about his success or failure; discussing with the teachers whether they have noticed any changes in the child's behaviour and gently reminding them of the importance of reinforcing desirable patterns of behaviour and ignoring, as far as possible, undesirable ones.

Case study

In order to illustrate and provide some support to the model, a case study is presented.[4] As only one of us (Gupta) was directly involved, the presentation uses the first person where appropriate.

The head-teacher of a large secondary school referred John as revealing several behaviour problems in school in previous weeks. He was an isolate in his peer group and tended to pick on other isolate children. He deliberately engineered situations so that he could get other children — particularly isolates — into trouble. He often truanted from school and despite their best efforts, the staff were unable to find reasons for this. Another problem was that of petty thieving. On one occasion he stole a number of articles from the chemistry laboratory; on another, over a number of days, he stole a quantity of felt-tip pens, pencils, and compasses and tried to plant them on another member of his form in order to incriminate him. According to John's father, he was a hoarder of trifles by nature. Of all the problems that he presented, both his parents and the school were most concerned about his habit of stealing, particularly that it might advance to more serious forms of theft. The school's impression of John's father was that he took a sound and keen interest in his boy and administered fair and reasonable corrective measures on him, and that the mother probably tended to spoil him so that he was led on occasions to play one parent off against the other. John was physically a small boy, who suffered from *diabetes insipidus*, a rare diabetic condition (which makes a patient very thirsty). Academically he was in the remedial class and his standard of work was not satisfactory: his last two reports were quite bad.

In line with the model described above, the first thing to do was to see the referrers to ensure their full co-operation, were it possible to help them to modify John's behaviour, and to make clear the demands that would be made on them. As it turned out, the school offered absolutely full co-operation.

Following this, John was seen. At the time of the first interview, he presented himself as a quiet, friendly, but quite nervous boy. Most of the time he rubbed his hands; there was a certain amount of tremor in them. As a rapport-building exercise — although this did not require much work as it was very easy to do — he was asked to complete the Mooney Problem Check-List (Mooney 1950). On this check-list, John underlined sixty-one problems which seemed to trouble him. He also indicated keenness to talk to someone about his problems.

Of the sixty-one problems that he underlined, twelve bothered him a lot, twenty-five bothered him quite a bit, and fourteen bothered him least. The ones which bothered him most were: being nervous, taking things too seriously, failing in so many things I try to do, trouble with arithmetic, being talked about, feelings too easily hurt, getting into trouble, needing to find a part-time job now, wanting to live in a different neighbourhood, deciding whether to go steady, getting into argument, not being as strong as other kids. It also emerged that one of his classmates, Paul, caused him considerable anxiety and unhappiness. During the interview, he burst into tears and asked that some of the problems should not be discussed with his parents. Under the question in the check-list 'What problems are troubling you most?', he particularly mentioned that he was bothered by his classmate Paul, and not being good at arithmetic. In view of John's eagerness to talk about his problems and the fact that it was so easy to build a working relationship with him, it was possible to discuss the two issues which seemed to be uppermost in his mind. While it required little effort to establish a rapport with him, this is not to imply that no further attempt was made during the interview to develop this relationship. It has been emphasized above that a warm, friendly, and trusting relationship is one of the essential features of this model.

It seemed quite apposite to start with the problem of petty thieving, since both the school and the parents were very concerned about this. During the first session, John entered into a contract that he would try not to steal — at least until he was seen again. The first session ended by giving him a small reward (a bar of chocolate) for being able to discuss his problems so openly and freely, and for entering into a contract. His permission was sought to mention to the head-teacher that he had agreed to try not to steal — at least until he was seen the next time. He was also asked if he was willing that I should discuss his difficulties with his classmate Paul and with maths with the head-teacher and ask him if something could be done about them. He was quite happy for me to raise these issues. Finally, he was asked if he would like me to see him again to discuss how things were with him. He agreed to this — in fact he was quite anxious to see me again.

Following this meeting with John, I saw Mr Fielding, the head-teacher. As promised to John, his difficulties with Paul and in maths were discussed. Mr Fielding knew that John was 'remedial', but he was not aware of the extent that these difficulties bothered him. Nor was he aware of the fact that John had a history of difficulty with maths since his junior school days. Mr Fielding agreed that he would look into both of these problems and would try to ensure that John got the right type of help for his maths and also that the teacher did not make unrealistic demands on him. Mr Fielding would also interview Paul to see what was happening between him and John. It was emphasized that Mr Fielding should inform all the teachers concerned about John's attempt at not stealing and also ask them that if they saw any change in his behaviour, they should make positive comments about it. Further, if at all possible, they should try not to be 'petty' with him. Finally, if by the end of the week there had been no incidence of stealing, the school should send a note home confirming this, and showing pleasure and approval

After a few days, and following the above discussion and advice, the parents were seen briefly. They were informed about all that had taken place and advised that they should also reward and praise John for his attempts at changing. During this meeting, John's parents informed me that they had three other older boys aged 14, 17, and 22. About John's early medical history, they said that when he was 10 months old he went into a coma for three days. The doctors at that time thought that he might die. They also said that John hated going to school. Of his interests, they said that he enjoyed history and sport, but was very behind with his maths — and they reiterated that he always had been.

These meetings were succeeded by a further appointment to see John after a week or so. When I saw him, the first thing he said was: 'I haven't stolen anything or told lies this week; I haven't truanted and haven't been in trouble with Paul either'. The behaviour was appropriately praised and rewarded. During the interview, John revealed that at one time he used to steal once or twice a week. However, he never used to steal in the junior school, but had started at his present school. He was asked if the target set for him to achieve had been difficult to accomplish, to which he replied 'no'. The interview with John was terminated with a further contract with him that he would refrain from stealing for another week or so. He promised that he would try to do so.

After having interviewed John, Mr Fielding was seen. On enquiry, he confirmed what John had told me at the interview. Mr Fielding also said that a letter had been sent to his parents about John's desirable behaviour in school. Mr Fielding added that other teachers had been quite sensitive over handling John.

On the third visit to school, Mr Fielding confirmed that during the second and third week, John had neither truanted nor had been in any trouble with any other boy. However, unfortunately, he had been involved in breaking into the school tuck-shop. Not only was John involved in this episode but also, according to Mr Fielding and his colleagues, John was the ring leader in this incident.

Armed with this somewhat disappointing information, John was seen again, as promised, for the third time. A lot of praise and encouragement was given for maintaining a regular attendance and for keeping out of trouble with other children. Shortly after, John volunteered to give his version of the stealing incident. According to John's account, he was bullied into taking part in this incident. The other children threatened that if he did not join them they would break his teeth. Shortly before the interview ended, John proffered an apology for taking part in the stealing incident and promised that in future he would definitely resist any bullying and avoid taking part in it. Were a similar situation to arise, rather than being intimidated, he would go and complain to Mr Fielding in future; John suggested this strategy himself. Again a lot of praise was given for volunteering to talk about the incident and for promising to refrain from taking part in future. As before, he was asked to continue to stay out of trouble, particularly with other children. He was also asked to continue to maintain progress with his school attendance. At the end of the session, he was promised that he would be seen again.

A passing comment is warranted here as to whether he was the ring leader in the stealing incident — the school's version of the story — or just bullied into taking part in it — John's account. My own impression was that it was hard not to accept John's version. John did not seem to have the personality attributes required to lead a gang of boys and to plan a break-in.

When after a fortnight John was seen again, he seemed happy and he remarked that he felt 'great'. He also added that he had not stolen anything, or hit Paul or truanted. Again he promised that he was going to try to maintain the progress that he had managed to achieve. As before, he received a lot of praise and a small reward for his excellent progress. However, during this interview he expressed concern that his new form-teacher was unaware of his medical condition, and did not realize that he needed drinks frequently and also needed to go to the lavatory regularly. He was assured that after the interview with him I would ask Mr Fielding if he could look into this matter. Before leaving him, I explained to him that I would not be seeing him as often as I used to in view of his overall improvement. I ended the interview by making arrangements to see him after two months. We also agreed that in the mean time I would be checking with the school about his progress.

After this interview when I saw Mr Fielding he confirmed that John had made good progress. I again emphasized the need to reinforce his good patterns of behaviour and to send notes to his parents on a regular basis about the excellent progress that he had been making. The importance of seeing him once in a while and praising him for what John had managed to achieve was also emphasized. In addition Mr Fielding was also asked if he could alert John's new form-teacher to his medical condition and to what it entailed.

Following this visit John and Mr Fielding were seen again after a two months' interval. During each of these visits, I was assured both by John and Mr Fielding that John no longer presented any of the problems for which he was originally referred. We concluded this case by agreeing that I would periodically phone to enquire whether he was still maintaining his progress. Follow-up phone calls confirmed that John had indeed maintained his behaviour changes and was no longer a 'problem boy'.

Conclusions

When reviewing the literature, evidence was presented which indicates not only that teachers show resistance against behavioural techniques, but also that

> some of those who attempt to use them give them up rather quickly, even when the techniques are working and the teacher has acknowledged that they are working. Behavioural consultants encounter teachers who refuse to continue behavioural techniques, saying that they were not really helping the child even though the child's behaviour had changed in the expected direction.
>
> (Rosenfield 1985: 153)

Fortunately the adapted behaviour modification model does not seem to suffer from the problems associated with traditional behaviour modification alluded to above. Clearly any claims made here, being based on personal experience with a reasonable but limited number of children, must be regarded as tentative and in need of further confirmation and research. However, it would appear that the adapted model has a number of advantages:

1 Above all, it is effective and helps to bring about changes in the desired direction, as our case study shows.
2 It has been found to be acceptable by all the teachers who were involved in trying to implement it in schools. Rarely did any teacher put up any 'barriers' against this model. Instead it ensured their full co-operation and support, since it did not make any unreasonable demands which are not manageable by teachers or which are in conflict with their belief system (cf. Rosenfield 1985; Huberman 1983).
3 A positive and highly satisfying by-product of the model is that it changes the teacher's perception of psychologists from impractical theory espousers to people who can help and advise them in modifying deviant and troublesome behaviours, given teachers' and parents' co-operation. With credibility gained, teachers are far more receptive to innovative ideas in other domains than they would otherwise be. It was apparent from their discussions about children that they had become far more positive in their interactions with them and

seemed to have begun to appreciate the value of listening sympathetically to children's difficulties and doing something about them. The pay-off is particularly rewarding for those psychologists whose preferred mode of working is the school-based consultancy model (for details of such a model see Burden 1978) rather than what is sometimes cynically described as 'the ''individual-child-crisis-type-referral system'' or ''motor-mechanic'' role that educational psychologists have been both trained for and expected to play in the past' (Burden 1978: 131).

4 Last, but not least, the adapted model also helps the practitioner to understand, in an applied setting, what makes a deviant child 'tick' — the traditional model does not present such an opportunity to study an individual child so closely.

In outlining the various benefits of the adapted model, the message is not that the traditional behaviour modification model should be abandoned in favour of the one presented here. Rather the intention is to make available to practitioners another approach which, in the authors' experience, is effective, acceptable, and appealing to teachers, in the hope that where traditional behaviour modification is not acceptable, this approach is likely to be.

Notes

1 'Traditional form of behavioural modification': a model which would include the following features:

1 choosing target behaviour,
2 observing the behaviour,
3 stating and evaluating your preliminary functional hypothesis with further behavioural observations, if necessary,
4 defining the target behaviour to be modified,
5 choosing a design for the demonstration of experimental control,
6 making base-line observations and plotting these on a graph,
7 assessing the reliability of your data,
8 specifying the treatment programme to be used,
9 conducting the treatment programme, keeping daily records of the child's behaviour,
10 demonstrating experimental control over the target behaviour,
11 phasing out the programme and, if possible, including procedures for increasing the durability and generalizability of treatment effects.

(For further details, see Gelfand and Hartmann 1975.)

2 The views expressed by us are our own and are not necessarily those of our respective employers.
3 See note 1.
4 For the sake of confidentiality, all the names in this case study have been changed.

References

American Psychological Association (1973) *Ethical Principles in the Conduct of Research with Human Participants*, Washington, DC: American Psychological Association.

Axline, V. (1964) 'The eight basic principles', in M. Haworth (ed.) *Child Psychotherapy*, New York: Basic Books.

Becker, W. C. (ed.) (1971) *An Empirical Basis for Change in Education: Selections on Behavioral Psychology for Teachers*, Chicago, Ill: Science Research Associates.

British Psychological Society (1985) 'A code of conduct for psychologists', *Bulletin of the BPS* 38: 41–3.

Burden, R. (1978) 'Schools' systems analysis: a project-centred approach', in B. Gillham (ed.) *Reconstructing Educational Psychology*, London: Croom Helm.

Caplin, M. D. (1966) 'The relationship between self-concept and academic achievement and between level of aspiration and achievement', *Dissertation Abstracts* 27: 979A.

Chazan, M. and Laing, A. F. (1985) 'Teachers' strategies in coping with behaviour difficulties in young children', *Maladjustment and Therapeutic Education* 3: 11–20.

Cooley, C. H. (1902) *Human Nature and the Social Order*, New York: Charles Scriber.

Davison, G. C. and Neale, J. M. (1974) *Abnormal Psychology: An Experimental Clinical Approach*, New York: Wiley.

Elliot, S. N., Witt, J. C., Galving, G. A., and Peterson, R. (1984) 'Acceptability of positive and reductive behavioral interventions: factors that influence teachers' decisions', *Journal of School Psychology* 22: 353–60.

Fargo, G. A., Behrns, C., and Nolen, P. (eds) (1970) *Behavior Modification in the Classroom*, Belmont, Calif: Wadsworth.

Gelfand, D. M. and Hartmann, D. P. (1975) *Child Behavior: Analysis and Therapy*, New York: Pergamon.

Gergen, K. J. (1971) *The Concept of Self*, New York: Holt, Rinehart, & Winston.

Gutkin, T. B. and Curtis, M. J. (1982) 'School-based consultation: theory and techniques', in C. R. Reynolds and T. B. Gutkins (eds) *The Handbook of School Psychology*, New York: Wiley.

Huberman, M. (1983) 'Recipes for busy kitchens', *'Creation, Diffusion, Utilization* 4, 4: 478–510.

Hyman, I. A. and Lally, D. (1982) 'A study of staff development programs for improving school discipline', *Urban Review* 14, 3: 181–96.

Kanfer, F. H. and Karoly, P. (1972) 'Self-control: a behaviouristic excursion into the lion's den', *Behaviour Therapy* 3: 398–416.

Kazdin, A. E. (1980) 'Acceptability of alternative treatments for deviant child behaviour', *Journal of Applied Behavior Analysis* 13: 259–73.

Kratochwill, T. R. and Someren, K. R. (1985) 'Barriers to treatment success in behavioral consultation: current limitations and future directions', *Journal of School Psychology* 23: 225–39.

Lambert, N. (1976) 'Children's problems and classroom interventions from the perspective of classroom teachers', *Professional Psychology* 7: 507–17.

Mead, G. H. (1934) *Mind, Self and Society*, Chicago, Ill: University of Chicago Press.

Meador, A. E. and Ollendick, T. H. (1984) 'Cognitive behaviour therapy with children: an evaluation of its efficacy and clinical utility', *Child and Family Behaviour Therapy* 6, 3: 25–44.

Meichenbaum, D. (1977) *Cognitive Behavior Modification: An Integrative Approach*, New York: Plenum Press.

Mooney, R. L. (1950), *Mooney Problem Check-List*, New York: Psychological Corporation.

O'Leary, K. D. and O'Leary, S. G. (1977) *Classroom Management: The Successful Use of Behavior Modification*, New York: Pergamon.

Presland, J. (1974) 'Modifying behaviour now', *Special Education: Forward Trends* 1, 3: 20–2.

Purkey, W. W. (1968) 'The search for self: evaluating students' self-concepts', in M. Argyle and V. Lee (1972) *Social Relationships*, Milton Keynes: Open University Press.

—— (1970) *Self-Concept and School Achievement*, Englewood Cliffs, NJ: Prentice-Hall.

Repucci, N. D. and Saunders, J. T. (1974) 'Social psychology of behaviour modification: problems of implementation in natural settings', *American Psychologist* 29: 649–60.

Rogers, C. R. (1951) *Client-Centered Therapy*, Boston, Mass: Houghton Mifflin.

—— (1961) *On Becoming a Person*, Boston, Mass: Houghton Mifflin.

Rosenfield, S. (1985) 'Teacher acceptance of behavioral principles: an issue of values', *TESE* 8, 3: 153–8.

Shapiro, E. S. and Lentz, F. E. (1985) 'A survey of school psychologists' use of behavior modification procedures', *Journal of School Psychology* 23: 327–36.

Tharp, R. G. and Wetzel, R. J. (1969) *Behavior Modification in the Natural Environment*, New York: Academic Press.

Thomas, J. B. (1983) *Self-Concept in Psychology and Education: A Review of Research*, Slough: NFER.

Ullman, L. P. and Krasner, L. (eds) (1965) *Case Studies in Behaviour Modification*, New York: Holt, Rinehart and Winston.

Winnett, R. A. and Winkler, R. C. (1972) 'Current behaviour modification in the classroom: be still, be quiet, be docile', *Journal of Applied Behaviour Analysis* 5: 499–504.

Chapter three

The role of the school consultant in dealing with behavioural problems

Carol Aubrey

Since the early 1950s management consultancy in industry, both in small firms and in large business organizations, has offered a professional service to assist in practical problem-solving in issues relating to organization policy and procedures, which hopefully leads to improved professional practice. Behind this service lies the assumption that an unsatisfactory condition exists which can be changed and improved.

Characteristics of a consulting service are

1 it is an independent service, provided by a change agent who enters a close, collaborative peer relationship with his client;
2 it is an advisory service, so responsibility for the competence and integrity of the advice is the consultant's, while responsibility for the ensuing change remains with the client;
3 it is a service which brings to bear a broad range of professional knowledge and skills, accrued from wide experience in a variety of settings, and informed by continued up-dating through research and observation of current methods and techniques;
4 it is a service whose successful completion and solution depends as much on the commitment of the client to the consultant–client relationship and to the agreed goal for change, as on the systematic problem-solving skills of the consultant.

Consultation can offer either an internal or external service. An internal consultant may be regarded as having a deeper appreciation of the organization and its complex, political relationships (and is cheaper!), while an external consultant may offer a great degree of objectivity and impartiality, or a specific expertise which is lacking in the organization. It is generally agreed that the consultant will take one of two specific roles: resource (or task) consultant or process consultant.

The *resource consultant* offers expert information and a service which leads ultimately to a change in performance of the organization or its subgroups. This assumes consultant expertise in the competent assessment of needs and the gathering of relevant information and observation, and consequent client implementation of his recommendations. It aims to bring about changes in the skills or understanding of organizational members, but does not have organizational development as a whole as the chief focus.

The *process consultant* is concerned to transmit his knowledge, techniques, and skills to the organization as a whole, to help it to take responsibility for its own problem-solving. This is achieved primarily through enabling the organizational groups or subgroups to become aware of, and to understand, the organizational processes and their consequences, in order to make the necessary adjustments that lead it to significant organizational change and development.

Two major aspects of the consulting relationship are

1 the analysis and solution of organization-related problems;
2 the relationship between the consultant and client, that is the organization which employs the service, or more specifically, the person who forms the personal relationship with the consultant.

Since change operates at four levels — level of knowledge, attitude, individual behaviour, and group or institutional performance — the consultant needs knowledge and skills in creating and developing interest in and gaining commitment to the implementation of change.

Existing use of consultation in education in UK

As Bell (1979) questioned, how much relevances has this for schools? He concluded that to the extent that there is very little scope within the British education system for the practice of buying in expert help — an outside, objective view of a specific problem — there is hardly any relevance. On the other hand, as he acknowledged, there are a few examples of this actually happening and certainly there is much lively discussion and debate about consultation and its utility, and some descriptions of existing practice.

Bolam (1978) suggested we have very little evidence of a systematic kind about the way in which educationalists are able to operate in a consultancy role. He examined two major potential sources of consultants — local authority advisers and college of education staff and their equivalents. He concluded that there were constraints for both of these sources. Advisers were in a superordinate role, which made it difficult to work together with school departments to help them to establish their own problem-solving and decision-making procedures. College of education staff, he felt, lacked credibility to teaching staff and heads and in any case while potentially they had time available, staff employment had to be justified primarily in terms of student–staff contact teaching hours. A third constraint, he noted, applied equally to advisers, university staff, or other potential consultants such as teachers and head-teachers: none has much experience of the role or of carrying it out.

Eraut (1977) pointed to two further aspects of the role of consultant in supporting school-based, in-service education, both concerning a consultant's credibility. First, there is the power and authority gap between teachers and providers; and second, there is an epistemological and communication gap. While the teacher thinks and talks about his profession and teaching in a mode which is both particularized and prescriptive, since this is what the role demands, those outside education, in this case consultants, avoid this.

Golby and Fish (1980) have enlarged on the 'largely unacknowledged set of complexities relating both to the identities and roles of the clients and to the vulnerabilities and strengths of the consultants — and vice versa!' Essential is the specification of roles, rights, and responsibilities:

> The LEA adviser . . . is certainly a powerful figure, but his recommendations come with political overtones and he is often interested in defending and promoting one curriculum area. . . . The curriculum consultant . . . has none of the adviser's power,

> has no curriculum territory to police and might enter fewer schools but probably enters them more often. . . .
> The lone, ex-head freelance might bring knowledge of past practice but outside any educational community might have limited access to new thinking. . . .
> The academic must be able to defend his interest not only in terms of the help he can give but in terms of what can be learned . . . from his reported experience.

In spite of such reservations, existing descriptions of school consultation in the UK have come from college of education staff and university academics working in the role of external consultant to individual schools or groups of schools. One of the best-known and earliest accounts of consultation in school is Richardson's (1973) account of her role as process consultant to the head-teacher and staff of Nailsea School, near Bristol, during its transition and expansion from an old grammar school into a comprehensive school. She regarded her task as studying the management of change through the interpersonal and intergroup behaviour of staff, and to help teachers gain a deeper understanding of these relationships. Her account comprises a piece of narrative, with glimpses of life in school, staffroom, and head-teacher's room, though she never visited a lesson and scarcely spoke to a child or parent. Data recording was highly personal and accounts of staff meetings and interviews with groups or individual staff members, apart from occasional jottings of dates or brief facts, or tape-recorded impressions and memories, were written up as soon as possible after the events. These data formed the raw material of both her book and outcome report, in the style of 'illuminative evaluation' (Parlett and Hamilton 1976). The methodology is borrowed from social anthropology and Richardson, as participant observer, described the operation of change on the context, organization, and practices of Nailsea School, the problems encountered, and the solutions developed, from various viewpoints, as well as the outcomes obtained.

Day (1984) described his external resource or task consultancy as being to support school-based curriculum development, in this case, in a project designed to enhance and monitor progress of children in seven first schools, involving parents in the reading process. The external consultant took overall responsibility for managing and evaluating the project in collaboration with heads and participating teachers, within the framework of 'action research' or case study (Cohen and Manion 1980). This seeks to describe the whole context, combining the use of traditional data collection as appropriate (in this case pre- and post-testing in reading and word recognition) with descriptive data of the illuminative type to report on the process, using such sources as information concerning the responses of pupils and parents. The writing of the evalutation report was co-ordinated by the consultant, who also conducted interviews with teachers and provided administrative support.

Shorter accounts include Collier's (1978) account of her role as process consultant to a British ex-patriate school. Her brief was to provide INSET education and training for the staff of the primary school, particularly the junior section for 7–11-year-olds and, like Richardson, Collier adopted the role of participant observer to assess the needs and analyse the organization-related problems of the primary school. This meant that evaluation goals involved not only descriptions of existing educational goals, settings, and personnel, but also judgements on the quality and appropriateness of these goals.

In addition to providing modelling of some group project work for groups of junior teachers, which resulted in eight weeks' in-service training (INSET) for twelve teachers, data were collected from sitting in on the whole school time-table for the first four weeks, talking to teachers, checking on aims, types of instruction, materials, modes of discipline and control, and responses of children and assessing the general atmosphere of the school. Tasks with the head-teacher, the bursar, the master in charge of discipline and with members of staff were initiated, minutes of staff meetings examined and other school documents were read as part of her goal of studying the existing school organization and practices. This lead to the high-lighting of four organization-related problems: the need for a better co-ordinated school policy, lack of continuity and disparity in staff qualifications, poor command of English language among the pupils and the isolation of the school from broad changes in educational thinking in the western world. The consultant claimed the enterprise was successful on the basis that the main recommendations in respect of policy change were implemented and that class teachers were seen to adopt the project work on the lines suggested, but acknowledged that longer-term success would be better judged in terms of effects after one year, or even after five years.

Murgatroyd and Reynolds (1984) described process consultation in two Welsh schools, one a state school and one a private school. No details were given of the observation, discussion, and analysis of the identified organization-related problems, nor of the subsequent intervention, monitoring, or evaluation of ensuing change.

Hopkins and Vickers (1986) described process consultation for a school self-evaluation project, in this case as a means of developing team-building, problem-solving skills, and action planning with a school staff. Their account includes a one-day workshop design with related experiential learning activities, their conclusion being that process consultation is a necessary adjunct to many educational innovations. The evaluation was in the form of a sentence completion task starting with the words, 'One thing I have learned . . .' completed by course members.

Hanko (1987) discussed the use of one year's school-based resource or task consultancy group work with up to fifty teachers for disruptive or disturbed children in six urban primary schools which aimed to offer assistance with management difficulties, together with long-term development and training in respect of wider issues. Weekly meetings of up to twelve members for each site, with one or two core school members who came for a year, plus many more short-term members, were set up to explore day-to-day difficulties presented by the children. As one teacher presented a case, the group would identify problems, look for alternative, action-related and workable solutions which were then tested out. This helped teachers appreciate how their understanding of individual children related to the learning dynamics of the whole class group and increased their skills in gaining support from parents. Consultant questioning was framed to focus on wider, underlying issues and to aid teachers in increasing their own means of interviewing to improve student learning. Thus with a minimum of factual input, a balance between consultant input and the judicious use of joint exploration was maintained with staff from infant to secondary school level. A course questionnaire monitored the usefulness of exploring other teachers' cases and, over a period of time, self-monitoring skills were reported to become more discernible, with a shift from a crisis-oriented concern to a more preventive awareness. Head-teachers confirmed, too, a raised professionalism in staffroom talk in general and more active participation at interprofessional clinic conferences. A long-term effect was the working out of plans by core members of all six schools to continue the support group for further staff the following year with only occasional attendance of the outside consultant. Also a number of schools applied to participate in the writer's subsequent investigation into the usefulness of consultancy provision.

As noted earlier, the accounts of school consultation come from university or college of education staff but not from school psychologists. Equally, it is interesting to note that the main constraints for the two major sources of consultants — lack of time, lack of credibility, and inability to work in a peer relationship of co-ordinate status with school staff — do not hold true for the local authority psychologist who, in many ways, is in an eminently suitable position for school consultation. As noted by Aubrey (1987), while management courses for school personnel, further education and local authority administrators and managers flourish and expand, utilizing relevant cognitive, behavioural and social psychological theory, and knowledge of organization development and change to create effective training goals, British psychologists do not receive adequate education and training in the form of a requisite knowledge base from a variety of domains together with necessary practical skills which would be needed to provide a flexible and comprehensive consultation service.

US school consultancy

By contrast, in the USA it is in the field of school psychology, particularly over the last ten to fifteen years, that models of school-based consultation have been used to describe a variety of goals and processes, developed in response to frustration with the short-comings of traditional modes of work, which have increasingly come to take a central place in training and practice. The need for new roles and practices for the US school psychologist has been described extensively and similar concerns have been expressed in the British literature over a similar period of time:

1 individual case work with children was neither effective nor cost-effective;

2 testing alone was liable to lead to classification and labelling rather than effective intervention;
3 the psychologist could contribute little to broader change in professional skills and techniques at classroom or school level while operating within an individual case model.

By contrast, consultation offered an *indirect* service provided by the consultant to someone else, the teacher or parent (the consultees), in *direct* contact with the child (client) displaying the problem. Thus it could apply as well to services offered to *groups* and as such was suitable for school-based, in-service training of teachers. Consultation is now regarded as one of the central roles rendered by the school psychologist. In a national survey Smith and Lyon (1985) discovered that 24 per cent of school psychological time was actually spent on consultation with significantly more time (40 per cent) desired for this activity.

Models which are described in the literature and most used by school psychologists are the mental health, organization development, and behavioural consultation models. Some writers include the problem-solving model but arguably, in a sense, all consultation models may be regarded as problem-solving models since there is a problem-solving sequence which is generally agreed will generate the best solution to a presenting problem for consultant and consultantee.

The type of service provided in the mental health and behavioural consultation models is not dissimilar to resource or task consultation or business consultation, which aims to bring about changes in the knowledge, attitude, or behaviour of individuals and groups, whereas organization development consultation, with the focus on organizational change through work with groups and subgroups in the organization, is a process consultation. These different models of school psychology consultation have different theoretical frameworks, different typical problems and applications, different intervention methods and goals, and different criteria for judging effective outcomes.

The earliest and best known model, *mental health consultation*, is associated with Caplan (1979). It was developed outside the context of school psychology, chiefly by clinical psychologists, in a move towards providing comprehensive community mental health services. This took place at a time of shift in emphasis towards *prevention* rather than treatment of mental illness which, in any case, was considered ineffective. The major goal is to help the consultee gain more insight into the emotional development and personality dynamics of clients. Most frequently, consultations involve consultee difficulties in affective relationships with children, through lack of knowledge, skills, or understanding or lack of professional objectivity. Caplan considered lack of professional objectivity or 'theme interference', as the result of over-involvement or distorted perception, to be the main reason for consultee difficulty. Strategies which Caplan offered to help resolve theme interference have lacked empirical support and behaviourally oriented psychologists have been more inclined to redefine the problem in observable, measurable terms amenable to intervention.

Behavioural consultation is associated with applied behavioural analysis techniques owed originally to Skinner (1953) and more recently to the social learning theory of Bandura (1977). Dissatisfaction with traditional psychometric and psycho-dynamic assessments and the effectiveness of behavioural interventions has led to their wide application in educational settings. Typically the goal of behavioural consultation is to assist the teacher in introducing specific changes in the classroom setting in order to modify learning or behavioural problems. Bergan (1977), whose name is associated particularly with this model, identified four stages of intervention:

1 problem identification,
2 problem analysis,
3 plan implementation,
4 problem solution.

The *organizational development consultation* model has its origins in the work of Kurt Lewin and the social psychology of group processes. It is closely linked to industrial psychology in terms of its emphasis on process strategies and goals for change. Its utilization in school psychology is associated particularly with Schmuck and Miles (1971; Schmuck *et al.* 1977) who emphasized change and improvement in school climate and organization to facilitate change and development as being essential to educational innovation. The primary goal is to increase the effectiveness of the functioning of school systems through open communication, the setting of organizational goals, and the use of group consensus, effective leadership in decision-making and conflict resolution.

The intervention procedures for the different models differ widely. Mental health consultation, which attempts to increase the insight and skills of the consultee, may use discussion with the consultee, group meetings where selected cases, or problems of concern are discussed, or even workshop/lecture settings where information and activities are presented by the consultant. In each case the aim of the intervention is to increase the sensitivity and understanding of the consultees, and the evaluation of feeling and concern about the children involved. The techniques used in organization development consultation utilize group training processes incorporating a variety of exercises and simulations to improve communication skills, negotiation of goals, identification and resolution of conflict, and practice of skills in conducting effective meetings. The consultant, here, acts as facilitator or catalyst but resists assuming a direct, expert role. In behaviour consultation, the intervention seeks to make some change or modification in the context or consequences of the problem behaviour, agreed between consultant and teacher. The process proceeds through a series of well-defined stages — problem definition, collection of base-line data, intervention, continued data collection and subsequent evaluation.

The effectiveness of school consultation

In terms of outcome, all three models have long-term criteria for success in increasing the consultee's competency to deal with similar problems. In mental health consultation, success will be judged on self-report or unstructured observation. Organization development consultation will use self-report supplemented by oberservation. Behavioural consultation will use objective, charted data showing base-line, pre-intervention data together with post-intervention rates or durations of problem behaviour. Medway (1979) in a review of research 1972–7 showed that behavioural consultation was particularly effective and had most empirical support. Medway and Forman (1980) found teachers preferred behavioural consultation, though psychologists regarded mental health consultation as more effective. While there is general agreement on the effectiveness of behavioural consultation, a basic problem with mental health consultation and organization development consultation is to determine whether increased understanding and insight generalizes to other situations, or whether improved interpersonal and organizational processes actually lead to improved learning experience for children.

Evidence from the USA indicates clearly that school consultancy as a response to behaviour problems in schools has proved effective. A recent national survey recording professional school psychology activities for one day by Lacayo *et al.* (1981) showed a third of time was spent on consultation activities. Fairchild (1976) compared two models — the traditional, clinical child assessment and the school-based consultation — in terms of the number of days between referral and follow-up and in terms of effectiveness, and found that on both counts consultation was more satisfactory. As mentioned earlier, the indirect service delivery model which allows time to be spent with consultees rather than clients is cost-effective, since it is beneficial that time is focused on the consultee who has most direct professional client contact and there may even be preventive implications since, in the long term, skills well-learned and insights gained may generalize to other clients. Supporting this rationale of maximum effectiveness, impact, and prevention, Ritter (1978) studied the effects over a seven-year period and found decreasing referrals over time with a consultation service, indicating that teachers were, in fact, increasing their own skills and techniques in dealing with clients.

Tyler and Fine (1974) and White and Fine (1976) showed that consultees preferred intensive involvement with the consultant while carrying out a mutually agreed intervention to ensure unforeseen obstructions could be tackled when they arose.

Wise (1979), examining the teachability of eleven consultative-related skills, found verbal skills to be the highest. Interpersonal and communication skills essential to effective consultation are relationship-building techniques of warmth, empathy, and genuineness. Engaging the active involvement of the consultee is a central element in successful consultation and as most teachers have received no training in consultation, they may, if not carefully prepared, look for a more dependent relationship and resent a consultant who seeks shared responsibility and mutual problem-solving rather than offering quick solutions which do not actively involve the teacher. Weissenburger *et al.* (1982) found the consultant's facilitativeness to be the main predictor of successful outcome.

The range and scope of problems

Consultation problems can be characterized as corrective, progressive, or creative.

Corrective problems

Corrective problems present the consultant with a *deteriorated* situation which needs ameliorating or correcting, in fact, troubleshooting. Such a chronic problem might involve the use of the techniques of applied behavioural analysis (behavioural consultation) to *increase* observable social or academic behaviours by the use of praise, modelling, establishing clear rules and shaping by reinforcing progressive approximations to the target behaviour, token reinforcement, self-specification and reinforcement. It might involve such techniques to *reduce* undesirable behaviours by extinction through ignoring, reinforcing incompatible, acceptable behaviours, 'time out' or withdrawal from social reinforcement, removal of privileges, self-instruction and self-evaluation or relaxation for anxieties or fears. Alternatively social skills training could be used to help socially isolated or rejected children to increase their initiating interactions by reinforcement.

In addition to ABA techniques, a variety of counselling techniques (mental health consultation) have been developed which seek to allow children to understand and gain better control over their emotions. Dreikurs (1968) showed teachers ways to determine the purpose of student behaviours by analysing their goals and the effects these have on the teacher. He suggested ways for teachers to use this to help children overcome the need to continue such behaviours.

Morse (1971) used the 'life space interview' where teachers and students worked to gain understanding of the meaning of troublesome incidents in order to seek ways of identifying and preventing the problem recurring.

Glasser (1969) described five steps for using 'reality therapy' — the three Rs: act responsibly, reasonably, and morally right — to achieve success and a feeling of self-worth by active listening. These were

1 get involved — be personal and friendly
2 emphasize present behaviour and consequences
3 help the student make a value judgement about his undesirable behaviour which suggests he has control and the responsibility to change his behaviour
4 help the student make a workable plan of action
5 get a commitment from the student — a signature, hand shake, contract — to fulfil the plan.

Gordon (1974) discussed the need to analyse the extent to which the teacher and pupil 'owned' the problem and showed how active listening could help teachers and students achieve a rational view of the problems and adopt a problem-solving attitude (problem-solving consultation).

Progressive problems

Progressive problems present the consultant with the task of working on and improving an existing condition. Consultation for this problem involves offering the institution a means of becoming more effective with the aid of realistic targets, which could involve potentially a range of technological, administrative, financial, or personnel changes. In the context of behaviour problems it is most likely that the targets of change will be school personnel. The consultant will have models and strategies for creating a more effective learning environment which will prevent most disruptive behaviours from occurring. The main task will be to examine the existing conditions, decide on appropriate input, and train staff in those more effective strategies in areas which it has been mutually agreed will be beneficial. These might include

1 teacher managing behaviours
2 teacher communication/interpersonal skills
3 teacher skills in presenting instructional materials or ordering learning
4 teacher–pupil relationships

Teacher managing behaviours

These involve not only appropriate curriculum planning and pacing to ensure children are successfully engaged in academic tasks, but also communicating and teaching effectively a set of workable rules and routines for classroom behaviour. Brophy and Putnam (1979) showed how classrooms which use these techniques function well as a result of careful planning at the beginning of the year, in terms of available space, storage of equipment and children's belongings and furniture, and planning paper flow and traffic patterns in advance.

Emmer *et al.* (1980) showed how smooth-flowing routines, rules, and procedures for room management were taught, practised, and further reinforced, where necessary. Kounin (1970) described how well-managed classrooms functioned through constant teacher attention to creating, maintaining, and re-training to provide conditions for efficient learning. Transitions were clearly signalled, cued, and taught so that children knew where to go and what to do with what equipment. Wragg (1981) noted that competent teachers began lessons at a brisk pace with a clear beginning and ending and thus pupils were certain about teacher expectation for task and behaviour. Kounin (1970) suggested that successful managers were distinguished by their strategies for minimizing disruption, for instance, 'with-it-ness', or vigilance in pupil monitoring, and 'overlapping', or managing to attend to more than one matter at a time, thus maintaining lesson momentum.

Teacher communication/interpersonal skills

The assumption here is that the effective teacher is not only an organizational leader for instruction, but also an authority figure. Wragg (1981), comparing student and experienced teachers, described how skilled teachers established dominance in the early days. Robertson (1981) drew attention to both verbal and non-verbal behaviour, which is significant in establishing teacher control and authority and sustaining attention through effective communication.

Teacher skills in presenting instructional materials

Again, Kounin (1970) suggested effective lessons provided variety and challenge in independent 'seat work'. More recent work has suggested learning is most effective when students have high levels of success in academic tasks, at least 70–80 per cent when teachers are present to monitor (Brophy and Evertson 1976) and 95–100 per cent for independent work or homework.

Studies have shown teachers can be trained to increase academic achievement or engaged time. Rosenshine's (1983) review of studies suggested teachers are most effective when they

1 structure the learning
2 proceed in small steps but at a brisk pace
3 give detailed and redundant instructions and explanations
4 provide many examples
5 ask a large number of questions and provide overt, active practice
6 provide feedback and corrections, particularly in the initial stages of learning new material
7 have a student success rate of 80 per cent or higher in initial learning
8 divide 'seat work' assignments into smaller assignments
9 provide for continued student practice so that students have a success rate of 90–100 per cent and become rapid and confident.

Teacher–pupil relationships

In respect of the teacher as a manager of group relationships, skills have been identified which increase the teacher's group leadership role. Reynolds (1976; Reynolds and Sullivan 1979) showed the effectiveness of giving pupils leadership responsibility. The teams-games-tournaments (TGT) approach enables members to contribute to team points awarded on a previously designed handicapping system for independent activities (Slavin 1980). This has positive effects both inside the classroom and out.

Training consultants for corrective and progressive problems

In-service training and workshop activities offer an effective means of introducing consultation to school staff and serve to produce the means for active skill development. Without training teachers will be without the necessary skills and knowledge to become effective and actively involved consultees who are prepared and ready to take part in conjoint problem-solving, to take responsibility for under-

Table 3.1 Consultation training

Friday Evening 6–9 p.m.

1. Introduction and Overview 6–7 p.m
   a. what is a consultation?
   b. why do it?
   c. how is it different from and better than other service delivery strategies?

7:00–7:15 p.m. Break

2. Models of Consultation 7:15–8 p.m.
   a. what is a model?
   b. mental health consultation
3. Demonstration Role-Plays 8–9 p.m.
   a. trainer with volunteer
   b. groups of 4

Saturday Morning 9 a.m.–12 noon

1. Listening Skills 9–10 a.m.
   a. reflect
   b. paraphrase
   c. summarize
   d. elaborate
   e. clarify
2. Feedback Skills 10–11 a.m.
   a. giving
   b. receiving

10:30–10:45 a.m. Break

3. Sample Methodology 11 a.m.–12 noon
   a. i.d. problem [identify problems]
   b. analyse problem — ABCs of behaviour
   c. generate solutions
   d. implementation
   e. evaluation

12 noon–1:30 p.m. Lunch

Saturday Afternoon 1:30–5 p.m.

1. Continue with Sample Methodology 1:30–2:15 p.m.
2. Sample Role-Plays 2:15–3:45 p.m.
   a. trainer with volunteer
   b. groups of 4
   c. problem-solving sessions

3:45–4:00 p.m. Break

3. Barriers to Implementing a Consultation Programme
   a. personal
   b. organizational

Source: Conoley and Conoley 1982: 142.

taking the agreed intervention and to provide the necessary data and monitoring for assessing programme effectiveness in dealing with the corrective problem.

On the other hand training for progressive problems will entail transmission of an organized body of research and information; appropriate audio-visual material to provide demonstrations of good practice; a sequence of techniques and activities for role-playing and simulation to give practice in skill development and feedback within the context of a small group; and opportunities for generalization of skills learned to classroom contexts.

Training procedures for school consultation borrow techniques and simulations from organization development consultation methods. These include techniques of active listening — acknowledging, paraphrasing, and summarizing, questioning to clarify and elaborate, giving and receiving positive and negative information in a tentative and non-judgemental way, which serve to highlight inaccuracies and inconsistencies in the consultee's perception, or to describe the behaviour of the consultee which appears to be impeding the consultancy process. Conoley and Conoley (1982) offered a useful illustration of a training programme in consultation (see Table 3.1).

Creative problems

These arise in a situation where no corrective or progressive problems present themselves to the consultant and no immediate intervention is required to increase output or performance, but where there is a feeling that the performance of the system as a whole could be enhanced and where potential exists for harnessing energies for organization development effort (organization development consultation). Here the consultant and consultee — and ultimately the whole school staff — will collaborate to improve organizational functioning by concentrating on interactional patterns, leadership, and communication which interfere with task performance.

The intervention focuses on group and sub-system dynamics, and on formal and informal norms and structures, and has the goal of planned effort at school self-study and improvement, or enhanced performance. With the rate of organizational and curriculum change in our educational system over the last ten years or so, it seems unlikely that this model will be much taken up and requested in schools. However, in a climate of increasing educational accountability and organized in-school review or self-evaluation, the technicians involved may prove valuable to staff in self-evaluating institutions. As acknowledged earlier, Hopkins and Vickers (1986) described development of skills such as team-building and problem-solving as part of their involvement in a school self-evaluation project.

The work of Schmuck *et al.* (1977) is a key to this model and their handbook gives detailed information on simulations and training procedures used to develop process skills. Appropriate activities and exercises are found in the series of annual Handbooks for Group Facilitators by Pfeiffer and Jones (1969 *et seq.*).

Application of the role of internal consultant

So far all the applications described have involved external consulting, where consultants are fully independent and autonomous experts from outside the organization.

By contrast, internal consultants already have an appreciation of the structures, organizational procedures, and formal and informal groupings and provided they have credibility in the eyes of the staff through both expert and referent power, internal consultants will be a valuable resource for consultation with respect to both short- and long-term problems.

In the UK typically it has been the educational psychologist who has advised schools about corrective and progressive behaviour problems, at least for the more disruptive and disturbing pupils who require more individualized and intensive intervention. The newer, applied behavioural interventions have offered opportunities for application in a variety of settings and psychologists' work has increasingly emphasized problem-solving strategies and clearly formulated objectives for observing and measuring behaviours. Such procedures have proved simple enough to be passed on to a range of professions who can obtain significant changes in academic and social skills. Individual preference and theoretical orientation will influence the type and extent of individual counselling which takes place, and the amount of involvement in school-wide strategies will depend on local policy and personal skills or preference. Although such material as PAD (Preventive

Approaches to Disruption) (Tweddle 1986) covers a range of procedures and strategies at the level of classroom management and lesson organization and some school-level considerations, psychologists in the main do not tackle creative problems or process consultation.

When the writer was asked to set up a part-time master's degree course in learning and behaviour problems in the secondary school from a systems perspective for experienced and senior staff, this offered an opportunity to prepare students for the role of internal consultant. The students, as agents of change, could adopt a problem-solving model to investigate corrective and progressive problems in their own school. The course had a traditional focus on institutional change and it was proposed that it should have two basic aims:

1 to obtain personal change in the individual student in terms of cognitive, behavioural, and affective/interpersonal skills;
2 to obtain institutional change in the student's 'home' school organization, in terms of an identified policy or procedure in respect of management of behaviour problems in schools.

Cognitive goals were to present students with a knowledge base drawn from a range of disciplines: organizational psychology, social psychology, sociology, applied behavioural analysis, programme planning and evaluation, organization development, management theory, and educational research.

Goals for behavioural change were to provide students with practical skills in applied behavioural analysis, classroom management and organization, social skills training, and counselling in the context of the use of tutorial time.

Goals for development of interpersonal skills included using strategies and simulations for effective communication, team building, problem-solving, uncovering and managing conflicts, decision-making and procedures for conducting effective meetings. These ensured students were equipped to deal with corrective, progressive, or creative problem-solving and as agents of change could assume the role of resource or process consultant in order to identify strengths and weaknesses in the home or school institution, and key problems which were hindering self-renewal and development.

This model of training, which supplements more established approaches to dealing with children and groups with involvement in school organizational change and development, owes much to Maher and Illback (1982a; 1982b), who attempted to provide an overview for the new conceptual and practical issues of organizational school psychology. Their model assumes that the school organization as consultee is instrumental in meeting the needs of the primary clients, or pupils. The primary task of organizational school development is the improvement of the school's policies, procedures, programmes, and practices so as to improve its performance in delivering appropriate education to all children.

Within this framework the school organization is defined in terms of an educational service delivery system organized in terms of five interrelated service units. Each unit comprises a service programme provided by service personnel.

1 The assessment service unit is concerned with screening and pre-placement testing programmes.
2 The instructional service unit is concerned with educational and instructional programmes in curriculum areas, such as mathematics or English.
3 The related service unit in the UK is probably concerned with pastoral, curriculum, and tutorial work.
4 The administrative service unit is concerned with pupil data, and with the organization and management of records and profiles.
5 The personnel development service unit is concerned with staff development and in-service training programmes.

The organizational school psychologist, or consultant, assists staff, management, and parents to identify priority needs and concerns related to the service units and then develops policies, procedures, or programmes that will enhance the identified concern.

In terms of education and training a range of performance evaluation methods have been used to assess the development of the cognitive, behavioural, affective, and interpersonal skills needed for organizational school psychology or consultancy, including the use of goal attainment scales as part of supervisory feedback to check progress in specific professional skills, the use of survey or questionnaire feedback from course work, and the use of behavioural contracts.

This account can do no more than serve as an introduction to consultation as a means of dealing effectively with behaviour problems in schools, and the variety of roles and activities available, each with its own methods, goals, and interventions.

Turning now specifically to the future role of consultancy as a response to behaviour problems in schools, we see on the one hand, classroom research over the last ten to fifteen years yielding accurate and detailed information about how competent teachers organize and manage their classrooms, and on the other hand, we know that few teachers have pre- or in-service training for effective classroom management or for coping with problem children or behaviour. At best the successful teachers often develop their own unsystematic 'tool bag' of 'tricks' gained through experience and trial-and-error learning, which is often difficult to describe accurately or to generalize consistently. This practice takes place in the UK in the context of the 1981 Education Act which has gone so far as to abolish all the old categories of special educational need, including maladjustment, leaving a single category based on the child's having significantly greater difficulty in learning than the majority of children of the same age. This suggests that behaviour difficulties warrant specific attention only when learning has been dramatically affected, while all the literature suggests that competent teachers are distinguished less by their responses to problem behaviour than by their skills in *preventing* it occurring.

If grant-maintained schools opt out of local authority control, school managers in the UK will be increasingly in a position to

> buy in the advisory services and in-service training either from their local education authorities — or from consultants of their own choosing.
>
> (*Times Educational Supplement*, 31 July 1987: 2)

References

Aubrey, C. (1987) 'Training for the role of school consultant as a means of dealing with behaviour problems in schools', *Educational and Child Psychology* 4: 14–29.

Bandura, A. (1977) *Social Learning Theory*, Englewood Cliffs, NJ: Prentice-Hall.

Bell, L. A. (1979) 'A discussion of some of the implications of using consultants in schools', *British Educational Research Journal* 5, 1: 55–62.
Bergan, J. (1977) *Behavioural Consultation*, Columbus, Ohio: Charles Merrill.
Bolam, R. (1978) 'School focused INSET and consultancy', *Educational Change and Development* 1, 1: 26–60.
Brophy, J. and Evertson, C. (1976) *Learning from Teaching: A Developmental Perspective*, Boston, Mass: Allyn & Bacon.
Brophy, J. and Putnam, J. (1979) 'Classroom management in the elementary grades', in D. Duke (ed.) *Classroom Management*, 78th Yearbook of the National Society for the Study of Education, pt 2, Chicago, Ill: University of Chicago Press.
Caplan, G. (1970) *The Theory and Practice of Mental Health Consultation*, New York: Basic Books.
Cohen, L. and Manion, L. (1980) *Research Methods in Education*, London: Croom Helm.
Collier, K. G. (1978) 'School-focused INSET: Questions posed by a three-month consultancy', *British Journal of In-Service Education*, 5, 1: 43–9.
Conoley, T. C. and Conoley, C. W. (1982) *School Consultation: A Guide to Practice and Training*, New York: Pergamon.
Day, C. W. (1984) 'External consultancy: supporting school-based curriculum development', in P. Holly and D. Whitehead (eds) *Classroom Action Research Network*, Bulletin 6, Cambridge Institute of Education.
Dreikurs, R. (1968) *Psychology in the Classroom: A Manual for Teachers*, 2nd edn, New York: Harper & Row.
Emmer, E., Evertson, C., and Anderson, L. (1980) 'Effective management at the beginning of the school year', *Elementary School Journal* 80: 219–31.
Eraut, M. (1977) 'Some perspective on consultancy in in-service education', *British Journal of In-Service Education* 4, 1–2: 95–9.
Fairchild, T. N. (1976) 'School psychological services: and empirical comparison of 2 methods', *Psychology in the Schools* 13, 2: 156–62.
Glasser, W. (1969) *Schools without Failure*, New York: Harper & Row.
Golby, M. and Fish, M. A. (1980) 'School-focused INSET: clients and consultants', *British Journal of In-Service Education* 4, 1–2: 83–8.
Gordon, T. (1974) *TET: Teacher Effective Training*, New York: McKay.
Hanko, G. (1987) 'SITE Project: Consultancy support and training courses for teachers of children with special needs in ordinary schools', *British Journal of In-Service Education* 7, 2: 125–8.
Hopkins, D. and Vickers, C. (1986) 'Process consultation in school self-evaluation', *Cambridge Journal of Education* 16, 2: 116–25.
Kounin, J. (1970) *Discipline and Group Management in Classrooms*, New York: Holt, Rinehart, & Winston.
Lacayo, N., Sherwood, G., and Morris, J. (1981) 'Daily activities of school psychologists: a national survey', *Psychology in the Schools* 18: 184–90.

Maher, C. A. and Illback, R. J. (1982a) 'Considerations for education and training in organisational school psychology', *Psychology in the Schools* 19: 194–9.

——— (1982b) 'Organisational school psychology: issues and considerations', *Journal of School Psychology* 20, 3: 244–53.

Medway, F. J. (1979) 'How effective is school consultancy? A review of recent research', *Journal of School Psychology* 17, 3: 275–82.

Medway, F. J. and Forman, S. G. (1980) 'Psychologists' and teachers' reactions to mental health and behavioural school consultation', *Journal of School Psychology* 18, 4: 338–48.

Morse, W. (1971) 'Worksheet on life space interviews for teachers', in N. Long, W. Morse, and R. Newman (eds) 'Conflict in the classroom: the education of children with problems', 2nd edn, Belmont, Calif: Wadsworth.

Murgatroyd, S. and Reynolds, D. (1984) 'The creative constancy: The potential of consultancy as a method of teacher education', *School Organisation* 4, 4: 321–35.

Parlett, M. and Hamilton, D. (1976) 'Evaluation as illumination', in D. L. Tawney (ed.) *Curriculum Evaluation Today*, London: Macmillan.

Pfeiffer, J. and Jones, J. (1969 *et seq.*) *Annual Handbook for Group Facilitators*, La Jolla, Calif: University Associates.

Reynolds, D. (1976) 'The delinquent school', in M. Hammersley and P. Woods (eds) *The Process of Schooling: A Sociological Reader*, London: Routledge & Kegan Paul.

Reynolds, D. and Sullivan, M. (1979) 'Bringing schools back in', in L. Barton and R. Meighan (eds) *Schools, Pupils and Deviance*, Nafferton, Driffield: Nafferton Books.

Richardson, E. (1933) *The Teacher, the School and the Task of Management*, London: Heinemann.

Ritter, D. R. (1978) 'Effects of a school consultation program upon referral patterns of teachers', *Psychology in the Schools*.

Robertson, J. (1981) *Effective Classroom Control*, London: Hodder & Stoughton.

Rosenshine, B. (1983) 'Teaching functions in instructional programs', *Elementary School Journal* 83, 4: 335–57.

Rutter, M., Maughan, B., Mortimore, P., and Ouston, J. (1979) *Fifteen Thousand Hours*, London: Open Books.

Schmuck, R. A. and Miles, M. B. (1971) *Organization Development in Schools*, Palo Alto, Calif: National Press Books.

Schmuck, R. A., Runkel, P. J., Arends, J. H., and Arends, R. I. (1977) *The Second Handbook of Organization Development*, Palo Alto, Calif: Mayfield Publishing.

Skinner, B. F. (1953) *Science and Human Behaviour*, New York: Macmillan.

Slavin, R. (1980) 'Co-operative learning', *Review of Educational Research* 50: 315–42.

Smith, D. K. and Lyon, M. A. (1985) 'Consultation in school psychology: Change from 81–84', *Psychology in the Schools* 22: 404–9.

Tweddle, D. (1986) (ed.) *Preventive Approaches to Disruption*, Basingstoke: Macmillan.

Tyler, M. M. and Fine, M. J. (1974) 'The effects of limited and intensive school psychologist consultation', *Journal of School Psychology* 12, 1: 8–16.

Weissenburger, J. W., Fine, M. J., and Poggio, J. P. (1982) 'The relationship of selected consultant/teacher characteristics to consultation outcomes', *Journal of School Psychology* 20, 4: 263–9.

White, P. O. and Fine, M. J. (1976) 'The effects of three schools' psychological consultant modes on selected teacher and pupil outcomes', *Psychology in the Schools* 13, 4: 414–20.

Wise, P. S. (1979) 'A training model of consultation', *Psychology in the Schools* 16, 4: 515–19.

Wragg, E. (1981) *Class Management and Control: A Teaching Skills Workbook*, London: Macmillan Education.

Chapter four

Preparing teachers for a support role in dealing with adjustment problems in secondary schools

John Presland and Philip White

Adjustment problems in secondary schools

Adjustment problems continue to be a matter for concern in British secondary schools, particularly those problems that are disruptive. In a survey of such schools (Merrett and Wheldall 1987), for instance, more than half of teachers said that they spent more time on problems of order and control than they ought. Both this survey, and those by McNamara (1987) and Steed *et al.* (1986), indicate that the behaviours that bother teachers most are those that sound mild but are very frequent, such as inappropriate talking, turning round in seats, disturbing the work of other pupils, and generally not attending to work. They can, however, be very disruptive. Steed *et al.* report that, in studies in which staff recorded incidents of behaviour that interfered seriously with the teaching process or the running of the school, 101 incidents were reported among fourth- and fifth-year pupils during two weeks, while 144 occurred in one week in another school.

Estimates of the number of individual pupils whose behaviour is 'disruptive' go up to at least 10–15 per cent (Davies 1980). The number of pupils who present very serious problems of this kind, though smaller, is still appreciable. Badger (1985) for instance, found that 38 pupils in a comprehensive school of over 1,200 were considered by some of their teachers to display behaviour which was exceptionally difficult to control within the normal school setting. There are indications that the number of instances in which schools feel that the situation is serious enough to suspend a pupil is rising. Thus Galloway (1982) found fifty-eight pupils suspended from the thirty-nine secondary schools in Sheffield in a twelve-month period during 1978/9 and reported evidence that the number was increasing. Recently Gale and Topping (1986) found that in nineteen schools in a metropolitan borough in the north who responded to questionnaires, 189 children were suspended in one school year.

While Docking (1987) points out the subjectivity of much of the evidence on which such estimates are based and quotes other studies with less dramatic findings, there is no doubt that the prevalence of disruptive behaviour in secondary schools is sufficient to cause alarm. Furthermore, not only does it interfere with lesson organization and learning, but also it is one of the sources of stress experienced by teachers and can undermine their effectiveness in this way (Sharp and Forman 1985; Cox and Brockley 1984; Kyriacou 1987; Dunham 1981; Kloska and Ramasut 1985).

Disruptive behaviour is, however, not the only kind of adjustment problem which should lead to concern. A study of truancy in fourth- and fifth-year pupils in secondary schools in Inner London (Thompson 1987) reported very high frequencies. Davies (1980) lists studies suggesting that truancy is a considerable problem and others which found adjustment problems generally to occur in up to 15 per cent of secondary pupils. While other kinds of adjustment problems do not cause the same level of excitement in the education world as disruptive behaviour, they affect the lives of pupils and must be included in thinking and planning for change.

What intervention techniques are effective?

A recent review of the evidence (Topping 1983) indicated that the only intervention techniques for adjustment problems which have been validated on any scale are those that are termed 'behavioural'. These approaches normally involve identifying specific changes in behaviour as objectives, altering the precursors and consequences of behaviours in a planned way to achieve these changes, and monitoring progress as objectively as possible. The commonest techniques included are well described by Cheesman and Watts (1985) and by Wheldall and Merrett (1984). While these methods have been most successful in primary and special schools, reviews of the evidence do reveal a number of studies showing useful results in secondary schools (Topping 1983; Presland 1980; Kolvin *et al.* 1981; Merrett and Wheldall 1987; McNamara 1987; Merrett 1981; Rees 1983).

In contrast, evidence validating other intervention techniques is very hard to find. While reviewers find a few encouraging studies of counselling techniques (Topping 1983; Kolvin *et al.* 1981), much more investigation is required to justify confident use. Techniques such as group work, drama therapy, and art therapy have hardly been subjected to objective investigation at all.

Where should intervention take place?

Before concluding that the main approach to intervention should be behavioural, it is important to consider the settings in which it is to take place, since it must have face validity in those settings.

Topping (1983) examines both the effectiveness and the cost of a wide range of types of provision and concludes that the most cost-effective occur within the mainstream school setting and a 'resource continuum'. A resource continuum implies a start within the pupils' usual class, with advice and support provided for teachers in dealing with the problems presented, proceeding if necessary to part-time withdrawal, full-time withdrawal to provision within the mainstream school, or withdrawal fully or in part to provision outside the school. The emphasis is on providing for needs in a situation as close as possible to normal attendance at ordinary classes.

Intervention techniques in mainstream settings

If priority is to be given to provision in mainstream schools, it is important to consider what methods have most face validity in that setting. As far as secondary schools in the UK are concerned, behavioural approaches do not stand up to this criterion very well. Those psychologists who attempt to help secondary schools implement behavioural techniques in the UK rarely have much cause to feel encouraged. One of the authors, who has organized workshops in which many teachers in primary and special education settings have carried out and monitored successful behaviour modification programmes, was unable to evoke any comparable applications in a workshop in a comprehensive school, and could not even recruit any teachers for one proposed in another. Harrop and McNamara (1979), who organized workshops involving one hundred secondary school teachers, found that only six carried out a behaviour modification programme in which success was both claimed by the teacher and supported by numerical data which participants were asked to collect.

What is it about secondary schools in the UK that makes them, apparently, reluctant to try out behaviour approaches, when the potential success of such approaches has been demonstrated? There are no clearly established reasons for this, but the following have been suggested:

1 It is seen as one more demand upon their time, and they have too many already.
2 Pupils are taught by a number of different teachers, and it is difficult to ensure consistency between them.
3 Many secondary-school teachers are reluctant to change their own behaviour, perhaps because they fear possible unknown fearful consequences, and find it very difficult to do so when they try.
4 Some teachers feel that responsibility for pupils' behaviour lies with the pastoral staff, or even outside the mainstream school.
5 Teacher praise and attention as rewarding consequences for acceptable behaviour become less effective for many pupils as they grow older and increasingly reject school.
6 The complex hierarchical organization of schools makes it difficult for the advising psychologist to have effective direct contact with those teachers experiencing the actual difficulties in handling pupils.
7 Peer group influences become increasingly more powerful than those organized by the teacher and may lead in directions different from those which the teacher wants.
8 Some teachers think the behaviour problems of pupils are intractable. Sometimes this is because it is believed their home backgrounds will interfere too much with any techniques used, and sometimes it is because the pupil is believed to be unaffected in any logical way by the consequences of his actions.
9 Some aspects of some behaviour modification methods may conflict in some respects with school rules and practices.
10 Many secondary-school teachers think behaviour modification is 'soft', and that difficult pupils should simply be

> punished or removed from the school. Those who do not think in this way might fear criticism or ridicule by these colleagues if they implemented the approaches.

None of these reasons *precludes* the use of behavioural approaches. One teacher *can* implement such approaches alone, *can* change his own behaviour, *can* decide to take responsibility for discipline in his own classroom, *can* decide to attack a problem which he fears is intractable, *can* open his mind to new methods, and *can* harden himself against criticism and ridicule. Most pupils *can* be influenced by praise if the teacher is not put off by the initial reactions; and there are other ways of rewarding acceptable behaviour anyway. Organizational difficulties *can* be overcome with sufficient determination. However, a collection of the problems listed is likely to make implementation more of a strain.

It seems, however, that less well validated methods are more likely to be acceptable in secondary schools. Counselling, for instance, though its actual techniques are little known, is very well thought of and is believed to be more 'humanistic' than behavioural approaches. Group work and drama therapy are unfamiliar in schools, but do not attract the hostility that at times greets behavioural approaches. Social skills training covers a wide range of approaches in which particular behaviours involved in relating to other people are specifically taught. Their connection with behavioural approaches is not altogether appreciated, which helps their acceptability.

Filling provision gaps in Wiltshire

Some of the issues above are well illustrated by events in Wiltshire. Until recently, Wiltshire schools were visited by educational psychologists, who have very limited time for supporting them in their efforts with pupils with adjustment difficulties. Child and family guidance centres also existed throughout the county, but concentrated largely on help in an outside-school context for those children whose parents could and would take them to the centre. Three off-site day adjustment centres operated on a full or part-time basis. Two of them catered for pupils who were mainly in the upper half of the secondary age range, while the other would take children of any age. A day special school took pupils of any age with adjustment difficulties from a limited area of the county, and there were two residential schools for pupils of secondary age. Use was also made of out-county schools, mainly non-LEA and residential.

Clearly Wiltshire did not have a complete continuum of resources, though this was approached more closely in some areas than in others. There was a major gap everywhere in that support within mainstream schools was extremely limited. In 1986, therefore, two schemes were begun to help fill this gap in different areas of the county. The first involved allocating a support teacher to each of four comprehensive schools. The second set up a team of three peripatetic support teachers to help both primary and secondary schools. Encouraging descriptions of schemes using support teachers had been provided by McPherson *et al.* (1986), members of Barnsley Special Education Team (1981), Ellis (1985), Sterne (1981), and Coulby and Harper (1985).

Planning a training course

In determining what kind of training the support teachers should have, a four-person planning team of special education advisers and psychologists first looked at the role they should, ideally, play in schools, then derived training objectives to prepare for these roles, and finally planned training activities to achieve those objectives. The activities were presented by a range of psychologists, advisers, and teachers from within the authority and by one outside speaker.

The support teacher role

We were unanimous in believing that a support teacher should not be somebody who simply removed problems from other staff. It was, rather, important that he or she should work as a member of a team of all relevant staff members. There is increasing evidence that schools can themselves be important determinants of how pupils behave (Rutter *et al.* 1979). It was important, therefore, that the team involved should include key people who could influence other staff, so that the school as a whole could work towards resolving problems.

The determination of the support teacher's role within the whole-school approach rested on the assumption that the class-teacher should remain in control and should, therefore, receive the necessary advice, help, and support to make it possible. It was important, therefore, that the support teacher should have expertise in:

1 assessing pupils' needs,
2 planning and, if necessary, adapting relevant negotiated programmes based on pupils' and staff needs,
3 teaching pupils by withdrawal work or supporting pupils in mainstream classes,
4 monitoring progress to ensure effective feedback to all concerned, including setting up and keeping appropriate records,
5 evaluating the work in conjunction with relevant agencies.

Objectives for training

Setting up a training course required identification of the intervention techniques that needed to be used. The issues discussed earlier are particularly relevant here. Behavioural approaches had to be included, because of their demonstrated effectiveness. It was hoped, also, that their implementation would be more feasible from within the school than from outside. In addition, it was important to include a range of other approaches which would have better face validity initially. Counselling, group work, drama therapy, and social skills training were, therefore, all included.

Techniques alone, however, were not enough. In view of the difficulties raised earlier, it was essential that the support teachers should have a knowledge, not only of the range of adjustment problems encountered in schools, but also of the attitude of teachers and others towards them. It was important that they should have a knowledge of the various kinds of provision made both nationally and locally and of the theoretical bases of various approaches to intervention, so that they could argue their case effectively with the sceptical. Attention also needed to be given to the organization and planning of the work and to liaison inside and outside the school, including with outside support services and parents. Persuading others, planning, and liaising should all be helped by an understanding of the organization and politics of schools. Since the work would be difficult and often frustrating, support teachers would also need to understand how stress could affect them, how it could be coped with and how help and support in facing it could be obtained. Finally, there were certain reading assignments so fundamental to preparation for this role that they were included as a major objective of the course.

The objectives so derived were set out in written form for all to see. They are listed below in the form of the skills, knowledge, understanding, and experiences which it was hoped the teachers would obtain. The teacher

1 has a knowledge of the range of adjustment problems encountered in schools and of the attitudes to them among teachers, other professionals, and parents,
2 has a knowledge of the range of provision made both nationally and locally,
3 has a knowledge of the range of theoretical approaches to adjustment problems,
4 has a knowledge of, and a good idea of how to use, a range of assessment, intervention, and recording techniques for adjustment problems and associated learning problems,
5 has an understanding of the organization and politics of schools,
6 can plan the organization of his or her work within a school,
7 has a knowledge of the work of a range of support services and can liaise effectively inside and outside the school, including with parents,
8 has an understanding of himself/herself in relation to the demands of the job and has devices for coping with stress and knowledge of how to obtain support,
9 has undertaken reading assignments on topics fundamental to the work.

Course activities and organization

The first run of the course was given to a group consisting of three support teachers allocated to individual schools and to peripatetic support teachers. Much of the earlier part of the course was also attended by the teachers in an off-site unit for pupils with adjustment difficulties. It was clear from the outset that the task was too large to fit into the three-week period allowed for it, and the course was, therefore, envisaged as a basic introduction, to be expanded by subsequent regular in-service training sessions when participants were in post.

The course consisted of twelve units, designed to cover the objectives outlined above as far as was possible within the time. The general pattern was to provide an input in the form of lectures or written hand-outs, to arrange practical exercises in the skills required, and to relate all knowledge and skills introduced to the task of planning how to carry out the support teacher role in the school(s) in which each participant would operate.

A term later, there was a second run of the course for one school-based and one peripatetic support teacher who were appointed too late for the first run. It was not possible to staff a repeat of the first run, so most of the information-bearing material was provided by hand-outs. Practical exercises and planning of the work were, however, much the same as in the first run, though there was less supervision of the activities.

The units of the course, which are also described elsewhere (Falconer-Hall and Harlatt, forthcoming), are outlined briefly below. The times indicated are those that were allocated for the first run, but those for the second run were similar.

1 *Preparation and briefing* (pre-course time and ½ hour on the course). A summary and overview of the course was provided and the role of the support teacher discussed. Participants were asked to visit the school (or *a* school) in which they would be working to study those aspects of its organization and communication which would be relevant to their work. A list of questions was provided to guide this study. Reading assignments were provided in which participants had to use specific books to answer questions or assemble information directly relevant to their role. One book provided a survey of policies, provision, and practices and associated research evidence (Topping 1983); another provided a systematic account of behavioural approaches (Cheesman and Watts 1985); another provided a systematic description of counselling skills (Munro *et al.* 1983); and the fourth (added at the second run) described a support teacher scheme in ILEA (Coulby and Harper 1985).
2 *The problem* (4 hours). The range of adjustment problems in mainstream schools was outlined and discussed, and attitudes to adjustment problems were explored mainly through the participants' looking at their own attitudes.

3 *Theoretical approaches to adjustment problems* (3¼ hours). Different approaches were discussed under three headings which were 'paired opposites' — humanistic v. behaviouristic, medical v. psychological, and systems v. individual client. Specific approaches included in this discussion were behavioural techniques, non-directive counselling as practised by Carl Rogers, various other techniques described as 'humanistic', social learning approaches, behavioural counselling, social skills training, and discussion groups.

4 *Patterns of provision* (2 hours). An outline was given of both national and local provision, including some detail on the use of support teachers. Visits were made to several kinds of local establishments for pupils with adjustment difficulties, participants reporting back to the group on their findings. Again, guiding questions were provided for these visits.

5 *Identification, referrals, and assessment* (3½ hours). Participants were guided to consider how these processes might be designed in relation to their individual job descriptions. Coulby and Harper's (1985) Five-Step Procedure for Individual 'Casework' was presented. Their five steps were referral, assessment, formulation, intervention, and evaluation, and this unit covered the first two. Requirements for a referral system were outlined, and techniques for identifying pupils at risk for adjustment problems discussed. The purposes of assessment were identified, and kinds of information and techniques required for it suggested. A range of referral forms and assessment instruments was shown. These included record forms of behaviour to be filled in by individual teachers, behaviour questionnaires, devices (such as the Bristol Social Adjustment Guides) for rating behaviour, pupil self-report forms (including the use of Repertory Grids) and techniques for identifying the social structure of a classroom (sociometry). Participants were invited to identify the kinds of information they would wish to collect on pupils in their individual working situations and to design their own referral forms.

6 *Assessment and intervention by behavioural methods* (8½ hours). The basic elements of a behavioural approach were outlined: identifying and describing behaviours to be changed; identifying influences affecting behaviours; observing,

measuring, and recording behaviours; selecting changes to make in the environment to change behaviours, and incorporating them into a detailed programme. There was then specific consideration of applying behavioural approaches in secondary schools, the use of contracts to influence behaviour and systems in which home and school co-operate. A range of recording forms was provided, and practice was organized in some of the component skills in a behavioural approach and in designing programmes.

7. *Assessment and intervention for learning* (4¾ hours). The connection between behavioural problems and learning problems was pointed out, and assessment techniques and organizational practices for supporting pupils with learning problems and intervention processes outlined. This was done within a model of instruction adapted from one by Child (1985). This model considers both assessment and the learning outcomes required in relation to the learner's physical attributes (health, physical handicaps, and so on), cognitive attributes (the knowledge, skills, and abilities already present) and affective attributes (interests, attitudes, self-concept, and so on). Progress from assessment to outcome is made through the structuring of a body of knowledge to help efficient learning, the sequencing and methods for presenting the knowledge, and the devices needed for motivating learning. The whole process is seen as taking place within the learning environment, which includes the perceptions, expectations, and understandings of the teacher and the physical and social features of the situation where learning is taking place, and organizational features within the school. Participants were guided to design schemes for assessment and recording of pupils' progress, including records primarily for pupils' use and to practise learning programmes.
8 *Other approaches to intervention* (8½ hours). These included counselling (2¼ hours), behavioural counselling (¾ hours, included in first run only), handling groups (1 hour), one approach to social skills training (2¼ hours), and drama therapy and role-play (2¼ hours). The main features of these approaches were outlined, and practical exercises in their application organized. Contributions on counselling and drama therapy included some account of the use of behavioural

techniques in combination with the approaches being presented.

9 *Organization and politics of schools* (1¼ hours). Participants were asked to look back at their records of visits to the school(s) in which they would be working and to consider how they would fit into this organization. At the first run, there was a presentation by a secondary-school head-teacher to supplement this, but not at the second run.

10 *Bringing things together* (17 hours). The material of the previous units was integrated into an overall scheme. The unit included consideration of the support services available both inside and outside the school and how the participants might make use of them; how the work of the support teachers would fit into the LEA's response to the 1981 Education Act, including a consideration of the various procedures set up by the authority; and interacting with parents. In designing overall schemes for organizing the work, much use was made of the work of Coulby and Harper (1985). Participants were helped to plan how they would organize their work in their individual schools, including consultation with relevant staff in those schools being involved in the process.

11 *Coping with stress* (4½ hours). Participants were offered guidance in identifying and managing stress, both in themselves and in the other staff they would be helping. Some discussion was included of teacher support groups (Raymond 1985). From early in the course, the group was itself encouraged to function as a self-help group, both during the initial training and afterwards.

12 *Evaluation of the course and identification of further needs for in-service training* (2–4 hours). This was by discussion and use of a questionnaire. The outcomes are discussed further in the next section.

Evaluation

An immediate aim in evaluating the course described above was to gather the opinions of participants on the administration and content of the course, and how they could be improved and adapted for use in a less presenter-intensive way. This was necessary to help produce a relatively self-contained package and delivery procedure which could be used effectively for future appointees. At this stage, no attempt was made to study changes in knowledge or behaviour resulting from the course. Only in the long term was it hoped to obtain feedback on the techniques which the support teachers use, their opinions of the effectiveness of these techniques, records of involvement with pupils and other teachers and pupil and parent reactions. Accounts of this feedback have, however, been written (Moore 1987; Falconer-Hall and Harlatt, forthcoming).

With such a small sample, confident generalizations are not possible. However, the overwhelming impression is that participants found the course arrangements satisfactory and the content almost universally relevant. Very few doubts were expressed about the value of the content selected and most criticism was directed at the actual style of presentation of individual sessions and the difficulty of balancing the need to inform and to provide intensive skill training against the need to keep within a limited time allotment. Despite these difficulties, one participant concluded critical remarks by writing, 'otherwise, the course was excellent, by far the best INSET I have attended'.

Suggestions for modified training for new entrants

The participants were asked for their views on how new entrants should be trained, and particularly about any modifications needed if the course had to be presented to them in a shorter form. Some participants felt that all the units should be retained for this purpose. Behavioural techniques, counselling, drama therapy, social skills training, the ILEA model, the pre-course reading, work on school management, and assessment and intervention for learning were all mentioned as priorities. Despite some critical comments, only one participant said that the visits to establishments for adjustment difficulties in the county should definitely be omitted.

When asked how best new appointees should be trained and helped to prepare for their work if it was impossible to staff a course similar to the one they had undertaken, replies varied. However, certain common ideas emerged:

1 The authority should not appoint 'inexperienced' staff to such posts unless intensive preparation was available.
2 The 'pre-course' reading should be required.
3 The course hand-outs should be rewritten to provide a self-instruction package with experiential and written elements — along Open University lines.
4 New appointees should work with existing post-holders for a set period.
5 Particular techniques or skills should be taught through 'day-release' workshops.
6 Regular support meetings of all the teachers should be held to provide supervision and support to new appointees.
7 The appointing school must be fully conversant with the support teacher's role and procedures and provide professional support from within its own structure.

Discussion and conclusions

Evaluation of the course as described above cannot be translated directly into recommendations for change. The data are opinions only and need not necessarily correspond with what is or is not effective training. It is, however, important to discover such reactions. First, they indicate whether a course has face validity and will, therefore, be taken seriously and acted upon. Second, they indicate a variety of ways of looking at the same material, which can promote rethinking. Let us look at these two functions in turn.

Participants' reactions indicated clearly that they felt they had gained a great deal of value from the course and any suggestions for improvement should not be allowed to obscure this finding. If they repeat this view widely, the course should come to have more status, and attendance will be sought by others. It is conceivable, for instance, that it would be of value to any school staff member with pastoral responsibilities, rather than just to support teachers. Both they, and those who provide funds for in-service training, need to appreciate its quality for this to be possible. Funding might also be affected by some of the critical comments. For instance, the constant reference by participants to needing more practice at skills taught might convince funders that a longer period should be allocated for the initial training and/or that follow-up training should be extensive.

Finally, views of participants on which more economical versions of the package would be appropriate for support teachers joining the authority in ones and twos should be helpful in providing something that is less likely to be rejected as inadequate. In Wiltshire several of these recommendations were implemented for the second run, where staffing could not be so intensive. The pre-course reading was maintained and extended; many of the course handouts were rewritten to provide elements of what will, we hope, be a largely self-instruction package; and regular support meetings and INSET activities have been held for all the support teachers, so that the new entrants have been able to make use of the experience of those trained previously as well as learn new skills. The existing support teachers also presented a session in the second run.

How should the course organizer use the feedback provided for rethinking the course? First, it looks as though the actual topics covered are what participants want, even though they had criticisms of methods of presentation. The exception was the use of visits to LEA establishments for pupils with adjustment difficulties. However, it could be argued that it *is* important for postholders to know what happens in such establishments, even if the knowledge does not improve their own work. The problem for the organizers would then be how to increase the face validity of this element — perhaps by identifying precisely the learning experiences expected from the visits and/or asking the establishments visited to structure the experience in particular ways.

Second, the course organization was regarded as largely satisfactory, at least for the first run, though there were a few suggestions which could be followed up. It should not, for instance, be too difficult to alternate the theory and practical sessions and to locate the former in the morning; nor to increase the social, group-forming elements, though this could be difficult in a packaged self-study format.

The main area for rethinking, however, is clearly methods of presentation. Though the organizers attempted to make the course as practical and as relevant to the posts as possible, the participants plainly thought there was room for improvement. Some things are, however, very difficult to change. Theoretical background, for instance, *is* theoretical. Contributors do not always follow guidelines, however well briefed. Time *does* limit the amount of practical work which can be carried out.

Of those changes recommended or implied, there are some that the organizers disagree with. For instance, the book on policies, provision, and practices (Topping 1983) which some participants criticized, is felt by the organizers to be the best account available of background information which is essential in such posts. Rethinking might, in such cases, best be resisted, unless a better method of presentation is suggested.

There remains a range of suggestions which can be implemented and where the case for alteration is stronger. Often, this refers specifically to particular individual contributions, and such information is both sensitive and probably of little value to readers who have not experienced the contribution and do not know the contributor. A number of general threads can, however, be drawn out of these comments:

1 A number of sessions were presented in a way that participants found difficult to understand, either because they introduced theories of some complexity (e.g. the unit on assessment and intervention for learning) or because they assumed too much pre-existing knowledge, e.g. the 1981 Act session and the session on published check-lists. Contributors need to be carefully briefed to avoid this and hand-outs need to be written in a style that is easy to understand.
2 Participants constantly commented that they would have liked a greater practical element. Probably this was most often because lack of time prevented it, rather than because there was too much theory. However, care must clearly be taken that only essential theory is included and that it should be by hand-out as far as possible, so that sessions can be devoted maximally to practical work.
3 Some activities, particularly the various school visits, were felt not to be organized in a way that most showed their relevance to the post-holders' work. Clearly, careful discussion with and briefing of those providing such experience is needed to increase relevance.

We hope that if these changes can be successfully implemented, future participants will have even more reason to think that they have been well prepared for their role than those who have attended the courses so far.

References

Badger, B. (1985) 'Behaviour problems: the primary-secondary link', *School Organisation* 6, 2: 185–93.

Barnsley Special Education Team (1981) 'A team approach to disruption', *Special Education: Forward Trends* 8, 1: 8–10.

Cheesman, P. L. and Watts, P. E. (1985) *Positive Behaviour Management*, London: Croom Helm.

Child, D. (1985) 'Educational psychology: Past, present and future', in N. Entwistle (ed.) *New Directions in Educational Psychology*, Brighton: Falmer.

Coulby, D. and Harper, T. (1985) *Preventing Classroom Disruption: Policy, Practice and Evaluation in Urban Schools*, London: Croom Helm.

Cox, T. and Brockley, T. (1984) 'The experience and effects of stress in teachers', *British Educational Research Journal* 10, 1: 83–7.

Davies, C. (1980) 'Disruptive pupils in secondary schools', *Links* 5, 3: 10–18.

Docking, J. W. (1987) *Control and Discipline in Schools*, 2nd edn, London: Harper & Row.

Dunham, J. (1981) 'Disruptive pupils and teacher stress', *Educational Research* 23, 3: 205–13.

Ellis, S. (1985) 'The work of the DO5 Schools Support Team', *Maladjustment and Therapeutic Education* 3, 2: 27–36.

Falconer-Hall, E. and Harlatt, L. (forthcoming) 'In-service training for support teachers', in T. Charlton and K. David (eds) *Teachers Make a Difference: Management of Behaviour Problems in Schools*, Basingstoke: Macmillan.

Gale, I. and Topping, K. (1986) 'Suspension from High School: The practice and its effects', *Pastoral Care* 4, 3: 215–24.

Galloway, D. (1982) 'A study of pupils suspended from schools', *British Journal of Educational Psychology* 52, 2: 205–12.

Harrop, L. A. and McNamara, E. (1979) 'Behaviour modification in the secondary school: A cautionary tale', *British Psychological Society Division of Educational and Child Psychology Occasional Papers* 3, 2: 38–41.

Kloska, A. and Ramasut, A. (1985) 'Teacher stress', *Maladjustment and Therapeutic Education* 3, 2: 19–26.

Kolvin, I., Garside, R. S., Nicol, A. R., Macmillan, A., Wolstenholme, F., and Leitch, I. M. (1981) *Help Starts Here: The Maladjusted Child in the Ordinary School*, London: Tavistock.

Kyriacou, C. (1987) 'Teacher stress and burnout: an international review', *Educational Research* 29, 2: 146–52.

McNamara, E. (1987) 'Behavioural approaches in the secondary school', in K. Wheldall (ed.) *The Behaviourist in the Classroom*, London: Allen & Unwin.

McPherson, E., Butcher, A. K., and Howarth, P. A. (1986) 'Working with school support teams', *British Psychological Society Division of*

Educational and Child Psychology Newsletter 21: 17–20.
Merrett, F. E. (1981) 'Studies in behaviour modification in British educational settings', *Educational Psychology* 1, 1: 13–38.
Merrett, M. and Wheldall, K. (1987) 'British teachers and the behavioural approach to teaching', in K. Wheldall (ed.) *The Behaviourist in the Classroom*, London: Allen & Unwin.
Moore, P. L. (1987) 'An evaluation of the newly established provision for pupils with adjustment difficulties in two secondary schools', unpublished M.Ed. dissertation, University of Bath.
Munro, E., Manthei, R. J., and Small, J. J. (1983) *Conselling: A Skills Approach*, 2nd edn, Auckland: Methuen.
Presland, J. (1980) 'Behaviour modification and secondary schools', in G. Upton and A. Gobell (eds) *Behaviour Problems in the Comprehensive School*, Faculty of Education, University College of Cardiff.
Raymond, J. (1985) 'The importance of teacher support groups in managing difficult behaviour', *Links* 10, 2: 31–7.
Rees, P. V. (1983) 'The use of behaviour modification techniques in a comprehensive school', *Maladjustment and Therapeutic Education* 1, 2: 53–62.
Rutter, M., Maughan, B., Mortimore, P., and Ouston, J. (1979) *Fifteen Thousand Hours: Secondary Schools and their Effects on Children*, Shepton Mallet: Open Books.
Sharp, J. J. and Forman, S. G. (1985) 'A comparison of two approaches to anxiety management for teachers', *Behaviour Therapy* 16, 4: 370–83.
Steed, D., Lawrence, J., and Young, P. (1986) 'The incident: a focus for looking at disruptive pupil behaviour', *Behavioural Approaches with Children* 10, 2: 34–8.
Sterne, M. (1981) 'The answer to disruptives?', *Education* 28 August: 180.
Thompson, S. (1987) 'Truancy "at epidemic level" ', *The Times*, 8 July.
Topping, K. (1983) *Educational Systems for Disruptive Adolescents*, London: Croom Helm.
Wheldall, K. and Merrett, S. (1984) *Positive Teaching*, London: Allen & Unwin.

Chapter five

Interventions with persistent absentees: an educational perspective

Ken Reid

John is 13. The school has labelled him a 'truant'. The fact is that he has attended school on three occasions in the first six weeks of the Autumn Term. He is also a member of a local counselling group for secondary-aged pupils run by the school psychological service. During his time in this group, he has revealed that he is afraid of his classmates because they tease and bully him. He has manifested a wide range of interrelated social and personal problems. Although well adjusted and growing in confidence as a member of the group, his non-attendance continues unabated. He appears to look forward to his counselling sessions. He hates school.

Janet is 15. She looks much older. At weekends she works on a fish stall in the market. She would like to have a full-time job. So would her parents, who need the money. Her father is unemployed; her mother works as a part-time cleaner in a factory. They live in a small terraced house on a large council estate. Janet is in the same group as John. Apart from their non-attendance and personal and social backgrounds, they have little in common. All Janet wants to do is to leave school as soon as possible.

Susan is 11. She 'loved' her primary school but feels lost at her local comprehensive. She is in a new registration form without any of her old friends. She is small for her age and feels highly self-conscious. She doesn't like some of her new lessons. At home she daren't tell her parents of her feelings because her father ignores her and her mother is too busy. Last week she skipped school for the first time. She went to see her aunt. She is fearful that her aunt will tell her mother. She doesn't know what she will do then.

John, Janet, and Susan typify the kinds of problems professionals will confront in their dealings with absentees. Absentees or non-attenders in this chapter include all illegal categories of non-attenders at school — truants, parental-condoned absentees, specific lesson absentees, and persistent absentees *per se*. They do not include school refusal cases which are a separate category altogether. Non-attenders are normally not aggressive or disruptive (Reid 1984b; 1984c), although a minority of difficult, disruptive truants do exist (Reid 1984a). Typically many absentees are loners, even isolates. Unusually they are leaders of a group. But a lot of absenteeism does take place in groups, perhaps increasingly so (Reid 1985).

School absenteeism is a national problem. The most reliable statistics suggest that around one in ten secondary-age pupils in England and Wales miss school daily. It is also a disproportionate problem. For example, far more fourth- and fifth-years miss school illegally than their counterparts in years one and two. More boys play truant. More girls are parental-condoned absentees. There are more absentees in inner-city and large urban areas than in semi-rural areas, suburban districts, or small towns. There are far more absentees in South Wales, the north-west, the north-east, central London, and parts of the Midlands than in the south, south-west and eastern regions of England. There are far more absentees in some schools than in others. Finally, far more absentees have parents with working-class rather than middle-class origins. They also tend to come from larger or one-parent families, disadvantaged housing, families in strife, and those which experience other forms of marital discord. In addition, the parents of absentees tend to earn less than the national average or find themselves unemployed (Reid 1985).

Similarly, inside schools absentees tend to be less well known by their teachers, to have related psychological, psychosomatic, or other health or behavioural problems, to gravitate towards the lower ability forms, to possess below average intelligence, to have lower self-concepts than many of their peers, and, often, depending upon their circumstances, to have fewer friends than their classmates (Reid 1983a; 1983b). Some absentees miss school for purely institutional reasons. Others for social or psychological ones. Many for combinations of all three (Reid 1983a; 1983b).

This much we know. What is less well known is how to persuade, coerce, or help a non-attender to return to school on a regular basis. The literature is full of a number of experiments which have been tried on a local, county, or school basis. While more success is claimed for some of these schemes than others, the fact remains that it is immensely difficult to know which intervention strategies are likely to succeed in any given set of circumstances. In fact, it is probably fair to say from the beginning that an analysis and evaluation of current practice would reveal a great deal of effort and diversity but little sustained improvement.

Generally speaking, most intervention strategies begin too late, when the pupil is too old and already at the persistent stage, and when the effects of cognitive dissonance have enabled the pupil to justify his or her non-attendance in his or her own mind at least. Far too many tutors in schools, educational psychologists, social workers, and others find themselves in positions where they have to scratch around searching for schemes which stand a chance of working; all too often without any real expectation of success.

There are several reasons for this state of affairs. First, there are numerous schemes which have already been tried with minimal effects. Second, the prognosis in individual cases is often bleak. Explicitly, there is little point in using behaviourist approaches (operant conditioning, reward schemes, etc.) when the absentee is hostile to the reward, the potential outcome, or the whole notion. That is he or she does not wish to return to school come what may!

Third, persistent school absenteeism is frequently a symptom of other problems — home, social, or medical. Fourth, some school absentees will not keep their appointments with professional agencies. Indeed, it is not unknown for some hostile or disruptive absentees to vent their anger on agents of the 'caring' services. Fifth, help from parents, social services, schools, education social workers, and educational psychologists tends to vary from region to region along with the degree of interest, commitment, viewpoints, policies, and referral patterns followed. There is little by way of a uniform policy throughout England and Wales. Moreover, a study of intervention policies with persistent absentees would be littered with (and probably hindered by) such factors as poor co-ordination, professional rivalries, and territorial imperatives (Reid 1986).

The formulation of an LEA policy for dealing with absentee behaviour in schools requires choices to be made between alternative strategies. Skinner *et al.* (1983) suggest that these revolve around whether the pupils concerned need to be segregrated from their peers for a short or long period of time, or remain integrated within the school setting. They consider that the main options can be seen in terms of

1 preventive pastoral care versus specialist provision on- or off-site;
2 on-site specialist provision versus off-site specialist provision;
3 short-term versus long-term provision (whether on- or off-site).

Clearly pros and cons can be made for each of these options on educational and pragmatic grounds and regional variations abound.

Apart from the question of *how* the issue is approached, there are a number of intervention strategies open to remedial agencies. Frankly, despite these opportunities, pressure of time, workloads, and immediate imperatives often force professionals to adopt an *ad hoc* response. This is true of pastoral staff, social workers, and educational psychologists although, interestingly, each professional group is often inclined to think the other has more time than themselves to deal with this particular phenomenon.

In the mid-1970s there was strong pressure on LEAs for specialist placements for disruptive pupils to be made available away from the classroom. Young *et al.* (1979; 1980) have argued that the 1974 local government reorganization was instrumental in creating a framework within which LEAs felt able to examine the issue in some detail and formulate a comprehensive strategy.

Many such schemes exist (Reid 1986). In the majority of cases the provision of off-site units was seen as the most appropriate response. A considerable number of on-site units, were, however, also established. In most cases pupils continued, and still continue, to be managed within the school setting along traditional lines, despite teachers' initial training limitations and, in some cases, obvious skill limitations (Reid 1987g).

There was not, and never has been, the same degree of pressure for special units for absentee pupils. But once units of various kinds had been established, many LEAs felt that they could be used with advantage for a wide variety of pupils including absentees (Skinner *et al.* 1983).

Traditionally many schools have been less concerned about their non-conforming absentees than many other kinds of educational groups. Recent legislation involving teachers' duties, school accountability, appraisal, and evaluation is beginning to change this attitude (Reid 1987h), as is research on school effectiveness (Reid *et al*. 1987).

Constraints of space prevent me from describing every intervention strategy in full. So many local projects are in process up and down the country that it is probably not feasible anyway. Therefore, I will now turn my attention to some of the better known schemes. These include

1 counselling groups in schools or in units
2 counselling individuals
3 establishing no-return units
4 setting up re-integration units
5 creating on-site units within and outside schools
6 establishing parent-absentee groups
7 setting up multi-problem groups
8 attempting peer counselling
9 instigating 'locational integration' units
10 creating short- and long-term off-site units of a variety of kinds
11 establishing IT day care centres
12 utilizing adjustment units
13 providing 'free' transport to escort absentees to and from school
14 sending pupils to alternative or 'free' schools
15 approving individual or group home tuition schemes.

Skinner *et al*. (1983) conclude that in the choice between preventive pastoral care and specialist provision for absentee pupils the majority of LEAs appear to have opted for specialist units. In choosing between on- and off-site units, the latter predominate by two to one. They believe that much of the debate has now shifted to the patterns of how schools use off-site centres, the most appropriate location, as well as the content of the education provided noting, incidentally, that units are generally set up for the 14–16 age group, often including disruptive absentees. Like many schools however, some LEAs appear to reserve the option of turning a blind eye and of not acknowledging that problems exist.

Thus intervention strategies tend to be a matter of local preference and of individual expertise. If a scheme works once, the notion grows that it is likely to work for a second time. This is perhaps not only pragmatic but also understandable and logical. The survey by Her Majesty's Inspectorate (HMI 1978) noted, *en passant*, that procedures for returning pupils to school were often less well developed than those for referral to units. They found that while the philosophies of practitioners within units varied, emphasizing different approaches such as social adjustment, remedial work in basic skills and general enrichment schemes for deprived pupils, the outcomes were similar. The prognosis for pupils of 14 or below was much better than for those who were older — adolescents who could make up their own minds. Indeed, irrespective of intervention strategy, writers continually draw attention to the different organization used by team leaders within the units (Grunsell 1980; Tattum 1982).

One scheme which is gaining in credibility operates in Wigan (Wilson 1988). There are three main elements to the scheme.

1 The use of group work, not only with young people but also with their parents.
2 There is a commitment from the social sevice and education departments to co-operative working, involving the pooling of resources and staff.
3 There is an appreciation of a need for a pro-active, rather than reactive, approach to the work in order to maximize the impact on the non-attenders and on the juvenile court.

Wilson considers that with the right attitudes and training the education welfare service and others can work successfully with the 'heavy end' of non-attenders in the community, rather than seeking their removal into local authority care or descending into the repeated use of threats which can ultimately prove to be so counter-productive in the majority of cases.

Summarizing, the literature reveals two forms of practice. One is the close co-operation of on- and off-site education centres and schools in identifying, working with, and reintegrating pupils in the 11–13 age group through a variety of social service, educational psychology or teaching schemes, school-based or otherwise, multi-disciplinary or in-house. The other is the existence of large numbers of 14–16-year-olds completing their education in on- and off-site educational centres following a complete breakdown in the pupil–school relationship, often preceded by years of tension and strain (Skinner *et al.* 1983).

Supporters of the first practice point to its advantages for pupils and schools. As yet however, there is very little hard evidence to indicate whether the reconciliation lasts until school-leaving age. Most teachers feel antipathy towards the alternative education programme. In particular, they object in principle to pupils being educated outside the mainstream. They think that alternative education encourages the premature labelling of pupils as 'deviants', 'failures', and 'truants'. Some teachers believe that well-managed schools should be able to contain and educate all kinds of pupils — including disruptive truants.

By contrast, supporters of the second practice highlight the special opportunities available in units for individualized programmes to be followed. They stress the advantages of the 'free' atmosphere, the positive gains at the absence of rules, the benefits of, for example, the use of individual contacts, the relaxed atmosphere, the improved teacher–tutor relationship and the all-round behavioural improvement which is often epitomized in the literature (Grunsell 1980; Reid 1986).

Teachers retort to these supposed benefits by asking whether there are any real gains for opting out, especially when a pupil misses out on a broad curriculum and external examination opportunities. But should it be necessary for absentees to have to be separated from their peers in order to receive an education programme suited to their needs and circumstances? Should absentees have to opt out to be treated with a modicum of respect and consideration (Sayer 1987)?

In fact, should teachers and administrators be asking themselves some further questions? Should they not be able to identify absenteeism earlier in schools? Should they not be more flexible in their approach so that they can encourage potential or actual absentees to remain or return to school? Should secondary teachers concentrate more on the first two years of schooling in their detection techniques given the failure of later intervention? Should school managers concentrate more on aspects of school organization (Reid 1982) and teacher management in order to prevent absenteeism? Should schools examine what type of curriculum and school ethos needs to be provided so as to retain potentially at risk pupils like absentees in schools in as productive a manner as possible (Reid 1987a; 1987b; 1987c; 1987d; 1987e)? Perhaps the introduction of school special needs policies following on from the Warnock philosophy will have some benefits in this respect (Galloway 1987)?

Of course, as indicated earlier, not all intervention strategies used with absentees currently lead to alternative education schemes being utilized. The specialized counselling of pupils in schools in groups by social workers or educational psychologists is one such example. Here pupils are withdrawn from individual lessons, or seen at lunch-times, or after school. Parent-absentee-professional groups meet in a range of venues at times to suit everyone. Multi-problem groups (absentees, disrupters, slow learners, handicapped pupils, etc.) are known to meet in and out of school hours.

The literature on alternative education schemes is generally encouraging. Reports on IT units, for example, are often highly positive (Pickles 1981; 1987). Moreover, the ultimate purpose of alternative education may be to analyse the shortcomings of mainstream schooling and by so doing, to feed back knowledge on curriculum innovation and methods of handling and teaching difficult groups of pupils which can be applied in the normal school setting (Skinner *et al.* 1983).

Nevertheless, the fact remains that most formal intervention strategies with absentees seem to fail. Most referred absentees fail to attend school regularly after their initial counselling interview and subsequent 'treatment'. The considerable claims that are made for alternative education programmes are made on the basis of dealing with a very small minority of the total population of absentees. In fact, the vast majority of absentees never reach the clinical stage and of those that do, all the evidence points to large numbers of failures up and down the country. Apart from anything else, most educational psychologists and/or social workers simply do not have either the time or expertise necessary in resolving non-attendance cases. Neither for that matter do the courts or teachers (Reid 1985).

And herein lies the root of the issue. Conventional wisdom suggests that intervention agents focus on the home, social and psychological aspects in remedial approaches. Research and practical experience show that in a majority of cases educational solutions are also needed; sometimes, quite frequently, more than anything else (Reid 1983a; 1983b).

Therefore approaches which favour non-educational solutions are normally inappropriate; what is needed is for outside agencies, as well as 'schools' themselves, to formulate meaningful institution-specific educational solutions.

The best way to stop non-attendance from escalating is to nip it in the bud. Schools have simply got to improve their detection schemes in accord with, for example, the Bicester scheme (Reid 1982), although other local schemes operate (Jones 1980). Factors which militate against good practice inside schools need to be eradicated. Far too many pupils, like John at the start of this chapter, miss school for comparatively trivial reasons which, psychologically, grow out of all proportion in their own minds.

Let us reflect on some of them. Bullying. Extortion. Being late. Being shouted at in class. 'Failing' a test or exam. Falling behind after being ill. The dislike of a teacher. Being 'sent to Coventry' by one's peers. Having a mother who is ill. Not having a school uniform. A fear of the water. Feeling stupid in PE kit. Having spots. And so forth. There is no end to this potential list.

The tragedy is that within many schools, despite the presence of pastoral staff and their systems of 'help', most teachers are too busy to understand or get at the root problems of actual or potential absentees' concerns. Consequently the pupils opt out: something which, in the initial stages at least, demands a certain amount of misplaced courage and leads to deviousness. The whole process means that teachers feel out of sympathy with pupils who have rejected the system, and so comparatively minor problems become exacerbated, reinforced, and develop.

Then for the hardened core, far too late, professional experts are called in to intervene. They are supposed to solve matters which teachers have ignored for months or years. Generally they fail. In reality, there are no magical panaceas.

Given this sad history of failure, I should like to propose a few elementary solutions. First, detection systems within schools must be improved. These should begin at the primary stage of education. Research (Reid 1985) indicates that roughly one in four or five absentees commence their non-attendance in their primary schools.

Second, school policies should be realistic rather than harsh or unbending. Is it better to modify the individual time-table of pupils (say girls' PE) than force them to participate and so withdraw? Should a pupil without a uniform be sent home? Should a pupil who has been away ill be assisted to catch up with her work? Should a pupil who needs extra help with reading, writing, or arithmetic receive it? Should a pupil who cannot get on with his peers be moved class or school?

Too many pupils have illegal but justifiable and/or understandable reasons for missing school. The pupil who is being badly taught. The pupil who cannot get on with a teacher who dislikes her. These are managerial issues which need resolving. Is every absentee wrong? Why do so many teacher/pastoral staff not listen to their pupils? In the late 1970s I remember researching in a school which had a 40-plus per cent rate of absenteeism. HMI later referred to the establishment as 'the worst truancy school in Britain'. Yet, in a matter of weeks, I became convinced that factors at work within the school were to blame. I also felt, but kept to myself, that the staff and their policies were to blame. The pupil management within the school was incredibly bad. Yet all the staff blamed the parents, the catchment area, the LEA, the head, the pupils themselves, the . . . Everything but themselves! Within three miles there were two larger comprehensives with above average rates of attendance in similar catchment areas.

Third, therefore, teachers need in-service programmes which lead them to understand the variety of complex, interwoven issues which are involved in non-attendance cases and how to combat and comprehend them (Reid 1987f). Other helping professionals need similar courses. Moreover, the best kind of intervention strategies, and those which operate and work most successfully (Gillman 1984), are those which are jointly planned by school staff and professional agencies together on a basis of mutual understanding. These require a disproportionate amount of time and energy. But there again, the rewards will be greater too. Sadly for the present time, the literature is deficient on illustrative case studies of good practice; something which is a challenge to professionals in several professions. There are signs however, that in a limited way, in isolated areas and schools, the formulation of good practice is already starting to happen, which must give us all some optimism for the future.

This makes good sense. It is surely futile for, say, psychologists to listen week in and week out to the failure of particular schools and not to report the information back. Not to do anything constructive with their knowledge. Not to instigate remedial policies which stand a chance of being effective.

Such creativity is probably infinitely better than using or resorting to alternative education schemes. It is similarly better than adding to statistics which prove that existing intervention strategies rarely succeed.

There are other positive benefits too. The improvement in the quality or relationships and team work between professionals from differing backgrounds and organizations. The gains in teacher–pupil relationships. The chance to improve the image and views pupils hold of their teachers and schools (Reid 1983b). The opportunity to eradicate or reduce absenteeism in schools on a large rather than a limited scale.

It is by following these bold innovative approaches that professionals like educational psychologists, social workers, and teachers will improve their own self-image and chances of job satisfaction. They may find that they assist school pastoral systems to work — rather than fail (Hamblin 1984; 1986; Reid 1986; 1987g; 1987i). They may prevent pupils like John, Janet, and Susan from even missing school in the first place. Or, if they did, make it easier to return.

But a final word of warning. To achieve these ideals there is going to have to be a massive attitudinal change amongst professionals — especially teachers; and realistically, this does seem a long way away. What is needed, therefore, are pilot research schemes which show that inter-disciplinary and multi-disciplinary approaches can work and prove effective. And these leads need to be followed up by professionals throughout the country.

References

Galloway, D. (1987) 'Absenteeism: Implications for pastoral care and provision for special educational needs', in K. Reid (ed.) *Combating School Absenteeism*, London: Hodder & Stoughton.

Gillman, B. (1984) 'School organisation and the control of disruptive incidents', in N. Frude and H. Gault (eds) *Disruptive Behaviour in Schools*, Chichester: Wiley.

Grunsell, R. (1980) *Absent from School: The Story of a Truancy Centre*, London, Writers & Readers.

Hamblin, D. H. (1984) 'The failure of pastoral care', *School Organization* 6, 1: 141–8.

——— (1986) *The Pastoral Curriculum*, Oxford: Blackwell.

HMI (1978) *Behavioural Units: A Survey of Special Units for Pupils with*

Behavioural Problems, London: Department of Education and Science.
Jones, A. (1980) 'The school's view of non-attendance', in L. Herson and I. Berg (eds) *Out of School*, Chichester: Wiley.
Pickles, T. (1981) 'Developing day-care', *Youth in Society* 52: 20–1.
——— (1987) 'Day-care — child-centred approach', in K. Reid (ed.) *Combating School Absenteeism*, London: Hodder & Stoughton.
Reid, K. (1982) 'The self-concept and persistent school absenteeism', *British Journal of Educational Psychology* 52, 2: 179–87.
——— (1983a) 'Retrospection and persistent school absenteeism', *Educational Research* 25, 2: 110–15.
——— (1983b) 'Differences between the perception of persistent absentees towards parents and teachers', *Educational Studies* 9, 3: 211–19.
——— (1984a) 'Some social, psychological and educational aspects related to persistent school absenteeism', *Research in Education* 31: 63–82.
——— (1984b) 'Disruptive behaviour and persistent school absenteeism', in N. Frude and H. Gault (eds) *Disruptive Behaviour in Schools*, Chichester: Wiley.
——— (1984c) 'The behaviour of persistent school absentees', *British Journal of Educational Psychology* 54: 320–30.
——— (1985) *Truancy and School Absenteeism*, London: Hodder & Stoughton.
——— (1986) *Disaffection from School*, London: Methuen.
——— (1987a) 'Attitudes: Parents, pupils and teachers — the implications for professionals and practitioners', in K. Reid (ed.) *Combating School Absenteeism*, London: Hodder & Stoughton.
——— (1987b) 'Absenteeism and the curiculum', in ibid.
——— (1987c) 'Effective pastoral care and school absenteeism', in ibid.
——— (1987d) 'The education welfare service', in ibid.
——— (1987e) 'The Hargreaves Report, school improvement and absenteeism', in ibid.
——— (1987f) 'Teacher education, disaffection and absenteeism', in ibid.
——— (1987g) 'Social work and school absenteeism', in ibid.
——— (1987h) 'Combating school absenteeism: main conclusions', in ibid.
——— (1987i) 'The creative interface of the Education and Social Services in cases of absenteeism', in ibid.
Reid, K., Hopkins, D., and Holly, P. (1987) *Towards the Effective School*, Oxford: Blackwell.
Sayer, J. (1987) 'Why have you come to school today? A pathology of presence', in K. Reid (ed.) *Combating School Absenteeism*, London: Hodder & Stoughton.
Skinner, A., with Platts, B., and Hill, B. (1983) *Disaffection From School: Issues and Interagency Reasons*, Leicester: National Youth Bureau.
Tattum, D. (1982) *Disruptive Pupils in Schools and Units*, Chichester: Wiley.
Wilson, J. (1988) 'Non-attenders', in K. Reid (ed.) *Helping Troubled*

Pupils in Schools, vol. 2, Oxford: Blackwell.
Young, P., Lawrence, J., and Steed, D. (1979) 'Local authority responses to disruptive behaviour in schools', *Policy and Politics* 7, 4: 387–93.
Young, P., Steed, D., and Lawrence, J. (1980), 'Local education authorities and autonomous off-site units for disruptive pupils in secondary schools', *Cambridge Journal of Education* 10, 2: 55–70.

Chapter six

Class-cutting: an ecological approach

Irwin Hyman

Class-cutting, for want of a better title, is a generic term to describe student behaviours which result in failure to attend class or school for any length of time. Lateness, failure to attend specific classes, and absence from school for the entire day are among the commonest disciplinary problems facing educators. As with most discipline problems, punishment has historically been the typical response by teachers and school administrators (Hyman and Wise 1979). Punishment, however, has quite limited efficacy to change behaviours, especially in the school setting where a complex set of variables often contribute to the misbehaviours (Hyman and D'Allessandro 1984; Hyman *et al.* 1979; Hyman *et al.* 1982a).

In an extensive review of research on the effectiveness of teacher training programmes to improve school discipline, Hyman and Lally (1982) reported on the voluminous literature documenting the worth of positive approaches to school discipline. The literature clearly demonstrates that prevention is the best way to eliminate the need for punishment. Yet schools continue to respond to problems such as class-cutting with a limited repertoire of punitively oriented responses. Suspension and detention are most frequently used as responses to class-cutting. The former is recognized as a rather absurd reaction since more time away from school is often the goal of students who are truant. In other words, the intended punishment becomes a reward. In some parts of the world, corporal punishment is quite popular and as equally ineffective as the latter two punishments.

Individual reasons for the continued use of ineffective disciplinary procedures are varied. Techniques such as corporal punishment and suspension are easy to carry out, they are inexpensive, they often result in short-term behavioural changes which reinforce the punisher and they require relatively little thought. Yet few colleges or universities which train educators recommend these limited responses to misbehaviour.

Most teachers in training are exposed to the vast research in development, learning, and behaviour which demonstrate the clear superiority of positive procedures to shape behaviour, enhance self-esteem, and provide the foundation for moral character development. Yet educators continue to rely on and defend punitive techniques which are sometimes actually abusive (Bogacki 1981; Hyman 1987; Hyman *et al.* 1987a; Hyman *et al.*, forthcoming). Obviously the undergraduate training of teachers has not convinced the majority to adopt effective preventive approaches to problems of school discipline such as class-cutting. The reasons for this are varied.

The purpose of this chapter is to explore briefly why many schools tend to be ineffective in dealing with the problem of class-cutting. This is first explained in terms of the reasons why educators continue to use methods which are ineffective in the long run. This is followed by a proposal to consider the problem theoretically from an ecological perspective. This section is purposely written for use with educators. It is a practical guide which professionals can use directly in helping teachers and administrators to design programmes. This does not deal with process factors involving methods of organizational development and consultation, which are discussed elsewhere (Hyman 1976; Lennox *et al.*, forthcoming).

Educator etiology and modelling effects

Traditional approaches to misbehaviour in school have tended to focus on the teacher as either victim of errant students or the cause of the student's misbehaviour. Despite university training in development, learning, and educational psychology at the undergraduate level, childhood experiences and the culture of the school have the greatest impact on teacher attitudes and subsequent behaviours towards misbehaviour. Most course work has tended to treat the problem theoretically, with little applied training which relates theory to practice. Few teachers receive courses which specifically address the theory, research, and practice of discipline, even though the ability of beginning teachers is very much judged on classroom management skills. Classroom control is a major standard for determining teacher tenure. Student teachers and new teachers quickly learn that punishment offers a 'quick fix'. This is taught by seasoned mentors who in turn learned from their own models. The culture of punitiveness is thus a transgenerational phenomenon which still permeates today's schools.

While the horrors recounted by Charles Dickens are relatively rare in modern education, it is not difficult to find them. This is evidenced in recurring cases of physical and psychological abuse which are well documented (Hyman 1987; Hyman *et al.* 1987a; Hyman *et al.* 1987b; Hyman *et al.*, forthcoming). Recognizing this problem, most developers of training have focused on encouraging teachers to use more enlightened and efficacious approaches to discipline. They attempt to train teachers to approach students in terms of motivating techniques but tend to ignore teachers as part of a culture in which the school, community, and traditions play an important role. This will be discussed later, but should be kept in mind.

During the last twenty years there has been a boom in the growth of programmes to improve teacher management of classroom behaviour (Hyman *et al.* 1982a; Hyman and Lally 1982; Stagliano and Hyman 1983). Most of these programmes might be categorized as micro-efforts because they reduce the problem to the smallest educational unit — the classroom.

Micro-approaches are quite popular with educators for a variety of reasons. Most have simple-to-read, practically oriented materials for teachers. The materials are often presented as part of well-oriented workshops which are conveniently organized to fit within school in-service training schedules. Many of the programme originators and workshop leaders are interesting speakers who entertain their audiences. Their polished presentations and slick materials are replete with individual examples relevant to the lives of teachers as they face daily problems of discipline. Yet do they really change the teachers' actual long-term behaviour? Probably not!

A crucial factor in the failure of teacher-focused discipline training has been the lack of attention to the powerful etiological factors which most determine teachers' responses to new approaches. For instance, many teachers do not believe that children should be rewarded for good behaviour. They reflect traditional assumptions that children should be good because they have a moral obligation to be good. Also these teachers may have been raised to believe that fear of punishment is the best motivator of proper behaviour in both children and adults. This type of person will generally actively resist implementing behaviour modification programmes in the classroom. If they are pressed to use behavioural techniques, they will overtly or covertly sabotage the programme. The failure will then be the result of a self-fulfilling prophecy. Despite these obvious limitations of school-wide training programmes for teachers, teacher-oriented training in school discipline tends to ignore idiosyncratic differences among staff which may well lead to failure at the school level. Yet these approaches continue to proliferate.

A series of studies on modelling behaviour clearly demonstrate the powerful role of childhood on the lives of people who eventually become teachers, child-care workers, psychologists and/or parents (Lennox 1982; Sofer 1983; Pokalo 1986; Mishkin 1987). These studies focused on the issue of corporal punishment and associated levels of adult punitiveness. Every study demonstrated that the level of punitiveness of adults in relation to the behaviour of their wards was significantly correlated with the amount of punitiveness they received during their own childhoods. Fundamentalist protestant religious orientation and childhood spent in conservative rural areas were also predictive of future punitiveness. The least punitive parents were those with educations past the master's level and having a history of little punitiveness directed towards them in their childhood and adolescent years.

Because of the importance of teacher differences in background, it seems obvious that discipline training should attempt to focus on issues such as class-cutting from two broad perspectives. First, individual training of teachers should attempt to provide options and approaches which are consistent with each teacher's own philosophic assumptions. This approach originated in the child variance concept proposed by Morse and Smith (1980). This work was then extended by Hyman and colleagues at the National Center for the Study of Corporal Punishment and Alternatives in the Schools (Hyman *et al.* 1982a; Hyman *et al.* 1983).

The Teacher Variance work by Hyman and his colleagues offers teachers insight into their own beliefs about children's misbehaviour. Scales of punitiveness and discipline orientation help teachers to choose one of six non-punitive approaches to problems such as class-cutting. These approaches are (1) behavioural, (2) psychodynamic/interpersonal, (3) classroom ecology, (4) sociological, (5) humanistic, and (6) biophysical. Teachers are encouraged to study in-depth the orientation with which they are most comfortable. They are presented with theory and then required to apply the theory to real-life situations.

The purpose of this chapter is to examine the problems of class-cutting from a broad ecological perspective, and therefore the Teacher Variance approach will not be discussed in detail. However, this approach to helping to individualize discipline training should be considered. If all teachers are able to improve the climate of their own classroom, there is little doubt that this will help to decrease class-cutting. This is based on the assumption that a major factor in avoidance is poor instruction and an unreceptive classroom environment. However, a variety of factors may contribute to the problem. Therefore it is appropriate to turn to a broader perspective with emphasis on a preventive approach, which also allows for the types of immediate solutions which educators want. Actually the approach presented fits somewhat within the framework of the sociological model of teacher variance.

An ecological framework

A number of years ago the writer was enlisted to develop a brief manual to help school administrators deal with the problem of class-cutting. The National Alliance for Safe Schools had begun to review the literature and list all of the recommendations available. However, there was no theoretical base and the list did not offer a systematic approach. This is typical of responses to dealing with school discipline problems.

Too often, disciplinarians act out a limited series of punishments without having a theoretical base for understanding why a particular approach does not work. They tend to ignore the system or culture in which misbehaviour occurs. Yet, twenty years of conducting in-service training suggests that educational practitioners have little appetite for digesting theory. Most frequently they want immediate answers to pressing problems. Therefore, as a sort of compromise, a 'bag of tricks' approach was developed within the framework of prevention theory. Educators contributed to a list of solutions to class-cutting. In order to add to the solutions provided in the literature, the investigators enlisted the aid of educators in a school for emotionally disturbed adolescents. This school had participated in a very successful project to reduce class-cutting.

The following material was developed to be used directly by educators. It is devoid of 'psychobabble' and addresses the educator directly. It is presented here in this format so that it will be of direct use to professionals working with educators. The first section deals with the problem of diagnosis.

In order to assess the problem, planners need to address a series of questions which are presented first. The outline presented should not be considered exhaustive. Each school can add to the diagnostic, preventive, and corrective suggestions presented.

Diagnostic considerations

Problems related to the home

A. Family structure

1 Is the family intact?
2 Who is responsible for discipline?
3 Does the student have family responsibilities that override concerns for being in school?
4 Does the parents' work schedule interfere with discipline?

B. Family power

1 Is one or both parents weak and unable to enforce school discipline?
2 Does the student use class-cutting as a way to get back at parents?
3 Is discipline regarding class-cutting overly punitive or overly permissive?
4 Do parents need the support of the school to enforce school attendance?

C Family values

1 Do parents value school attendance?
2 Are parents able to communicate effectively their value of the school to the child?
3 Are parents undermining school authority?

Problems related to school

A School organization

1 Is there a clear set of guidelines regarding class-cutting?
2 Are students and parents aware of the consequences of class-cutting?
3 Are guidelines just sent out once a year, sent home with students, discussed in class, etc.?
4 Are guidelines followed in an overly legalistic manner which prevents fairness by ignoring individual circumstances?
5 Are guidelines inconsistently followed or ignored by individuals or groups of staff?
6 Does the school have appropriate staff to handle class-cutting? This includes checking attendance, intraschool communication, truancy officers, etc. Can computers be used to speed data use?
7 Are there appropriate physical barriers to class-cutting?
8 Are there sufficient and appropriate staff for monitoring the halls, athletic fields, etc.?
9 Are there adequate personnel to discourage suspended or expelled students and others from entering school and encouraging students to cut classes?
10 Does the school have a motivational system to encourage attendances, for example awards, free time?
11 Does the administration encourage good attendance by teachers by using the same approaches to positive motivation as teachers may use with students?
12 Do students have the opportunity for restitution rather than punishment?
13 Do staff understand individual reasons for class-cutting or do they generalize, for example 'It's all the parents' fault'?
14 Are there provisions and facilities for in-school suspension and after school detention?
15 Does the principal attempt to make school an interesting and rewarding place for students?

B Students and peer group

1 What subgroup cultures exist and how does each encourage or discourage class-cutting?

2 Do students perceive staff as favouring particular subgroups in terms of the enforcement of rules?
3 Have staff attempted to use differential motivational techniques to reach various peer groups?
4 Have novel approaches such as peer counselling, peer tutoring, etc. been used?
5 Have students been involved in planning discipline codes, monitoring the fairness of administration of rules, etc.?

C Teachers and teaching

1 Are significant numbers of teachers 'burned out' and therefore unconcerned about class-cutting?
2 Are there systems of rewards or recognition for teachers who motivate students to attend?
3 Are teachers involved in problem-solving and planning regarding class-cutting?
4 Do teachers receive adequate information and consultation concerning students with severe class-cutting problems?
5 Do teachers feel that they are supported by the administration in difficult cases?
6 Are teachers provided with time and encouraged to work with parents on class-cutting? Is this done through other staff such as guidance counsellors or truant officers? If so, do they facilitate or truncate communication between parents and teachers?
7 Are teachers teaching with adequate supplies of interesting texts and supplementary materials?
8 Are students being taught at appropriate grade levels?

Problems related to the community

A Values

1 Does the community at large support and value the school and the need for students to be in school?
2 Are there hostilities between segments of the community and students?
3 Can industry and business be tapped to help provide incentives for good school attendance?
4 Does the community allow sweet shops, video hire shops, snooker halls, etc. to cater to school-children during the school day?

B Control

1 Is there a co-operative relationship with the police regarding school-aged young people on the streets during school hours?
2 Are there or could there be juvenile officers assigned to the school?
3 Is there a rational and helpful system of juvenile justice for dealing with chronic truants?

C Opportunities

1 Are there adequate work study opportunities for students who can't or won't function in a full academic setting?
2 Do students perceive adequate work opportunities upon graduation?
3 Are community recreation activities overly available during school hours?

Prevention and remediation

In a latter section of this chapter there is a 'bag of tricks' which have been used with various levels of success. Each school district is unique and what works in one place may be a failure in another. If long-range solutions are required, it is necessary to diagnose the reasons for cutting classes and then determine levels of intervention. The level of intervention should be matched with the place where the problem resides. For instance if significant numbers of students are cutting school in the remedial level track, it is possible that the course work is perceived as babyish and dull to the students. Increasing punishments for cutting might be much less effective than improving instruction and materials.

For purposes of intervention, five categories are included: prevention, primary and secondary level correction, punishment, and restitution. They cannot be precise and therefore overlap may be anticipated; however, they may act as rough guidelines.

Prevention

Based on current research concerning schooling, it can be assumed that if schools are safe, if teachers are enthusiastic, if materials are interesting and if good school spirit exists, cutting will be minimal

(Hyman and D'Allessandro 1984). Educators can begin by asking themselves, 'If things were really good, how would they be?' Prevention depends on the development of students' internalized controls, a desire to achieve, and a co-operative spirit with school authorities, parents, etc.

Primary level correction

These interventions are aimed at infrequent offenders. They usually consist of mild forms of punishment, the use of incentives, or parent contracts. They target situational cutters.

Secondary level correction

Interventions here often include specialized services and programmes. Correction techniques may include alternative schools, short- or long-term counselling, close co-operation with parents, etc. While punishment may be needed, educators recognize that these students are in need of and may profit from help.

Punishment

Punishments such as in-school suspension, after-school detention, fining parents, etc. are often used with chronic truants. Often the courts need to be involved. Punishment is generally not effective if it is overused. Most educators would agree that suspension and expulsion for class-cutting are not helpful with chronic truants. This is supported by the limited research available.

Restitution

This approach is rarely used in contemporary schools. It provides students with the opportunity to 'make up' for their misdeeds. It requires creativity and time but interestingly is being used with increasing frequency by the courts, especially as an alternative to incarceration.

Using the problem-solving matrix

The problem-solving matrix summary of the narrative is presented on p. 117. This matrix (see Table 6.1) is meant to provide a

Table 6.1 Problem-solving matrix for class-cutting

Diagnosis category	*Levels of intervention*				
	1 Prevention	*2 Primary correction*	*3 Secondary correction*	*4 Punishment*	*5 Restitution*
Home					
A Family structure	HA1	HA2	HA3	HA4	HA5
B Family power	HB1	HB2	HB3	HB4	HB5
C Family values	HC1	HC2	HC3	HC4	HC5
School					
A Organization	SA1	SA2	SA3	SA4	SA5
B Students and peer groups	SB1	SB2	SB3	SB4	SB5
C Teachers and teaching	SC1	SC2	SC3	SC4	SC5
Community					
A Values	CA1	CA2	CA3	CA4	CA5
B Control	CB1	CB2	CB3	CB4	CB5
C Opportunities	CC1	CC2	CC3	CC4	CC5

systematic method of approaching the problem of class-cutting. Depending on time and resources, the following approach may be used in its entirety or in sections.

1 Gather data concerning the source of the class-cutting problem. This can be done for individuals or for the entire school. Data collection is best served by use of a questionnaire. Sources could be students, parents, staff, etc. While actual data gathering is strongly advised, it is recognized that it may not be possible because of limitations in qualified staff, staff time, resources, etc. An alternative would be the use of a representative committee. An outside consultant can be extremely helpful in beginning stages (Lennox *et al.*, forthcoming). This diagnosis as to the major source or sources should be determined and the major target area identified. Also recognize that the diagnosis categories presented here are not intended to be definitive and other categories may be added.
2 Decide what levels of interventions are possible considering resources available.
3 Use the coding in the matrix to check for appropriate levels of interventions which might work in your school. Add additional interventions through brainstorming.
4 Consider the advantages and disadvantages of each approach. You may determine additional strengths and weaknesses.
5 Set up committees to implement the programmes. Try to collect data on class-cutting in a way that are easily retrievable. Computerization would be ideal.
6 Evaluate if your approaches are working. If not, gather additional data on why they are not working and correct them.

Additional considerations

This chapter is meant to provide a process for examining and solving the problem of class-cutting. If the problem is severe it may be systemic within the school and may require outside consultation in order to offer an objective view of the situation. The intervention approaches suggested here have strengths and weaknesses which are summarized below.

Prevention

Prevention provides the best long-term solution to most problems. The major advantage is that prevention has a pervasive effect that reaches beyond individual cases. Over the long run, prevention is almost always the most cost-effective solution.

The major drawback regarding prevention is that initially it requires great effort. Also it requires people to function in specific ways which can cause resentment and resistance. For instance, enthusiastic teachers may be highly valued by students and administrators. But who defines enthusiasm and how do you teach this to all school staff if it is perceived as necessary to improve class attendance?

Correction

Methods of primary correction work when all parties hold the same values. They are easily used, effective, and have few drawbacks. Secondary correction suggests that students have become chronic in class-cutting behaviour. Successful programmes of secondary correction often require help from mental health professionals. The advantage of correction techniques is that they focus on individuals and may get to the root of the problem. However, they may not appear cost effective when the time of highly trained personnel is primarily focused on individuals.

Punishment

Research and experience indicate that punishment is the least effective way to change behaviour. Its advantage is that it is usually relatively cheap, can easily be administered by untrained staff, and students sometimes prefer it in order to wipe away the misdeed. It is effective only when it taps the student's sense of guilt. Chronic truants have often been frequently punished without any appreciable effect.

Restitution

Restitution is a useful alternative to punishment. Its major advantage is that it may be related to the misdeed and let the student 'do something good'. Restitution requires a great deal of planning and assigning work tasks may interfere with union rules involving building maintenance workers.

Working with the home

In cases of class-cutting it is usually necessary to contact parents. Surveys suggest that teachers most often identify uncooperative parents as the chief culprits in cutting. The great advantages in working with parents is that you may be intervening at the root of the problem. For a variety of reasons, teachers may not be willing to work with parents and need training and motivation in this area.

Working with the community

It is very helpful to obtain community involvement. It extends the reach of the school. However, it usually requires a lot of public relations and political efforts and most school people feel that they are too busy with their own problems. It is helpful to assign a staff member to the task of community relations officer if the outreach is to be successful.

Following are the actual interventions suggested for use with the matrix. (Here the 'Community' part of the matrix is not being discussed.) Note, again, that these are intended as a beginning and offer examples to the approach. They will not work if not adapted to local conditions and if results of these and new solutions are not continuously evaluated.

Interventions for the matrix: home

HA1: Family structure — prevention

- Facilitate provisions for pre-school service so that high-school students are not responsible for caring for younger siblings during the school day.
- Offer parents' workshops in parenting, discipline, etc.
- Be sure parents receive copies of guidelines regarding class-cutting.

HA2: Family structure — primary correction

- Offer small group parenting seminars for parents of students who are beginning to cut class.
- Provide parents with booklets on corrective techniques.

HA3: Family structure — secondary correction

- Help parents by using daily communication techniques.
- Set up behaviour modification system with parents.

HA4: Family structure — punishment

- Support parents' efforts to punish students for class-cutting.
- Have school psychologist or guidance counsellor check that family understands the role of punishment.

HA5: Family structure — restitution

- Help parents determine what types of restitution are applicable.

HB1: Family power — prevention

- Help parents determine role in discipline.
- Help parents to understand if they are being manipulated by student.

HB2: Family power — primary correction

- Offer small group parenting seminars on various topics which deal with control of teenagers.
- Keep parents informed of all cutting and help them use corrective techniques.

HB3: Family power — secondary correction

- Work with parents to assure correction techniques are followed appropriately.
- Use techniques similar to those in HA3.
- Suggest family therapy if necessary.

HB4: Family power — punishment

- Use techniques similar to those in HA4.
- Determine if punishment is too severe and non-productive or too weak.
- Determine if student is winning power struggle by class-cutting.

HB5: Family power — restitution

- Use techniques similar to those in HA5.
- Support parent in charge of discipline with suggestions and encouragement.

HC1: Family values — prevention

- Send newsletter home to parents containing the events of the month and include items on improved attendance.
- Increase parent involvement by having teachers send positive reports home instead of only negative ones.
- If parents are afraid of school authorities or resent the intrusion, develop better attitudes through communication.
- Start a 'Discipline Helpline' (Fina 1985).

HC2: Family values — primary correction

- Permit special several-day outings (special vacations, hunting trips, etc.) with parents for students with perfect attendance. Arrange for completion of missed school work.
- Help parents to understand the appropriate use of rewards and punishment.

HC3: Family values — secondary correction

- Help parents to understand the value of positive methods of motivation. If overly permissive in family, help them to understand the results.

HC4: Family values — punishment

- Assure parents that punishment may have to be used and that they should not feel guilty. On the other hand, if punishment is excessively used and is too harsh, help parents to understand that it becomes counterproductive.

HC5: Family values — restitution

— Convince parents of the value of restitution.

Interventions for the matrix: school

SA1: School organization — prevention

— Take all possible steps to assure that school is a safe, rewarding, and pleasant place to be.
— Develop clear set of guidelines (discipline code or a booklet of rules and responsibilities).
— Develop and use periodically an attitude scale to determine school climate.
— Be certain students are aware of the rules, keep them clear, concise, well publicized, appropriate, and consistently enforced.
— Use fewer substitute teachers as child-minders and provide a stimulating agenda of films, discussions, and impromptu guest (other staff) speakers.
— Incorporate ethnic and group pride into school pride by having competition between schools rather than between groups.
— Combine form-base with first period.
— Ascertain whether teachers have something to gain from student class-cutting and truancy.
— Display attendance graphs periodically with one class competing against the other.
— Permit exam exemption for students with perfect attendance or straight As if they desire.
— Have an attendance lottery, with each student having the opportunity to win by random drawing of student's number.
— Offer rewards for perfect attendance by the staff.
— Offer rewards to teachers who are able to maintain high attendance in their classes.

SA2: School organization–primary correction

— Provide teachers or staff with time and facilities to telephone parents or class-cutters.

— Reward improved or perfect attendance with tangible and social means, such as stickers, publicity, luncheons for parents and students, or tickets to sporting or social events.
— Have form teacher review with each student the previous year's attendance record — often students are not fully aware of how much time they have really missed.
— Schedule special presentations, assemblies, guest speakers, and fun aspects of the course on days of peak class-cutting or truancy.
— Eliminate half-day sessions and early dismissals as the students feel that they are not worth coming in for.
— Phone call by counsellor, teacher, deputy-head, or vice-principal to parents or guardians for class-cutting and truancy.
— Check for health problems that might be embarrassing or interfering with class work, such as poor hearing or vision, hyperactivity, dyslexia, glandular disorders, etc.
— Develop work study programmes for those who are beginning to resent school because of inability to do work or who express excessive boredom.
— Use a computerized phone system to contact parents of truant students.
— Send post cards home to inform parents of class-cutting.

SA3: School organization — secondary correction

— Set up alternative school for chronic truants.
— Set up crisis centre for students who cut class because of situational factors such as fear of coming to school, fear of class assignments, etc.
— Set up discipline helpline.
— Offer wake-up call if student is habitually late.
— For students unable to adhere to a full-day schedule or with special family problems, shorten the day schedule or provide evening or Saturday classes.
— Have students telephone school at 6:00 am each morning; if they do not check in, have attendance officer phone them at 6:02 am.
— Make mini-courses part of the curriculum for those who are having difficulty concentrating for long periods of time.

— Establish contracts for those who are chronic truants to improve their attendance gradually.
— Provide group counselling for chronic truants.
— Provide for school safety for those who are afraid to come to school.
— Provide locks on doors so students can't wander into unauthorized spaces between classes.

SA4: School organization — punishment

— Use after-school detention.
— Develop in-school suspension but check literature on proper use.

SA5: School organization — restitution

— Provide chores as an alternative to punishment.

SB1: School students and peer groups — prevention

— Use student team teaching to involve students in the class.
— Have a student-operated information booth for the dissemination of school policy and for student input.
— Bring a former student back to stress the importance of attendance on getting the most out of school.
— Involve all students in ongoing projects to promote healthy school climate.

SB2: School students and peer groups — primary correction

— Set up 'study buddy' systems for students beginning to cut class.
— Check neighbourhood patterns and get beginning truants to become part of groups of students who help them get to school.

SB3: School students and peer groups — secondary correction

— Have peers counsel truants and class-cutters.
— Make one truant responsible for another (wake up calls, make up assignments, etc.)

SB4: School students and peer group — punishment

— Have a student review group to determine punishments (this should be used with caution and close monitoring).

SB5: School students and peer groups — restitution

— Have students help other students as alternatives to punishment, such as teaching a less able student.

SC1: School teachers and teaching — prevention

— Tell students that future employers will check their school record for job reliability.
— Never follow a predictable routine, so that exams and quizzes may not be selectively cut.
— Put disliked tasks immediately before tasks the students enjoy as an incentive to concentrate on the assignment.
— Add vocational courses for students with low academic interest to help make school experience meaningful.
— Use liberal verbal praise for improvement instead of negative reinforcement for truancy.
— Schedule competitions and tournaments between classes not only on lesson material but also for perfect attendance.
— Use educational games or competitions whenever possible to teach or reinforce presented material.
— Take register at the end of class to avoid dead time at the beginning.
— Be alert to the student who is bored or truly unable to keep up with the majority.
— Permit students to have an active part in the general lesson plans.
— Keep class material stimulating to promote good attendance.
— Provide in-service training for teachers on new creative teaching methods.
— Add 'effort grade' and number of classes missed in each subject to the report card.
— Start class on time.

SC2: School teachers and teaching — primary correction

- Begin lesson with something important; do not take class time to go over it again for the late arrivals. Make it their responsibility to find out what happened.
- Telephone parents of students who cut class and try to find out why.
- Schedule conference with student and discuss class-cutting in a non-punitive way.
- Set up contract with student.
- Use problem-solving interview with student.
- Find out student's interests and encourage special reports.

SC3: School teachers and teaching — secondary correction

- Refer to school psychologist.
- Design special curriculum for chronic truant.

SC4: School teachers and teaching — punishment

- Detention scaled to truancy or class-cutting.
- Give partial credit instead of full credit for course if attendance is poor.
- Deny extra-curricular attendance when student is not present for the entire school day.
- Grade reduction for excessive truancy or class-cutting if legal.
- Denial of make-up work for unexcused absences, receiving a zero for the day's work if the class is skipped.

SC5: School teachers and teaching — restitution

- Have student do classroom chores to make up for cutting.
- Have student help another student.

Summary and conclusion

This chapter has been written expressly for those professionals who would like to apply an ecological approach to the problem of class-cutting. Very practical suggestions are offered. These can be used directly with educators. However, the success of this approach is dependent upon the skills and sensitivity of those providing leadership for change. Rigid adherence to the solutions offered here can end only in failure. The process of change is critically important and it is assumed that organizational consultation skills are needed for success (Hyman 1977; Lennox *et al.*, forthcoming). The focus on prevention may be difficult to implement with educators who are oriented towards punitiveness. Therefore professionals are urged to proceed with patience, caution, and perseverance.

References

Bogacki, D. (1981) 'Attitudes toward corporal punishment: Authoritarian personality and pupil control ideology of school personnel', unpublished doctoral dissertation, Temple University, Philadelphia, Pa.

Fina, A. (1985) 'Measuring the effectiveness of a telephone counselling service designed to help callers solve discipline problems', unpublished doctoral dissertation, Temple University, Philadelphia, Pa.

Hyman, I. (1976) 'A bicentennial consideration of the advent of child advocacy', *Journal of Child Clinical Psychology* 5, 3: 15–20.

——— (1987) 'Psychological correlates of corporal punishment and physical abuse', in B. Germain and M. Brassard (eds) *Psychological Maltreatment of Children and Youth*, Elmsford, NY: Pergamon.

Hyman, I. and D'Allessandro, J. (1984) 'Good old fashioned discipline: The politics of punitiveness', *Phi Delta Kappan* 66, 1: 39–45.

Hyman, I. and Lally, D. (1982) 'The effectiveness of staff development programs to improve school discipline', *Urban Review* 14, 3: 181–96.

Hyman, I. and Wise, J. (eds) (1979) *Corporal Punishment in American Education: Readings in History and Practice*, Philadelphia, Pa: Temple University Press.

Hyman, I., Bilus, F., Dennehy, M. N., Feldman, G., Flanagan, D., Maital, S., and McDowell, E. (1979) 'Discipline in American education: An overview and analysis', *Journal of Education* 161, 2: 51–70.

Hyman, I., Flanagan, D., and Smith, K. (1982a) 'Discipline in the schools', in C. Reynolds and T. Gutkin (eds) *A Handbook for the Practice of School Psychology*, New York: Wiley.

Hyman, I., Stern, A., Lally, D., Kreutter, K., Berlinghof, M., and Prior, J. (1982b) 'Discipline in the high school: Organizational factors and roles for the school psychologist', *School Psychology Review* XI, 4: 409–16.

Hyman, I., Lennox, N., Lally, D., and Marchon, S. (1983) 'Teacher variance: A multidimensional approach to discipline', unpublished manuscript, Temple University, Philadelphia, Pa.

Hyman, I., Clarke, J., and Erdlen, R. (1987a) 'An analysis of physical abuse in American schools', *Aggressive Behavior* 13: 1–7.

Hyman, I. Zelikoff, W., and Clarke, J. (1987b) 'The effects of severe disciplinary practices in the schools', paper presented at the Annual

Convention of the American Psychological Association, New York City, 31 August.

Hyman, I., Zelikoff, W., and Clarke, J. (forthcoming) 'Psychological and physical abuse in the schools: A paradigm for understanding PTSD in children', *Journal of Traumatic Stress* I, 2.

Lennox, N. (1982) 'Teacher use of corporal punishment as a function of modeling behavior', unpublished doctoral dissertation, Temple University, Philadelphia, Pa.

Lennox, N., Hyman, I., and Hughes, C. (forthcoming) 'Institutionalization of a consultation based service delivery system', in J. Graden, J. Zins, and M. Curtis (eds) *Alternative Educational Delivery Systems: Enhancing Educational Options for all Students*, Washington, DC: National Association of School Psychologists.

Mishkin, A. (1987) 'Corporal punishment: Why some parents use less severe discipline practices than they experienced as children', unpublished doctoral dissertation, Temple University, Philadelphia, Pa.

Morse, W. and Smith, J. (1980) *Understanding Child Variance*, Reston, Va: Council for Exceptional Children.

Pokalo, M. (1986) 'Caregivers' attitudes toward the severity of punishment for forty-four misbehaviors in mental retardation institutions', unpublished doctoral dissertation, Temple University, Philadelphia, Pa.

Sofer, B. (1983) 'Psychologists' attitudes toward corporal punishment', unpublished doctoral dissertation, Temple University, Philadelphia, Pa.

Stagliano, P. and Hyman, I. (1983) 'Analysis of state departments of education activities regarding violence and vandalism in the public schools', *Phi Delta Kappan* 65, 1: 67–8.

Chapter seven

The behavioural treatment of school phobia

Nigel Blagg

The nature of school phobia

School phobia is a distressing and puzzling phenomenon that was first described by Broadwin as a special kind of truancy.

> The child is absent from school for periods varying from several months to a year. The absence is consistent. At all times the parent knows where the child is. It is near the mother or near the home. The reason for the truancy is incomprehensible to the parents and to the school. The child may say that it is afraid to go to school, afraid of the teacher or say that it does not know why it will not go to school.
>
> (Broadwin 1932)

Miller *et al.* (1974) point out that school phobia is more prevalent than any other childhood phobia. Graziano *et al.* (1979) indicate that although the problem affects less than 1 per cent of the school population, the ratio of papers on the topic to that of other phobias is at least 25:1. These authors go on to suggest that the high referral rate of school phobia is probably a reflection of the high cultural value and legal requirements of school attendance.

The majority of treatment studies have selected school phobics from middle-class families while truants have been generally reported as coming from lower socio-economic groups. This has led to some writers' suggesting that purported differences between phobics and truants are clinical artefacts, being merely correlates of the social class differences that tend to exist between the two groups. Indeed, some educational psychologists and sociologists have doubted the relevance of distinguishing different types of non-attenders, arguing that it may be more useful to look at the characteristics of the school environments that may be generating attendance difficulties (Reynolds and Murgatroyd 1977; Kavanagh and Carroll 1977).

Hersov's (1960–61) classic study delineating school phobics from truants on a whole range of characteristics was perhaps weakened by sample bias. Nevertheless my replication of Hersov's study (Blagg 1979, reported in Blagg 1987 and Blagg and Yule, forthcoming) confirmed and extended Hersov's findings even though the phobic and truant samples were evenly matched for social class.

A number of researchers have emphasized that school phobia can be a precursor to major psychiatric problems in adulthood (Berg *et al.* 1974; Tyrer and Tyrer 1974). Certainly the condition, or rather set of conditions, does cause enormous upset and suffering to those children affected as well as their families and school-teachers. Taking all these issues into consideration there does seem to be a strong need to identify the most efficient and effective strategies to treat this problem. A recent book (Blagg 1987a) addresses this area, reviewing what is known about school phobia and drawing together the common elements in the successful psychodynamic and behaviourally based treatments. However, this chapter will mainly confine itself to a consideration of behavioural treatment approaches.

Behavioural treatment approaches

The earliest treatment studies were largely psychoanalytically based (Johnson *et al.* 1941; Klein 1945; Warren 1948; Thompson 1948; Van Houten 1948; Bornstein 1949; Suttenfield 1954; Coolidge *et al.* 1957; Sperling 1961). However the publication of Wolpe's (1954) work on systematic desensitization stimulated interest in behavioural treatment and from the early 1960s a large number of behavioural case studies were reported in the literature. As Berecz (1968) pointed out, the earliest studies were over-simplistic 'one shot attempts to prove the effectiveness of certain techniques'. Nevertheless these early studies were important in developing and refining the behavioural art.

Increasingly behavioural work has adopted a more explicit problem-solving approach to therapy (Yule 1977). Great care is taken to gather all of the relevant information about the problem. The presenting difficulties are carefully defined and clarified;

hypotheses are proposed to account for observations and clear, deliberate interventions are introduced, monitored, and evaluated. Over the years a wide range of techniques arising out of both classical and operant conditioning paradigms have been developed and successfully applied to both young children and adolescents. Moreover, as this chapter will indicate, many behaviour therapists now acknowledge the importance of using a range of principles and techniques in any one case in order to address an extensive range of child, family, and school issues. In this way the unique needs of each case can be recognized and effectively treated (Kennedy 1965; Hersov 1977; Blagg 1977; 1979; 1987; Yule *et al.* 1980; Phillips and Wolpe 1981; Blagg and Yule 1984).

The basic assumption underlying treatments derived from the classical conditioning paradigm is that some form of anxiety is responsible for school phobia. If this anxiety can be eliminated the problem will be alleviated. The major treatment techniques derived from this model include systematic desensitization, emotive imagery, flooding and implosion (see also Chapter 8).

Systematic desensitization (SD) is a procedure that involves exposing the child to a sequence of carefully graded fear-provoking situations starting with minimally worrying stimuli, building up to the most feared issues and contexts. At each stage in the hierarchy the child is helped to overcome any stress and anxiety by concentrating on a behaviour that is antagonistic (reciprocally inhibiting) to the anxiety (Wolpe 1954). The approach can be carried out in the therapist's office working with imagined scenes to simulate real-life circumstances (SD imaginal), or alternatively the child can be worked through a series of real-life situations (SD *in vivo*). In either case the approach is highly dependent upon a thorough and skilful analysis and clarification of all of the anxiety-provoking circumstances surrounding the school phobia case. In many cases, children, parents, and teachers are not always consciously aware of all the fears and worries, and even if they are they may find it hard to express them clearly. Accordingly the therapist has to be systematic in addressing a wide range of content issues as well as subtle in considering many process issues.

The earliest reported behavioural treatment of a school phobic (Lazarus 1960) utilized SD (imaginal). A 9½-year-old girl had suddenly started refusing school with night terrors, enuresis, and stomach pains after she had experienced three closely spaced traumatic incidents. A school-friend had drowned, a second friend had died of meningitis, and the child had also witnessed a fatal road accident. These issues had precipitated in the child a fear of losing her mother. A seven-item fear hierarchy was constructed around lengthening separation experiences. The child was helped to confront and overcome fears at each stage in the hierarchy by using imagined scenes paired with muscle relaxation. The child returned to school quite happily after ten days, and the night terrors and enuresis disappeared. Apart from occasional bed-wetting all therapeutic gains were maintained over a fifteen-month period.

Chapel (1967) and Croghan (1981) also report on the successful application of SD (imaginal) to school phobic cases. Although the pupils in both studies overcame their problems, neither case was that clear cut. Chapel used hypnosis as a means of reciprocally inhibiting anxiety. The boy needed daily 30-minute sessions for one week to achieve a sufficiently relaxed state to start SD (imaginal) treatment. He then needed eighteen 20–30-minute desensitization sessions over a six-week period before returning to school. Even then, however, an unspecified amount of out-patient treatment was still required for the rest of the academic year. In spite of this, the school phobic problems recurred after a long summer holiday, requiring another fifteen sessions to rectify. To some extent 'flooding' may have also played a part in treatment as the boy was ultimately forced to remain at school throughout the day.

Although Croghan (1981) emphasizes SD (imaginal) as the main approach to treating a 17-year-old boy who had been a phobic for five years, the improvements could have been equally well explained in cognitive behaviour therapy terms. Apart from desensitizing the boy to current worries like preparing for school in the mornings, he also helped him to re-interpret and restructure painful memories of the incident that had precipitated the problem five years previously (a 'major and humiliating showdown' with two boys with whom he had refused to fight).

A number of therapists (Schermann and Grover 1962; Eysenck and Rachman 1965; Miller 1972) have successfully demonstrated the usefulness of combining SD (imaginal) and SD (*in vivo*). In some cases children are prepared for *in vivo* sessions by prior imagined sessions. In other cases SD (imaginal) is used as a way of reinforcing and consolidating the child's success at each stage of the *in vivo* hierarchy. Sometimes, however, *in vivo* sessions become necessary because of drawbacks of using imagined scenes. The technicalities of the imaginal approach effectively minimize the role of parents and teachers in treatment, giving rise to the danger of developing a dependency situation on the therapist. The approach is extremely time consuming but perhaps most important of all, as Yule (1977) points out, it can be difficult to find a behaviour that is both antagonistic to anxiety and easily controllable by the child at the therapist's request. For instance, some children find it very hard to learn muscle relaxation techniques, others are not responsive to hypnotherapy. Some children find difficulty in visualizing imagined stimuli, or else fail to experience anxiety in relation to imagined stimuli. Whether these problems reflect inadequacies in the therapist or skill deficits in the child is a moot point (Yule *et al.* 1980).

Interestingly, a study by Tahmisian and McReynolds (1971) illustrates some of these issues. A twelve-step SD (imaginal) procedure was used to desensitize a 13-year-old girl with separation anxiety triggered by attendance at a summer camp. The child made no progress towards returning to school. The parents constantly gave in to her when she was upset. Accordingly they were assigned a major role in treatment, helping the child through a fifteen-step *in vivo* hierarchy. Operant procedures were also employed in that the child's protests were ignored in a planned way while co-operative behaviour was rewarded. After three weeks, regular school attendance was resumed and maintained at a four-week follow-up.

Garvey and Hegrenes (1966) and Olsen and Coleman (1967) cite examples of the effective use of SD (*in vivo*). Both studies actively involved the fathers in the treatment and utilized the therapeutic relationship as a means of reciprocally inhibiting the anxiety responses at each stage of the hierarchy.

Emotive imagery

Emotive imagery is a rather specialized technique that some behaviour therapists have found to be a powerful alternative to the normal relaxation procedures used in SD. In this procedure, the therapist develops imagined scenes which conjure up in the child feelings of excitement, self-assertion, and general 'positive effect' as a means of inhibiting anxiety. The procedure was first reported by Lazarus and Abramovitz (1962). They described the case of an

8-year-old girl who had become school phobic and enuretic after a series of emotional upsets in class. A hierarchy of feared school situations was developed in which the Enid Blyton character Noddy was placed. The child was requested to protect and reassure Noddy. The treatment was highly successful. The child returned to school after only four sessions, and the enuresis disappeared after two months without being specifically treated.

Van der Ploeg (1975) also made use of this technique in treating a 14-year-old school-phobic boy with urinary frequency problems. The boy was trained in deep relaxation and systematically desensitized imaginally using both relaxation and stories of sailing experiences designed to create powerful emotive images. After fifteen office sessions, the treatment shifted into an *in vivo* mode involving increasing exposure to school. The school phobia and urinary problems were overcome in one month. All treatment gains were maintained at an eighteen-month follow-up.

Implosive therapy

In contrast to these procedures involving varying kinds of *graded* exposure to threatening circumstances, flooding and implosion involves an immediate confrontation of the maximally feared situation without any prior preparation. The child is held in the intensely feared situation until the anxiety begins to show signs of visible waning on the classical extinction model (Stampfl 1967; 1968; Stampfl and Levis 1967). The basic assumption in this procedure is that if the child experiences anxiety as a result of a conditioned response to certain conditioned stimuli, the vivid presentation of the stimuli in the absence of any primary aversive stimuli should eventually lead to the extinction of the anxiety response.

Implosive therapy achieves this by confronting the child in imagination, vividly describing and exaggerating the child's worst fears. The approach is exemplified by Smith and Sharpe (1970) who treated a 13-year-old boy who had been refusing school for sixty days. A careful behavioural analysis revealed that the boy was particularly worried about failing in mathematics and literature classes. His greatest fear was the thought of being called on in class and being unable to answer the teacher's questions correctly with resulting ridicule by both the teacher and classmates. Treatment involved the boy in visualizing highly threatening classroom scenes involving derision and ridicule without any escape. For instance, the literature classroom scene was presented thus

> The room is dark and strange and the chairs have been pushed to the sides of the room. Students begin silently filing into the room. It is too dark to identify them. Tension grows as Billy wonders what will happen. The students encircle him, pressing ever closer and begin to murmur 'Crazy Billy' . . .
>
> (Smith and Sharpe 1970)

The approach produced remarkably rapid results. By the fourth session of implosive therapy Billy was attending school full time. A follow-up at thirteen weeks showed that he was attending school regularly, enjoying improved social relationships, and achieving better grades in his school work. The authors went to a lot of trouble to involve the parents in treatment. They explained to them the theoretical rationale behind the treatment and kept in daily telephone contact with them and the school-teachers. It seems likely that operant factors also played a role in treatment, as the parents were urged to remove secondary gains at home for being off school like watching television and going to bed late. The school-teachers were also advised on ways of encouraging and reinforcing desired behaviours.

Flooding

Perhaps the most controversial procedure for treating school phobia is that of flooding. In this approach fears and phobias are directly confronted in real life, again without any prior preparation. The approach is naturally very stressful for the child, family, and school-teachers and also for the therapist. Parents and teachers need a lot of convincing that a controlled, forced immediate confrontation is the best way ahead, and many practical management issues need to be thought through to ensure successful treatment. The approach should not be entered into lightly. If mishandled the outcome could be an even more anxious child and parents presenting even greater obstacles to treatment. The process of classical extinction often results in a temporary worsening of the problem before it begins to wane. Giving up treatment as a result of heightened anxiety could well reinforce and 'shape' more extreme protest behaviour in the child. Probably because of these issues, flooding is normally reported as one part of a more comprehensive treatment package (Kennedy 1965; Rines 1973; Blagg 1979; Blagg and Yule 1984; Blagg 1987). However, before considering these packages mention should be made of studies involving predominantly operant procedures.

Operant approaches

Operant approaches do not assume that anxiety has caused the school phobia. Although the 'shaping' approaches used are reminiscent of SD (*in vivo*) no formal fear hierarchies are established and the child is not trained in relaxation procedures. Basically operant-based treatments of school phobia involve

1 maximizing incentives for attending school by ensuring that extra positive reinforcements are built into the school day;
2 minimizing incentives for remaining at home by removing positive reinforcers like greater personal freedom, television, and extra adult attention.

In some cases, tangible artificial reinforcers like sweets are used in the early stages of treatment programmes; however, wherever possible natural reinforcers in the child's life are reorganized and rescheduled to ensure greater likelihood of generalization and maintenance of treatment gains. Quite frequently a 'shaping' procedure is used in which the child is rewarded for increasing approximations to the ultimate desired behaviour of a return to full-time schooling. In effect, this frequently means a graded reintroduction to school, starting with some kind of part-time attendance leading to full-time normal schooling, the focus of treatment being the reinforcement of each step taken en route.

The approach is particularly well illustrated in a highly detailed case study reported by Ayllon *et al.* (1970). The authors report the case of an 8-year-old girl who had shown a gradual onset of school phobia. There did not appear to be clear-cut precipitants of the problem, but observations of the child at home over thirteen days revealed that she was being very strongly reinforced for staying at home. The child enjoyed a very close relationship with her mother and tried to follow her to work each day. However, typically she ended up staying with an undemanding neighbour. Treatment involved

1 prompting and shaping school attendance,
2 removal of pleasant consequences for not attending school,
3 the development of a home-based motivational system,
4 the production of aversive consequences in the mother whenever the child stayed at home.

Initially the child was taken to school each day by a therapist and obliged to spend an increasingly longer time in school, starting with the last hour of each day. Gradually the child was taken to school earlier and earlier. The backward-chaining approach allowed the natural contingencies like going home time to reinforce school attendance. Sweets were also used as an added incentive. By the seventh day the child was able to stay in school without support, but was unwilling to go voluntarily, and when the pressure was removed for five days she refused school again. At this stage it was realized the child was being reinforced by individual attention from the mother after the other children had gone to school. This benefit was removed but the child still refused school. As a result a star chart was introduced for all of the children in the family, with one star being earned for each day's voluntary school attendance, with five consecutive stars resulting in special treats (sweets). The child's attendance improved but was still not fully satisfactory. Ultimately the therapist put pressure on the mother by expecting her to leave home ten minutes before the children. If they arrived at school within fifteen minutes of the mother they earned their star. If not, the mother was greatly inconvenienced by having to walk back home (one mile) in order to take the child to school. This was necessary on only two occasions. The second time the mother was visibly irritated and literally forced the child to go to school without allowing an opportunity for discussion. Thereafter normal attendance was resumed and maintained when the star was withdrawn one month later. A follow-up after nine months revealed no symptom substitution; the child's social behaviour had greatly improved and her attendance and schoolwork were excellent.

The study is interesting in demonstrating therapist persistence and attention to detail, with the treatment intervention being tested, adapted, and developed to suit the needs of the case. In some ways the treatment could be construed in classical conditioning terms, with the therapist acting as a desensitizer in the 'shaping' procedure with treatment being finally effected by 'flooding'. The study does highlight the crucial importance of assessing parental motivation to resolve the problem. In this case the mother was ultimately forced into a more committed stance by being in effect punished for the child's poor attendance. One wonders whether a more rapid treatment outcome would have occurred had she been obliged to be more forceful in the early stages.

An earlier paper by Hersen (1968) placed so much emphasis on the mother's role in reinforcing and maintaining the school refusal pattern of her 12-year-old son that treatment was directed entirely at training the mother in contingency management over ten one-hour sessions spread over ten weeks. During these sessions she was helped to recognize and understand the way she was unknowingly reinforcing the boy's inappropriate behaviour. Gradually she learnt to change her pattern of reinforcements, with the result that the boy's attendance normalized and he rarely reported feeling ill.

Several studies have shown the effectiveness of formalizing contingency management into written contracts (Cantrell *et al.* 1969; Welch and Carpenter 1970; Vaal 1973). The approach known as contingency contracting rests upon the careful selection of reinforcers and punishers. A clear, unambiguous, tightly defined behavioural contract is then developed and agreed upon between the child and the other parties. These three studies demonstrated that this approach could work quickly and effectively with mildly anxious children whose parents were unwittingly reinforcing their school avoidance pattern.

Social skills training

King (forthcoming) makes the useful point that in some cases school phobia can be regarded in part as a failure to comply with parental instructions. He goes on to argue that in such cases parents may need particular help with the nature and quality of their instructions and suggests that they may be helped by Forehand's (1979) parent-training model. This involves attention to issues like the need to gain the child's attention; the avoidance of long chains of instructions and too many explanations accompanying commands.

Although many school phobics suffer from relationship problems with their peers, relatively little attention has been paid to systematic social skills training. However, a recent paper by Esveldt-Dawson *et al.* (1982) provides a fascinating example of a treatment approach where social skills training formed the major part of the intervention. The subject was a 12-year-old girl with school phobia, a fear of unfamiliar males, multiple somatic complaints, and limited interaction with peers. The girl was hospitalized and close attention was paid to the nature of her avoidance behaviours and the absence of normal pro-social approach responses. Treatment centred on a series of role-play situations. Each role-play session was preceded by a five-minute talk on phobias and how the training programme could help. The therapist then modelled the appropriate behaviours before asking the child to act out a scene. The child was encouraged for progress and areas requiring further improvement were identified and specific advice given with further modelling practice. Attention was paid to many areas like body posture, nervous mannerisms, eye contact, the verbal content of messages and responses, and appropriate emotional affect in social interactions. Twenty-four treatment sessions produced rapid improvements across many areas. Social skills improved both with peers and strangers and normal school attendance was resumed and maintained at seven and twenty-one week follow-ups.

Combining classical and operant-based approaches

The majority of behavioural studies utilize a number of different treatment techniques while explicitly reporting only one or two of the approaches. Nevertheless, some studies have openly acknowledged the combined involvement of very different treatment elements in the management of a single case (Patterson 1965; Lazarus *et al.* 1964; Kennedy 1965; Rines 1973; Blagg 1977; 1981; 1987; Yule *et al.* 1980; Phillips and Wolpe 1981).

The study by Lazarus *et al.* (1964) is of special interest as the authors appear to recognize and attempt to resolve the conceptual conflict in using classical and/or operant-based procedures. The case reported was that of a 9-year-old boy with a long history of unresolved separation anxiety in school situations. He finally became school phobic after a series of stressful events (an operation with complications, witnessing a drowning and, finally, being upset at the death of a close friend of his sister). SD (imaginal) was first tried but abandoned because of the boy's difficulty in describing his true feelings. A mild tranquillizer was prescribed by the family doctor to reduce anticipatory anxiety first thing in the morning and SD (*in vivo*) was implemented with a variety of techniques used to desensitize the boy at each stage (humour, distraction, encouragement, emotive imagery). At the same time positive incentives for being in school were organized and gains for being out of school were eliminated. After fifteen treatment sessions the boy appeared minimally anxious; accordingly a reward system was introduced to reinforce the child's return to full-time schooling without the help of a therapist. Nevertheless, the boy remained dependent on the therapist's presence on the school premises until eventually the mother became rather forceful, emphasizing that school attendance was compulsory and would, if necessary, be enforced by agents beyond her control. This allowed the therapist to withdraw and three weeks later tangible rewards were no longer necessary to maintain regular school attendance.

On the basis of this study the authors suggest that the level of anxiety in the child should dictate the treatment strategy with low levels indicating an operant approach and high levels of anxiety requiring systematic desensitization. However, the authors do not indicate how to go about assessing the level of anxiety. As Lang (1970) has shown, observed levels of anxiety do not necessarily correlate with subjective self-reports or physiological measures. As Blagg (1987) emphasizes it is very difficult sometimes to distinguish between learned, operant-derived, tyrannical tantrums and genuine fear reactions. Furthermore, SD (*in vivo*) may result in the strengthening of avoidance responses and the reinforcement of dependent behaviour by allowing the child to return home after each treatment session. On the other hand, Lazarus *et al.* (1964) argue that the use of a purely operant approach, in which attention is withheld until the child returns to the classroom, could be therapeutically disadvantageous if the problem is viewed within a classical conditioning paradigm. Premature exposure to the most feared situation could then heighten anxiety and strengthen the avoidance response. This point certainly applies if escape from the situation is possible. However, if the child is held in the fear-provoking situation until anxiety begins to wane on the classical extinction model, and the child is then reinforced and encouraged for progress, the classical and operant models are no longer in conflict. Indeed, this is basically the approach used by Kennedy (1965), Rines (1973), Blagg (1977; 1981; 1987), and Blagg and Yule (1984).

Kennedy's (1965) highly successful treatment approach has attracted special attention because it was the first large-scale behavioural treatment series to be reported in the literature. Kennedy distinguished between type 1 and type 2 school phobics according to ten differential symptoms referring to issues surrounding the timing and nature of the onset of the phobia, expressed worries about death, parental characteristics, and family communication patterns. The type 1 cases who had shown a sudden onset following an illness were regarded as easier to treat and responsive to a rapid return to school approach. Type 2 cases who had shown an incipient onset with many family problems were regarded as needing longer-time supportive therapy.

Kennedy applied his treatment package to fifty type 1 cases, thirty-seven of them being 11 years or younger. The approach achieved a 100 per cent success with cases taking only three days to treat and treatment gains maintained over long-term follow-up. Kennedy utilized both classical and operant models but avoided the problems referred to in the study by Lazarus *et al.* (1964). In essence Kennedy's approach involves blocking the escape route and enforcing school attendance (desensitizing by classical extinction). However at the same time special treats and privileges are organized both at home and at school to reinforce appropriate behaviour. Physical complaints are treated in a low-key matter of fact manner so that they are not reinforced and eventually peter out. In order to achieve these aims, good interprofessional relationships and the ability to inspire confidence in the parents is regarded as essential. Although the results of the study look highly exciting, Kennedy does imply that many of the type 1 cases selected for treatment would have returned to school no matter what treatment they had received. Furthermore, follow-ups were not really that rigorous. In addition there are difficulties in using Kennedy's typology. Some of the items involve subjective judgements and one of the items is an outcome of treatment rather than a basis for initial diagnosis. In spite of this, Kennedy's work has certainly been a landmark in the treatment of school phobia.

A subsequent study by Rines (1973) suggests that Kennedy's

approach can be equally well applied to more problematic type 2 cases and should not just be reserved for the less serious type 1 cases. Rines treated a 12-year-old girl who showed seven of the ten type 2 features. Both parents and clinicians had reluctantly accepted the inevitability of hospital treatment. However, before deciding on final disposition, it was somewhat sceptically agreed to give a direct behavioural approach a two-month trial. Within this time period the child was attending school regularly. A follow-up at the end of the year revealed that the child's school attendance was normal and academic progress was excellent. Nevertheless the family pathology continued and the child continued to experience social problems.

Comprehensive behavioural management

Two brief papers by Blagg (1977; 1981) describe a comprehensive behavioural strategy for the rapid diagnosis and treatment of school phobia. Once again, both operant and classical conditioning paradigms are used in a way that avoids conflict between the models. Blagg's strategy has much in common with Kennedy's, although the former is more comprehensive and systematic and considers the fundamental question about whether or not the child is attending an appropriate school before engineering a rapid return. A highly detailed step-wise guide to the diagnostic and rapid treatment procedure is described in Blagg (1987). The essential elements can be summarized thus:

1 The elimination of medical issues by taking the child to the family doctor for a full check-up, preferably out of school hours. In the few cases where a paediatric referral is necessary this should be organized as swiftly as possible with the minimum of fuss.
2 The establishment of the appropriate school for the child to attend. Occasionally, insurmountable difficulties relating to the child's peers, teachers, or schoolwork indicate a change of school before any treatment programme can be instituted.
3 A wide ranging and detailed analysis of child, family, and school-related issues leading up to and surrounding the development of the school phobia. This is a crucial stage which is not only concerned with exposing issues, but more importantly

with exposing child, parent, and teacher perceptions of each other's worries and concerns. This is a delicate exercise that relies heavily upon establishing good relationships with the child, the family, and the school. This in turn involves attending to many process issues like the need to assess client motivation, intervene as quickly as possible, and be sensitive to the timing and pacing, style and setting of the interview.

Beyond this there are many content issues that need to be addressed including the child's attendance pattern and schooling history, associated symptoms, out-of-school activities, attitudinal, personality, intellectual, and academic characteristics, developmental history and home and school-related anxieties. With respect to the family, the structure and patterns of influence and control need to be thoroughly articulated, sources of stress and anxiety identified, and costs and benefits of the school phobic's problem assessed with respect to each family member as well as close friends. Naturally the school also requires close scrutiny. Although the child may harbour irrational fears the latter are likely to be intertwined with realistic worries. For example, many school phobics experience genuine concerns about difficulties with certain aspects of their schoolwork. Others may suffer from bullying or excessive teasing. A change of class, school, or teacher are often common precipitants of a school phobic episode. In each case the precise circumstances and details need to be clarified. It is often vital to make significant changes in the school environment before confronting residual irrational fears. As Blagg (1987) elaborates, there are many recurring themes although each school phobic case is unique.

4 Formal and informal desensitization of the many exposed child, teacher, and parental anxieties through the use of humour, discussion, and emotive imagery. At this stage parents can be helped to prepare for the inevitable confrontation by rehearsing ways of behaving each morning. The child can be helped to rehearse replies to painful enquiries from other pupils and teachers about the persistent absence. Reassurance can be given about the availability of extra help with schoolwork and any special measures regarding the use of quiet rooms or activities during lunch hours and breaks can be explained. Teachers can also be helped to plan and rehearse

ways of treating the child especially on arrival at the school in the mornings.

5 A controlled, enforced school attendance using an escort procedure where necessary, effectively blocking the avoidance behaviour and desensitizing the child's anxieties through classical extinction. Wherever possible, the family should maintain the responsibility for taking the child to school. However in certain cases outside support may be indicated. In such circumstances great care needs to be taken to ensure that the escort chosen is someone who can (a) assist the family as long as is necessary, (b) be minimally inconvenienced by the procedure, (c) remain confident, calm, and unruffled in the event of severe tantrums and protest behaviours in the child and stress and worry in the parents.

6 The use of operant procedures, both at home and at school, to (a) focus parent and teacher attention on avoiding certain antecedents likely to lead to specific behaviour difficulties, (b) eliminate particular teacher and parent behaviours likely to reinforce and maintain fear reactions, protests, psychosomatic complaints, and avoidance behaviours, and (c) maximize ways of rewarding regular voluntary school attendance and other social and academic behaviours being targeted in treatment.

There are so many issues to explore with school phobics that Blagg (1987) recommends the use of a comprehensive school phobia record form that can act as an *aide-mémoire* in history-taking.

Blagg and Yule (1984) applied the approach outlined above to a treatment series of thirty school phobics who conformed to the diagnostic criteria suggested by Berg *et al.* (1969):

1 Extreme difficulty in attending school with refusal and absence from school for at least three days.
2 Accompanying marked emotional upset such as temper tantrums, sleep disturbance, psychosomatic complaints.
3 Child remains at home with knowledge and permission of parents.
4 Absence of significant antisocial problems like persistent lying, wandering from home, stealing, destructiveness, or disapproved sexual activity.

Children suffering from gross physical illness, bronchial asthma, suicidal tendencies, anorexia and psychotic conditions were excluded from the study.

In what would appear to be the only reported comparative treatment study dealing exclusively with school phobics, Blagg's comprehensive behavioural treatment approach was compared with psychiatric hospital in-patient treatment and home tuition supported by psychotherapy. The in-patient treatment was applied to sixteen school phobics and the home tuition group contained twenty cases. All cases in the study conformed to Berg *et al.*'s (1969) diagnostic criteria. Unfortunately the study did not permit random allocation to treatment groups, and inevitably the question arises as to whether or not the three treatment groups were closely matched. Accordingly the subjects were systematically compared on a whole range of factors. There were no statistically significant differences between the groups on sex, social class, intelligence quotient (Wechsler 1974), reading age (Burt 1974), pattern of associated symptoms, school and home-related anxieties, family size, parental attitude, and employment rates. Unlike Kennedy's (1965) study, most children were in the 11–16-year-old age range. Only five of the behavioural and one of the hospitalized group were younger than 11 years. All three groups were closely matched for the number of previous episodes of school refusal; however the behavioural group was significantly younger at the start of treatment than the other two groups. The mean age for the behavioural, hospitalized, and home-tutored groups was 13.0 years, 13.5 years, and 14.3 years respectively.

Applying Kennedy's criteria as far as possible, just over half the children in the behavioural group, three-quarters in the home-tutored group, and approximately one-quarter in the hospitalized group were classified as type 2 cases, that is they were more seriously disturbed. These differences were not statistically significant.

Thus although the cases were not randomly allocated, the three treatment groups were remarkably similar at the start of treatment. Nevertheless, there were dramatic differences in the treatment outcome between the three groups. Whereas twenty-eight out of thirty of the behavioural group overcame their difficulties and maintained their progress over two years, only two of the home-tutored children and six of the hospitalized children achieved a similar success. The treatment outcome pattern favouring the behavioural group was maintained when only type 2 cases were considered and when all children below 11 years were eliminated. The outcome for the behavioural treatment series was better than any previously reported study dealing with children in this older age group.

The extremely poor outcome figures for the home-tutored group combined with clinical observations suggested that this form of intervention may have inhibited spontaneous remission or, even worse, reinforced the children's problems. Furthermore, it is important to emphasize that the most successful treatment group received the least therapist time. The behavioural group took on average 2.5 weeks to treat, compared to 45.3 weeks for the hospitalized children and 72.1 weeks for the home-tutored cases. These significant differences in treatment duration conceal even greater variations in financial costs. Hospital in-patient treatment may run into hundreds of pounds per week. Home-tuition with psychotherapy is also a highly expensive option especially if it goes on for months and months.

Although the behavioural approach paid attention to the same diagnostic issues in each case, the treatment programme was flexibly adapted to suit the unique individual needs of each child and context. In common with the other behavioural interventions that use a mixture of techniques it is difficult to isolate the most effective elements in the total treatment package. At the same time there do seem to be certain universal ingredients in successful behavioural treatments and a detailed review by Blagg (1987) notes that these same ingredients also characterize other successful treatment approaches derived from a psychodynamic model.

Conclusions

Assuming that the child is registered at an appropriate school and medical issues have been eliminated the essential treatment elements in school phobia appear to be

1 The establishment of good relationships between the family, the child, and the school.
2 The clarification of the real and imagined home and school events that have caused distress.

3 Practical measures to deal with realistic concerns and the use of a variety of techniques to reduce irrational anxiety.
4 An early confrontation of the feared situations through a carefully controlled, enforced school attendance.

Given the overwhelming research evidence favouring approaches based on these principles, it is surprising that some children are still being treated by hospitalization or home-tuition with psychotherapy. Furthermore, in the knowledge that a direct behavioural attack on even the more difficult, older Kennedy type 2 cases can produce such quick and effective results, the premature use of special units or residential schools seems to be highly questionable.

References

Ayllon, T., Smith, D., and Rodgers, M. (1970) 'Behavioural management of school phobia', *Journal of Behaviour Therapy and Experimental Psychiatry* 1: 125–38.

Berecz, J. M. (1968) 'Phobias of childhood: etiology and treatment', *Psychological Bulletin* 70: 694–720.

Berg, I., Marks, I., McGuire, R., and Lipsedge, M. (1974) 'School phobia and agoraphobia', *Psychological Medicine* 4: 428–34.

Berg, I., Nichols, K., and Pritchard, C. (1969) 'School phobia — its classification and relationship to dependency', *Journal of Child Psychology and Psychiatry* 10: 23–41.

Blagg, N. R. (1977) 'A detailed strategy for the rapid treatment of school phobics', *Bulletin of the British Association for Behavioural Psychotherapy* 5: 70–5.

——— (1979) 'The behavioural treatment of school refusal', unpublished PhD thesis, Institute of Psychiatry, University of London.

——— (1981) 'A behavioural approach to school refusal: Behaviour modification in education', *Perspectives* 5, School of Education, University of Exeter.

——— (1987) *School Phobia and its Treatment*, London: Routledge.

Blagg, N. R. and Yule, W. (1984) 'The behavioural treatment of school refusal: a comparative study', *Behaviour, Research and Therapy* 22: 119–27.

——— (forthcoming) 'A replication of Hersov's Study'.

Bornstein, B. (1949) 'The analysis of a phobic child', *Psychoanalytic Study of the Child* 3 and 4: 181–226.

Broadwin, I. T. (1932) 'A contribution to the study of truancy', *Orthopsychiatry* 2: 253–9.

Burt, C. (1974) *The Burt (Rearranged) Word Reading Test* (revised edn), London: University of London Press.

Cantrell, R. P., Cantrell, M. L., Huddleston, C. M., and Wooldridge,

R.L. (1969) 'Application of contingency contracts to four school attendance problems', *Journal of Applied Behavioural Analysis* 2: 215–20.

Chapel, J. K. (1967) 'Treatment of a case of school phobia by reciprocal inhibition', *Canadian Psychiatric Association Journal* 12: 25–8.

Coolidge, J. C., Hahn, P. B., and Peck, A. L. (1957) 'School phobia: neurotic crisis or way of life', *American Journal of Orthopsychiatry* 27: 296–306.

Coolidge, J. C., Brodie, R. D., and Feeney, B. (1964) 'A ten-year follow-up of sixty-six school phobic children', *American Journal of Orthopsychiatry* 34: 675–84.

Croghan, L. M. (1981) 'Conceptualising the critical elements in a rapid desensitisation to school anxiety: a case study', *Journal of Pediatric Psychology* 6: 165–9.

Esveldt-Dawson, K., Wisner, K. L., Unis, A. S., Matson, J. L., and Kazdin, A. E. (1982) 'Treatment of phobias in a hospitalised child', *Journal of Behaviour Therapy and Experimental Psychiatry* 13, 1: 77–83.

Eysenck, H. J. and Rachman, S. (1965) *The Causes and Cure of Neurosis*, London: Routledge & Kegan Paul.

Forehand, R. (1979) 'Parent behavioural training to modify child non-compliance: treatment generalisation across time and from home to school', *Behaviour Modification* 3, 1: 3–25.

Garvey, W. P. and Hegrenes, J. R. (1966) 'Desensitisation techniques in the treatment of school phobia', *American Journal of Orthopsychiatry* 35, 147–52.

Graziano, A. M., DeGiovanni, I. S., and Garcia, K. A. (1979) 'Behavioural treatment of children's fears: a review', *Psychology Bulletin* 86, 4: 804–30.

Hersen, M. (1968) 'Treatment of a compulsive and phobic disorder through a total behaviour therapy programme: a case study', *Psychotherapy* 5: 220–5.

Hersov, L. A. (1960–61) 'Persistent nonattendance at school', *Journal of Psychology and Psychiatry* 1, 2: 130–6.

Hersov, L. A. (1977) 'School refusal', in M. Rutter and L. A. Hersov (eds) *Child Psychiatry: Modern Approaches*, Oxford: Blackwell.

Johnson, A. M., Falstein, E. L., Szurek, S., and Svendsen, M. (1941) 'School phobia', *American Journal of Orthopsychiatry* 11: 702–11.

Kavanagh, A. and Carroll, H. C. (1977) 'The pupil attendance in three comprehensive schools: A study of the pupils and their families', in H. C. Carroll (ed.) *Absenteeism in South Wales: Studies of Pupils, their Homes and their Secondary Schools*, Faculty of Education, University College of Swansea.

Kennedy, W. A. (1965) 'School phobia: rapid treatment of fifty cases', *Journal of Abnormal Psychology* 70, 4: 285–9.

King, N. (forthcoming) *Children's Phobias*, Chichester: Wiley.

Klein, E. (1945) 'The reluctance to go to school', *Psychoanalytic Study of the Child* 1: 263–79.

Lang, P. (1970) 'Stimulus control, response control and desensitisation of fear', in D. Levis (ed.) *Learning Approaches to Therapeutic Behaviour Change*, Chicago, Ill: Aldine Press.

Lazarus, A. A. (1960) 'The elimination of children's phobias by deconditioning', in H. J. Eysenck (ed.) *Behaviour Therapy and the Neuroses*, Oxford: Pergamon.

Lazarus, A. A. and Abramovitz, A. (1962) 'The use of emotive imagery in the treatment of children's phobias', *Journal of Mental Science* 108: 191–5.

Lazarus, A. A., Davidson, G. C., and Polefka, D. A. (1964) 'Classical and operant factors in the treatment of a school phobia', *Journal of Abnormal Psychology* 70: 225–9.

Miller, L. C., Barrett, C. L., and Hampe, E. (1974) 'Phobias of childhood in a prescientific era', in A. Davies (ed.) *Child Personality and Psychopathology: Current Topics* vol. 1, New York: Wiley.

Miller, P. M. (1972) 'The use of visual imagery and muscle relaxation in the counter-conditioning of a phobic child: a case study', *Journal of Nervous and Mental Diseases* 154: 457–9.

Olsen, I. A. and Coleman, H. S. (1967) 'Treatment of school phobia as a case of separation anxiety', *Psychology in the Schools* 4: 151–4.

Patterson, G. R. (1965) 'A learning theory approach to the treatment of the school phobic child', in L. P. Ullman and L. Krasner (eds) *Case Studies in Behaviour Modification*, New York: Holt, Rinehart, & Winston.

Phillips, D. and Wolpe, S. (1981) 'Multiple behavioural techniques in severe separation anxiety of a twelve year old', *Journal of Behaviour Therapy and Experimental Psychiatry* 12, 4: 329–32.

Reynolds, D. and Murgatroyd, S. (1974) 'Being absent from school', *British Journal of Law and Society* 1: 78–80.

Rines, W. B. (1973) 'Behaviour therapy before institutionalisation', *Psychotherapy: Theory, Research and Practice* 10: 281–3.

Schermann, A. and Grover, V. M. (1962) 'Treatment of children's behaviour disorders: a method of re-education', *Medical Procedures* 8: 151–4.

Smith, R. E. annd Sharpe, T. M. (1970) 'Treatment of a school phobia with implosive therapy', *Journal of Consulting Clinical Psychology* 35: 239–43.

Sperling, M. (1961) 'Analytic first aid in school phobias', *Psychoanalytic Quarterly* 30: 504–18.

Stampfl, T. G. (1967) 'Implosive therapy: I. The theory', in S. G. Armitage (ed.) *Behaviour Modification Techniques in the Treatment of Emotional Disorders*, Veterans Admin. Battle Creek, Michigan.

——— (1968) 'Implosive therapy: a behaviour therapy?' *Behaviour Research and Therapy* 6: 31–6.

Stampfl, T. G. and Levis, D. J. (1967) 'Essentials of implosive therapy, a learning theory-based psychodynamic behavioural therapy', *Journal of Abnormal Psychology* 72: 496–503.

Suttenfield, V. (1954) 'School phobia: a study of five cases', *American Journal of Orthopsychiatry* 24: 308–80.

Tahmisian, J. A. and McReynolds, W. T. (1971) 'Use of parents as behavioural engineers in the treatment of a school phobic girl', *Journal of Counselling Psychology* 18: 225–8.

Thompson, J. (1948) 'Children's fears in relation to school attendance', *Bulletin of the National Association of Social Workers* 24: 1.

Tyrer, P. and Tyrer, S. (1974) 'School refusal truancy and neurotic illness', *Psychological Medicine* 4: 416–21.

Vaal, J. J. (1973) 'Applying contingency contracting to a school phobic: a case study', *Journal of Behaviour Therapy and Experimental Psychiatry* 4: 371–3.

Van der Ploeg, H. M. (1975) 'Treatment of frequency of urination by stories competing with anxiety', *Journal of Behaviour Therapy and Experimental Psychiatry* 6: 165–6.

Van Houten (1948) 'Mother–child relationships in twelve cases of school phobia', *Smith College Studies in Social Work* 18: 161–80.

Warren, W. (1948) 'Acute neurotic breakdown in children with refusal to go to school', *Archives of the Disturbed Child*, 266–72.

Wechsler, D. (1974) *Wechsler Intelligence Scale for Children — Revised*, Slough: National Foundation for Educational Research.

Welch, M. W. and Carpenter, C. (1970) 'Solution of a school phobia by contingency contracting', *School Applications of Learning Theory* 2, 11–17.

Wolpe, J. (1954) 'Reciprocal inhibition as the main basis of psychotherapeutic effects', *Archives of Neurological Psychiatry* 72: 205–26.

Yule, W. (1977) 'Behavioural approaches to treatment', in M. Rutter and L. Hersov (eds) *Child Psychiatry: Modern Approaches*, London: Blackwell Scientific.

Yule, W., Hersov, L., and Treseder, J. (1980) 'Behavioural treatments of school refusal', in L. Hersov and I. Berg (eds) *Out of School*, Chichester: Wiley.

Chapter eight

The management of school phobia

Hazel Baker

Brief history of the work on school attendance problems

Non-school attendance in its varying forms is probably as old as schools. One definite reference is nearly 400 years old:

> Then the whining schoolboy, with his satchel
> And shining morning face, creeping like snail
> Unwillingly to school.
>
> (*As You Like It*, II, vii: 145–7)

If, as seems possible, there is an autobiographical element in this description, the condition appears sometimes to have a very satisfactory outcome as measured by Shakespeare's adult achievement.

Moving forward in time, Broadwin (1932) and Partridge (1939), both studying truancy, distinguished a group of children they called neurotic. Johnson (1941) first used the term 'school phobia'. Warren (1948) produced a study to differentiate between truants and school phobics. This was developed in the noted work of Hersov (1960a), who became with Berg the major authority in Britain.

The main work in the USA was carried out by Eisenberg (1958), who considered the chief problem to be a separation anxiety in relation to the mother. Bowlby (1958) is the most prominent follower of this view here and links it with his mother–baby attachment theory. Where there is lack of security in the primary attachment, the child will continue to feel anxiety at any physical or emotional separation from mother.

Kennedy (1965) divided school refusers into type 1 and type 2; type 1 responding to brief treatment and type 2 needing more prolonged and complicated treatment. The more recent work in the country has been carried out by Berg *et al.* (1969), who divides cases into acute and chronic types.

Until recently, workers used the terms 'school refusal' and 'school phobia' indiscriminately. There are now attempts to limit school phobia to cases where a definite phobic reaction to school is evident.

Hsai (1984) suggests cases fall on a continuum with school phobia at one end, where the child 'can't' go to school, and at the other end, school refusal, where the child 'won't' go to school. The point at which a child is on this scale at any particular time has obvious implications for treatment. In what follows the term 'school phobia' will be used unless quoting from studies which use the term 'school refusal'.

Definition and classification: differentiation from truancy and the masquerade syndrome

The best definition of school phobia remains that of Berg (1969). He lists

1 severe difficulty in attending school, often amounting to prolonged absence;
2 severe emotional upset shown by such symptoms as excessive fearfulness, undue tempers, misery or complaints of feeling ill without obvious organic cause, on being faced with the prospect of going to school;
3 staying at home when they should be at school with the knowledge of the parents at some stage in the course of the disorder;
4 absence of significant antisocial disorder such as stealing, lying, wandering, destructiveness or sexual misbehaviour.

Berg *et al.* (1969) also classified school phobics into two main groups: the acute school phobics who had had at least three years' trouble-free attendance at school before the illness began and the chronic school phobics who had long-standing difficulties. This division corresponds broadly with the classification of Kennedy (1965). His type 1 or neurotic school phobia has an acute onset: the parents have a good relationship, but the child often fears illness or death of the mother. Type 2 or way of life school phobia has a prolonged or incipient onset: there is poor communication with parents and the father takes little interest in the family.

The differences between school phobia and truancy are very important as the managements are quite different. These differences were first described by Hersov (1960a). Truants are children who absent themselves from school without the parents' permission or who are kept at home by the parents because they can be of help in the family, whereas school phobics have severe difficulty attending school, and severe emotional upset at the prospect of having to go to school. They stay at home with the parents' knowledge and have no significant antisocial traits. Truants do not go to school because they do not want to go to school. School phobics want to go to school, but cannot. Truants are often dull children who find school difficult and have parents who may be unreliable and lacking in routine. There is little warmth, direction, or cohesion in the home. Truants are usually emotionally normal, although they may suffer emotional disturbance due to faulty training. They are often delinquent. The families frequently do not value education and tend to be anti-authority, hence, they do not take the truanting behaviour very seriously until the law is involved. The children may use physical symptoms as an excuse when caught, but these are obviously feigned and not, like those of the school phobics, neurotic.

There are intermediate types, sometimes called 'ego-weak children'. They complain of vague physical symptoms associated not only with school attendance, but also with other strange situations. Once in school, they appear happy. They are often physically immature and voice fears of growing up. These ego-weak children merge with the chronic school phobics.

Chronic school phobics are usually of low average intelligence. They find difficulty in forming a good adult-type identification and normal adolescent rebellion is lacking. Unfortunately the family is often inadequate and connives at keeping the child protected, dependent, and immature. The children, when refusing school, may be taken to visit Granny or have a trip on Dad's lorry. Thus they are getting plenty of secondary gain for their phobic behaviour. It is often very difficult to persuade such families to co-operate fully in treatment.

The acute school phobic is usually from a more stable and adequate family and before the onset of symptoms appears emotionally normal and of least average intelligence. The onset is sudden, with panic or acute physical symptoms, which usually disappear at weekends or holidays.

A different variant is called the masquerade symptoms (Waller and Eisenberg 1980). In this the child has a real physical illness, usually very slight, which is used as an excuse for prolonged absence from school and may, if allowed to continue, develop into full-blown school phobia when the child has recovered. In genuine chronic physical illness separation anxiety and maternal over-protection often cause a child, who could benefit from school attendance, to be kept at home.

Presenting picture

All studies show that an equal number of boys and girls suffer from this disorder. It becomes more common at and after puberty, although it can occur at any age. The main initial symptom is anxiety, which may amount to panic. This is usually centred on school or some aspect of school, but may be generalized. As time goes on, the anxiety may spread to other situations, such as riding on a bus, going into shops, going out of the house, or meeting visitors in the house, until finally the children are confined to their own room and sometimes their bed.

There is very often some depression. Bernstein and Garfinkel (1986) found 50 per cent of their sample had symptoms of both anxiety and depression. Physical symptoms are nearly always present. These are usually obviously due to anxiety and include nausea, vomiting, diarrhoea, headache, and so on. However, the condition may present with a dramatic physical symptom such as acute abdominal pain, a convulsion, or a severe paralysis.

A 12-year-old boy became so emaciated and dehydrated by diarrhoea and vomiting that he had to be admitted to hospital for rehydration and it was some months before he was physically strong enough to be treated for his school phobia.

General points on management

It is first essential to exclude genuine physical illness and for both child and parents to be reassured that the child is perfectly healthy. This often means co-operation with a paediatrician. It is also important that the school knows that the child is not physically ill and what action to take if symptoms occur in school. One boy had three times been put in an ambulance and sent to the local casualty department following hysterical convulsions. These were starting to occur whenever he was faced with a difficult situation. When they stopped procuring secondary gain for him, they ceased. Symptoms occurring in school should receive as little attention as possible so long as they do not inconvenience other pupils. When necessary, the child may have to be taken to the medical room for a time.

It is important also to exclude real psychiatric illness. If there is any doubt about the presence of psychotic symptoms or severe depression, psychiatric help should be sought. Schizophrenia is rare in school age children, but it does occur. Depression is much more common (Bernstein and Garfinkel 1986). The school phobia is sometimes merely a symptom of such a depression which needs treating for itself. This does not mean that once the depression is under control ordinary methods of management of school attendance do not apply. As with any other illness, return to school after recovery may be difficult. Psychiatric supervision is necessary. Suicide does occur in children and adolescents and, in less extreme circumstances, putting pressure on a severely depressed child can greatly impede recovery.

When all genuine illness is excluded a plan of management must be made. It is very important that all persons and agencies dealing with the child agree on this plan and work together. If one agency can be 'played off' against another, anxiety will increase. This co-operation will involve the school, the family doctor, paediatrician, psychologist, psychiatrist, education welfare officer, social worker, and any other professional with whom the family is in contact. It is very necessary to obtain the parents' full confidence and co-operation.

Cases of school phobia should be regarded as emergencies and seen at the earliest possible moment. Time spent at home increases secondary gain and reinforces a deviant behaviour pattern. The person taking on management should be readily available in person or on the phone to deal with problems as they arise. The aim should be full-time school attendance as quickly as possible and once this is achieved, time off school to see doctors, dentists, or for any other reason should be avoided at all costs (Hsai 1984).

Interventions in the school

The child and parents will nearly always ask for a change of school. This is hardly ever desirable and if effected may lead to repeated changes, ending by the child attending possibly seven schools in two years. However, the confidence of the family will be lost if their request is not taken seriously and the suitability of the present school to this specific child investigated. Both parents and child then need firmly reassuring that all other alternatives are less desirable.

The child's needs within the school should then be assessed. Chazan (1962) found educational difficulties in two-thirds of his cases. He felt that they all required some form of remedial teaching to help them function adequately. This necessitates arrangement with the school, and the child and parents then being reassured that extra help will be available.

Next, a teacher should be found to whom the child can communicate and with whom the child feels comfortable. The child must know when and where this teacher will be available, so that the child can report small problems as they arise. The head-teacher, year head, or form tutor should be asked to communicate to all members of staff who teach the child that there is a problem and that they should avoid singling the child out in any way or using anything approaching sarcasm. Such remarks as 'well, where have you been hiding?' or 'long time no see' have been reported and can do much harm. Combined with this need to find a key teacher, there should be the allocation of a refuge, a place the child can go if feeling overcome by panic or when fearing a possible break down in tears. This place can be the medical room, a named teacher's office, the school secretary's room, or the library. Whenever children retire there, they should not be left alone for long periods, but encouraged to return to class as soon as possible.

The next stage is to find if the phobia originated in or is focused on any particular element of school. This is often games, showers, or assembly. If children can initially be excused these problem areas, they can be dealt with later when their general attendance is satisfactory. If, after a period of attendance, they then complain of anxiety over a second situation, repeated exemptions should be avoided and they should be encouraged to extend rather than restrict their participation in school activities.

Another source of anxiety for children who have relationship difficulties is the playground where they are ostracized or bullied. Often discreet alternatives to full playground participation can be found such as the library, school clubs, or a job tidying, collecting, or distributing for a member of staff. With young children an infant or junior head-teacher can sometimes arrange an older befriender for the phobic child to stay with at play-time and ward off bullying. The younger child will use the older as a role model and very soon be able to cope alone.

Another point needing attention is the journey to and from school. Is there bullying on the school bus? Is the child afraid of being attacked in the street on the journey? Usually ways can be found to protect children for a time until their confidence builds up. A friend's parents might give the child a lift, an older child could walk with him, a different or longer route could be chosen or public transport used rather than the school bus.

All this process needs doing very quickly, if possible at the time of the first interview and by telephone, so that the child and parent can be sent directly to see the key teacher or head-teacher and resume attendance the next day. It is often advisable to discuss with the child and ask the teacher to confirm at this initial interview the reason the child will give to his peers for his absence. Fear of being questioned on this subject is often a bar to returning when all else has been smoothed out (Kennedy 1965).

In the majority of cases who are seen early, these simple adjustments to the environment are all that is needed initially. However, close contact and support are needed for some months to guard against recurrence and ensure future maturation proceeds normally. When children have been off school for a long time and there are many emotional and physical symptoms, treatment, usually behavioural, may be needed and should be offered, but it is surprising how often, when a gradual return to school is discussed (see pp. 160–5) children will opt for immediate return full time. This avoids the embarrassment of explaining why they are not attending full time and makes catching up with work easier. These children especially need prolonged follow-up and support which should, of course, be available after school hours or in the holidays.

Interventions with parents

All workers investigating the family situations in school phobic children have found evidence of disturbed family dynamics (e.g. Hersov 1960a; Davidson 1961; Baker and Wills 1979).

Hersov describes the fathers as inadequate and half the mothers as over-indulgent. Davidson describes the mothers as immature and dependent on the maternal grandmother. Baker and Wills found the mothers to be older than would be expected and the child often an only child or the youngest. Other factors in the home are illness or death of a family member or close friend, stress in the marriage, or a move of house with loss of social support. The result is that family relationships are more intense and tend to be turned inwards. There is little investment of emotion in the outside world. The crucial relationship is between the mother and child. This is usually very strong, but ambivalent with a lot of hostility on both sides. For some of the above reasons, the child is often very precious or special in some way.

It is necessary to take these factors into account even if a totally behavioural approach to management is planned. If the parents will not or cannot co-operate fully, work with the child will be very difficult. First, their attitude to the child and his problems should be investigated. They may be expecting too much of him, academically, athletically or socially, criticizing his failures rather than rewarding any slight success. Some time is needed to convince the parents of the value of positive reinforcement and for the need of small frequent rewards such as five pence for each house point, rather than a new racer bike if he gets top marks in tests at the end of the school year.

Investigation of the parents' own problems needs to be carried out tactfully, without in any way suggesting 'it is all their fault'. A mother who is too involved with her child will benefit from taking a part-time job or joining a voluntary group. Parents need encouraging to improve their own social life together and let the children grow away. It needs pointing out that a generation gap is healthy. The family should not 'do everything together'. If the parents have a life of their own, the child will feel free to move away and build his own personality.

Parents are helped by being told that school phobia usually occurs in 'good families', families where the child feels safe and secure. The outside world is seen as dangerous and threatening by comparison. School is the first step to this outside world and if home is too comfortable, it is more difficult to take that step. The parents also need support to cope with the child's rebellious and often aggressive behaviour and to be reassured that this is part of the normal process of growing up and will pass when he has settled at school.

It is worth taking time to help the parents fully understand what is going on, so that they can co-operate and will not think that authority figures are operating on them and their child in the interests of some mysterious 'them', but that all is being carried out in the best interests of their child. They can easily become hostile or even paranoid and thwart any attempt at getting the child back to school to the extent of disappearing out of the area. One lady moved around the country for all her daughter's secondary school life, appearing briefly in Wales, Kent, and Scotland as well as the Midlands. Each time she and the girl were laboriously traced, the pair again vanished. When the girl reached the age of 16, they returned to their original area and at once both settled in steady jobs.

When the family problems appear entrenched, family therapy should be offered, but this should not be used as an excuse to delay measures aimed at returning the child to school.

Interventions with the child

Where simple measures as already described between the child and the school do not achieve full-time attendance, more formal 'treatment' of the child is needed.

Confidence and self-confidence

It is very important, even if using a strictly behavioural approach, first to achieve good rapport with the child. He is going to be encouraged to do things he is afraid of, things he does not want to do and often, things in which he sees no point. This means listening sympathetically to his complaints and taking seriously his fears. Also it involves increasing his confidence and self-esteem by stressing his good points, taking seriously his ambitions and day-dreams and finding points where these can be realized. In this way, he can be given hope and see sense in attending a school where he is unhappy to prepare for a future that is highly desirable. For example, he can be helped to see how his interest now in computer games could lead to good maths and science A levels, which will be needed if he is to achieve his ambition of becoming a spaceman or an RAF pilot.

Dealing with anxieties and using cognitive therapy

Reality and cognitive therapy in children are described by Glasser (1965), Kendall (1981), and Brulle *et al.* (1985) among other workers. The child is asked to contemplate the reasons for and the results of his behaviour. In milder cases this can be directly correlated with his failure to attend school, but usually it is necessary to break down his anxieties into specific events. He is asked to relate events at school that have worried him. This may range from 'name calling' or 'thumping' by peers, to teachers shouting at or punishing him for something he has not done.

How he feels about these events and ways he can react to them are rehearsed in detail. It is best if, in doing this, he can be helped to laugh. Spontaneous laughter is the best counter-stimulus to anxiety. This is achieved quite easily in inventing names he can call back to his tormenters and verbal responses or body gestures with which he can reply to aggression. This use of humour in the rehearsal sequence helps him to reply with laughter and to laugh with his peers and sometimes at himself. In this way, he may acquire a very important social skill. It is best to warn teachers of advice given and to discuss with the child his limits in retaliatory behaviour! Also the roles set for the child should be coping models where allowances are made for mistakes, which again can be made humorous, not mastery models where performance is ideal (Kazdin 1974).

With older children it is possible to discuss the relationship between thought and feeling. They have come to see school as 'bad', so they feel bad about it and have feelings of emotional discomfort and often physical discomfort when attending. They are 'sick to death of it'. It is 'a pain in the neck' to them. (A more earthy word than 'neck' may be used.) Some good things about school such as swimming, art, or soccer can be discussed, and mental focusing on these used to counter bad feelings about school in general. The child can live through the whole day, or even week, looking forward to his favourite activity.

In follow-up interviews the child should be asked to keep a diary of bad experiences and bad feelings, noting when they occurred and how he dealt with them. These are discussed. He is praised for what he achieved, however little, and ways of improving his performance discussed and rehearsed. The mere fact of writing it all down or remembering the event for writing down seems to reduce the anxiety at the time.

Social skills training

School phobics often have poor peer relationships. The ability to improve on these and to communicate with confidence with other pupils and with adults will depend on the level the child has reached in social perspective skills. These levels are described by Selman and Byrne (1974), Shantz (1975), and Selman (1976). At level 0 the child does not comprehend the view of another. If he enjoys an activity, he regards it as enjoyable for all. At level 1 the child can realize that another may have different ideas from himself, but has great difficulty in taking the role of another. At level 2 the child has difficulty in seeing his own and another's point of view simultaneously, although he knows that they are different. At level 3 the child can see both points of view at once and can see the situation from the outside as an independent observer.

Help in these areas can first be discussed at a one-to-one interview. The child can describe interpersonal events in which he has not been comfortable and his own feelings and then those of the other person are explored. He can be helped to understand how his behaviour affected first the feelings then the behaviour of the other person. He can be encouraged to watch other people and try and imagine how they feel, to notice at school those children in the playground who feel lonely and might need a companion and discuss how to approach them; also to notice those who are happily playing in a group and will not like to be interrupted. He can try and understand the teacher's feelings or those of his parents and notice how his behaviour affects them.

He can then progress to role-playing different social scenarios with the therapist. If possible, this should go on to role-play in a peer group with video play-back. Such methods are very useful, not merely for helping the child feel more confident in school, but in learning to cope in a mature way with out of school situations including family relationships.

Behavioural methods

Where more structured therapy is needed, several surveys have shown the behavioural approach to be superior to the psychotherapeutic in getting the child back to school (Kennedy 1965; Miller *et al.* 1974). Treatment may be by desensitization, implosion, or operant methods. Often elements of all three are used.

Desensitization was well described by Wolpe (1958) and its application to school phobia was elaborated by Prout and Harvey (1978) among others. The school is seen as the anxiety-provoking stimulus. The child is first taught to relax, using a calming mental picture of his own choosing. This may be difficult and take time. Children are usually bored and irritated by golden sands and lapping seas. Imagining a favourite play activity or television programme may produce the desired effect. Children usually relax fairly easily and, in entrenched cases, light hypnosis may be helpful. The child then needs to construct a hierarchy of situations associated with school that cause anxiety. This could start with getting up in the morning and putting on school clothes and progress through easy stages to entering school and sitting in the classroom. Later situations like games, the playground, or specific lessons can be added. While relaxed, the child is asked to imagine these situations in increasing order of anxiety until he feels tense, then he is asked immediately to return to relaxation. When the child can imagine a situation without tension, he is exposed to it in real life, usually first with a trusted adult. This can be a professional or a family member. Getting into the school building should be achieved as soon as possible. If it is not achieved quickly in school hours, as a start, some schools will arrange an hour's attendance with teaching, when the other children have gone home. It is sometimes helpful to arrange part-time attendance for a favourite lesson. The approach needs to be flexible, but aiming at progress each day with increasing periods of normal education. Usually once classroom attendance has begun, the time spent in school escalates very quickly.

At the same time as the child is being introduced to school, all secondary gains in the home are stopped. If the child has been off school some time, these will be considerable. Time spent at home should be as boring as possible. No television or hi-fi in school hours should be allowed, no shopping trips with parents, no playing with pets, no reading other than school books. On the other hand, small rewards in the form of activities tailored to the child and taking place at weekends or evenings can be allowed, contingent on increasing school attendance.

The parents obviously have a key role in this process and need support and encouragement. Some children are so attached to the mother and there is so much separation anxiety that this has to be tackled first. One boy of 10, who had been off school several months, when first seen, had many physical symptoms and spent his days on the sofa in the living-room cuddling a hot water bottle, waited on by his mother. He could not bear her to leave him. While relaxed he was asked to imagine mother leaving him to go into the kitchen to make a pot of tea and leaving him in the living-room. Next he imagined mother going to the front door, then mother visiting a neighbour's house, then mother going to the local corner shop. His mother was then asked to carry out these situations in reality and to be absent for gradually increasing lengths of time, until he stayed in the house without her for one hour. After this, return to school with the use of desensitization was quite rapid. He had a few booster sessions of relaxation the weeks before he was due to start at secondary school, where he settled happily.

As can be seen, operant methods are introduced with desensitization as school phobia is much more complex than a simple phobia (Ayllon *et al.* 1970). Rewards are given for each advance towards normal full-time attendance. At first, these are treats at home, but gradually achievements at school, academically, athletically, and socially produce natural rewards. It is very helpful if the school can co-operate by taking every opportunity to find small achievements to reward in school in the early stages.

Implosion therapy advocated by Kennedy (especially for his type 1 cases) is the best treatment for cases with a very short history, especially in younger children. The child is pressurized to attend school after any real problems in the reality situation are righted. This method is often used by mothers and teachers in infant school without recourse to any outside advice. However, in older children or in longer-standing cases, it is better to use relaxation and imagination of the particular school situation first; and only when the child has experience of this, to use pressure for full-time normal attendance (Smith and Sharpe 1970).

Where return to school is not achieved

Inevitably, not all children will return to school with the above measures. These are usually depressed children, children who have been off school for a very long time with physical illness, and cases of the masquerade syndrome with severe physical symptoms. There are various types of provision for such children.

Special teaching unit

Most areas have some form of unit in which the child can be taught in a sheltered environment with only a small number of similar children and with a high teacher–pupil ratio. Attendance is flexible and the atmosphere relaxed. Where the child is very disturbed, a member of the teaching staff can visit the home, form a relationship with the child, and take him to the unit for an initial visit. It should be made clear to the child and family that such provision is only temporary and the aim is to return the child to school. Attendance at such a unit effects the separation of the child from home and establishes a regular routine of attendance for education at a location outside home.

Hospital unit

Where the child has had long periods in hospital or admission for investigations in the masquerade syndrome, he will have attended the hospital school. If there are difficulties about immediate transfer to normal school, he can continue to attend the hospital school on a day basis until attendance at normal school is achieved. If the child says he is too ill for school, it can be pointed out that there is no way he is too ill for hospital. At all costs 'rest' or convalescence at home should be avoided.

Psychiatric unit

Where the child has a severe psychiatric condition, he will need to attend either a day or residential psychiatric unit. Berg (1970) describes great benefit in cases with dependence on mother and separation anxiety. These cases can be handled better in a psychiatric unit than a school. In the milieu of a unit the child can develop social skills and independence.

Where the parents cannot co-operate with home management and constantly give in too easily to the child, residential treatment should be considered. The parents' and the child's consent is necessary for admission and considerable powers of persuasion are usually needed. In fact, discussion of residential treatment in psychiatric unit or school often results in return to school. This is not to say that residential treatment should ever be used as a threat. There should be a real intent to use it and a place available before it is discussed with parents and child. If the child refuses and returns to school, continuing support to him and the family should be provided.

Residential school

Occasionally a residential school is considered, much less frequently now than formerly. Few schools have the facilities needed to treat these very disturbed children and entrance to them depends on a statement which often takes many months that the child may waste at home.

Evaluation and outcome

Most follow-up studies of school phobics use return to school as the main measure of success of treatment. Studies comparing behavioural treatments with other methods, usually psychotherapy, found that behavioural interventions were vastly superior in returning children to school (Blagg and Yule 1984). Kennedy (1965) treated fifty type 1 school phobics with implosion and had them all back in three days. They were still at school at one-year follow-up. However, this treatment was unsuccessful in six children of type 2. These latter children later received supportive therapy.

Apart from Kennedy no worker has studied in great detail the relative value of different types of management. In no study are cases selected randomly for different management programmes. Nowhere are blind procedures used. Neither Berg (1970) nor Baker and Wills (1978) carried out reliability studies on categorization.

Blagg and Yule did not use random selection or allocation. Although study of the three groups they reported on showed no significant differences on a number of factors *after selection*, the results cannot be regarded as totally reliable.

Inevitably, overall success based on return to school varies widely between surveys and is dependent on the severity and type of disturbance, time already off school and method of intervention. Adolescents ill enough to be hospitalized will obviously not respond to short-term behavioural techniques, as will young children with very short histories of refusal.

Some workers have tried to evaluate the long-term outcome of school phobic children and followed them up into adult life. Retrospective studies of neurotic adults have often found that these adults had a previous history of school phobia (Tyrer and Tyrer 1974; Berg *et al.* 1974). Examination of admissions to a psychiatric unit for school phobia showed that 30 per cent were emotionally disturbed apart from their school phobia (Berg *et al.* 1974). Other retrospective studies showed that neurotic disturbance tends to occur more often in school phobics when they grow up than would be expected (Warren 1960; Coolidge *et al.* 1964; Waldron 1976; Waller and Eisenberg 1980).

Berg and Jackson (1985) carried out a detailed survey of 168 patients treated in an in-patient unit for school phobia; ten years on average after their discharge, they found 50 per cent were well. These tended to be of higher intelligence, treated when they were under 14 years old and well, or much improved on discharge. However 13 per cent had needed psychiatric treatment, 5 per cent in hospital. It is assumed that children needing in-patient treatment were fairly severely disturbed. Baker and Wills (1979) followed up seventy-one children after they had left school. These were treated as out-patients, so presumably were less disturbed than those in Berg's survey. In the 1979 study 10 per cent of the children needed further psychiatric treatment, but not in hospital. In this study emotional adjustment was measured by function in work or higher education; fifty-seven of the children were functioning well. Those who did poorly were those needing further psychiatric treatment.

These last two studies emphasize the need to treat vigorously the underlying neurotic condition as well as getting the child back to school. As in many other conditions, it is necessary to treat the whole child and often the whole family, not just the presenting symptom.

> No man [or child or symptom] is an island, entire of itself.
> (Donne, *Devotions*, c. 1600)

References

Ayllon, T., Smith, D., and Rogers, M. (1970) 'Behavioural management of school phobia', *Journal of Behavioural Therapy and Experimental Psychology* 1: 125–38.

Baker, H. and Wills, U. (1978) 'School phobia: classification and treatment', *British Journal of Psychiatry* 132: 492–9.

——— (1979) 'School phobic children and work', *British Journal of Psychiatry* 135: 561–4.

Berg, I. (1970) 'A follow up study of school phobic adolescents admitted to an inpatient unit', *Journal of Child Psychology and Psychiatry* 11: 37–47.

Berg, I. and Jackson, A. (1985) 'Teenage school refusers grown up: a follow up study of 168 subjects, ten years on average after inpatient treatment', *British Journal of Psychiatry* 147: 366–70.

Berg, I., Nichols, K., and Pritchard, C. (1969) 'School phobia and its relationship to dependency', *Journal of Psychology and Psychiatry* 10: 123–41.

Berg, I., Marks, I., McGuire, R., and Lipsedge, M. (1974) 'School phobia and agoraphobia', *Psychological Medicine* 4: 428–34.

Bernstein, G. A. and Garfinkel, B. D. (1986) 'School phobia: the overlap of affective and anxiety disorders', *Journal of American Academy of Child Psychiatric Disorders* 25: 235–41.

Blagg, N. R. and Yule, W. (1984) 'Behavioural treatment of school refusal: a comparative study', *Behaviour Research and Therapy* 22, 2: 119–27.

Bowlby, J. (1958) 'The nature of the child's tie to his mother', *International Journal of Psycho-Analysis* 3a: 350–73.

Broadwin, I. T. (1932) 'A contribution to the study of truancy', *American Journal of Orthopsychiatry* 2: 253–9.

Brulle, A. R., McIntyre, T. C., and Mills, J. S. (1985) 'School phobia: its educational implications', *Elementary School Guidance Counseling* 20: 19–28.

Chazan, M. (1962) 'School phobia', *British Journal of Educational Psychology* 32: 200–17.

Coolidge, J. C., Brodie, R. D., and Feeney, B. (1964) 'A ten year follow up study of sixty-six school phobic children', *American Journal of Orthopsychiatry* 34: 675–84.

Davidson, S. (1961) 'School phobia as a manifestation of family disturbance', *Journal of Child Psychology and Psychiatry* 1: 270–87.

Eisenberg, L. (1958) 'School phobia: a study in the communication of anxiety', *American Journal of Psychiatry* 114: 712–18.
Glasser, W. (1965) 'Reality therapy: a new approach to psychiatry', New York: Harper & Row.
Hersov, L. A. (1960a) 'Persistent non attendance at school', *Journal of Child Psychology and Psychiatry* 1: 130–6.
——— (1960b) 'Refusal to go to school', *Journal of Child Psychology and Psychiatry* 1: 137–45.
Hsai, H. (1984) 'Structural and strategic approach to school phobia/school refusal', *Psychology in the Schools* 21: 360–7.
Johnson, A. M. (1941) 'School phobia', *American Journal of Orthopsychiatry* 11: 702–11.
Kazdin, A. E. (1974) 'Covent modelling, model similarity and reduction of avoidance behaviour', *Behaviour Therapy* 5: 325–40.
Kendall, P. C. (1981) 'Cognitive behavioural interventions with children', in B. B. Lahey and A. E. Kazdin (eds) *Advances in Clinical Psychology*, New York: Plenum Press.
Kennedy, W. A. (1965) 'School phobia: rapid treatment of fifty cases', *Journal of Abnormal Psychology* 70, 4: 285–9.
Miller, L. C., Barrett, C. L., Hampe, E. and Noble, H. (1974) 'Comparison of reciprocal inhibition psychotherapy and waiting list control for phobic children', *Journal of Abnormal Psychology* 79: 269–79.
Partridge, J. M. (1939) 'Truancy', *Journal of Mental Science* 85: 45–81.
Prout, H. T. and Harvey, J. R. (1978) 'Applications of desensitization for school related problems, a review', *Psychology in the Schools* 15: 533–41.
Selman, R. L. (1976) 'Towards a structural analysis of developing interpersonal relations' concept: research with normal and disturbed preadolescent boys', in A. B. Pick (ed.) *Minnesota Symposia on Child Psychology* vol. 10, Minneapolis, Minn: University of Minnesota Press.
Selman, R. and Byrne, D. (1974) 'A structural developmental analysis of levels of role taking in middle childhood', *Child Development* 45: 803–6.
Shantz, C. V. (1975) 'The development of social cognition', in E. M. Hetherinton (ed.) *Review of Child Developmental Research*, vol. 5, Chicago, Ill: University of Chicago Press.
Smith, R. E. and Sharpe, T. M. (1970) 'Treatment of school phobia with implosive therapy', *Journal of Consulting and Clinical Psychology* 35: 339–43.
Tyrer, P. and Tyrer, S. (1974) 'School refusal, truancy and adult mental illness', *Psychological Medicine* 4: 416–21.
Waldron, S. (1976) 'The significance of childhood neurosis for adult mental health: a follow up study', *American Journal of Psychiatry* 133: 532–8.
Waller, D. and Eisenberg, L. (1980) 'School refusal in childhood — a psychiatric-paediatric perspective', in L. Hersov and I. Berg (eds) *Out of School*, New York: Wiley.
Warren, W. (1948) 'Acute neurotic breakdown in children with refusal

to go to school', *Archives of Diseases in Childhood* 23: 266–72.
——— (1960) 'Some relationships between the psychiatry of children and of adults', *Journal of Mental Science* 106: 815–26.
Wolpe, J. (1958) *Psychotherapy by Reciprocal Inihibition*, Stanford, Calif: Stanford University Press.

Chapter nine

Approaches to the remediation of learning difficulties: a current assessment

Gilbert Gredler

Over the past several years there has been increasing concern about the education of children and the best ways to provide educational services for students' learning difficulties. In the USA this concern has been exemplified in part by the passage of federal legislation. An example is PL94-142, which has mandated certain types of support help for children with a variety of learning problems. Enactment of the 1981 Education Act by the House of Commons in Britain has served as a similar impetus for development of educational support services. Concurrently there has been an increase in the number of articles and research studies dealing with the remediation of learning problems.

Any reader of the remediation literature has to be impressed by the variety of approaches available to help children with learning problems. Countless intervention methods purport to offer improved achievement in children with reading problems. Individuals have advocated, at one time or another, use of colour-cued words, changes in the English alphabet, 'directive teaching', task analysis, computer-assisted instruction, a delay in school entrance, special class placement for one year, remediation of deficient processing abilities, and dozens of behavioural and motivational approaches.

The purpose of this chapter is to review some major issues in the interpretations of research studies and a number of remediation approaches that offer promising results will then be discussed.

Major issues in interpretation of remediation studies

An important question which comes to the fore first is 'Can it be determined if there really are intervention methods which are superior to others and should be recommended to help remediate learning difficulties?' Answers to such questions should take into account the definition of the diagnostic process that is accepted by educational and psychological personnel. If the nature of the learning difficulty is conceptualized in different ways by various professionals then selected intervention processes will vary depending on the belief structure of the individual making the choice.

The relationship between diagnosis and remediation should be clarified. Several models of diagnosis and remediation are competing for favour and each one has advantages. One model emphasizes that the act of diagnosis is quite separate from any remediation which might follow.

In such a paradigm, diagnosis determines only the existence of a problem, but a specific plan of remediation and intervention does not flow from the assessment data except in a general way (O'Donnell 1972). For example, a group of children are screened as to their reading performance. All students with wide discrepancies between reading achievement and grade placement in school are then given extra help from a remedial reading teacher during the school year. The remedial teacher then works out her own plan of attack. Thus the diagnostic process is only undertaken to identify a problem, but a specific plan of remediation does not flow out of the diagnostic data.

In contrast, diagnosis may be conceived as a process where the actual intervention steps flow from what is discovered during the diagnostic phase. Knowledge gained from the assessment process is important because the results obtained help determine what will be done in the intervention phase. For example, if the educator believes in the importance of remediating processing deficits so as to improve reading performance, then the child who is found to have a serious visual perceptual deficit might begin a programme aimed at strengthening the various components of visual perceptual processes.

Diagnosis and remediation may also be considered as overlapping. For example, a remedial lesson can become a springboard for further diagnostic hypotheses about a child's reading problem. The continually ongoing relationship between the two facets is stressed. According to this position diagnosis cannot exist without remediation also being involved (O'Donnell 1972).

The most extreme position is one in which the treatment is dictated by the diagnosis as illustrated below:

> Diagnosis is conducted for the *sole purpose* of prescription development to be used in remediation or in circumvention of the problem. Having established the learning mode as a result of diagnostic activities, the teacher then draws upon a rich background of training and experience to determine which instructional strategies to match to the student's learning mode — the instructional strategies are, in a sense, PRESCRIBED by the result of the diagnostic activities, especially the learning mode.
>
> (Poteet 1973: 58–9)

Acceptance of the view of the educational primacy of the child's learning problems has led to the idea that the relationship between educational deficits and academic performance is the only area to be investigated; and that the diagnostic/remediation process is basically the province of the classroom-teacher and resource-room personnel.

While the importance of the teaching process cannot be denied, restriction of the diagnostic/remediation analogue to the academic skills area alone is ill-advised. A more meaningful definition of the diagnostic process would emphasize *assessment* of the individual child. Such assessment would involve the 'systematic collection, organization and interpretation of information about an individual and the situation in which he finds himself' (Sundberg *et al.* 1973). We are interested in valid ways of measuring behaviour and confirming hypotheses. How do children with learning disabilities meet their educational and personal problems and what are their concerns about their difficulties? In the *assessment* of children, positive attributes of the individual are also given primacy. Emphasis is also placed on the ways that children are reacting to the situations in which they find themselves. Emphasis is not merely on the intrapsychic aspects of the individual.

When the diagnostic process is defined as coterminous with

remediation then some educators believe it is efficient to have the same individual diagnose, suggest hypotheses about the remedial strategies, and then carry out the specific intervention programme (O'Donnell 1972). The fallacy of this approach is that only educational diagnostic activities are stressed and the diagnosis/intervention process is in danger of becoming too narrow and proscribed.

Adequate conceptualization of the assessment/remediation process is therefore paramount if the needs of the child with learning problems are to be adequately served. To develop *adequate* working hypotheses about an individual child and attempt to explain and provide *appropriate* intervention strategies involves various levels of inferential thinking about the problem situation. Three such levels of inferential thinking have been proposed by Sundberg *et al.* (1973). These levels range from making minimum inferences about a child's problem to being able to provide an overall conceptualization of the problem situation and therefore being able to implement a sophisticated assessment intervention programme. These various levels are elaborated on further below.

Level I

At this level brief information already available about a child can result in an immediate decision. For example, if children are below the age limit to begin school, the result is that they must wait until next year to enter when they are old enough. At a more sophisticated level, Level I inferences could involve the use of a behaviour rating check-list such as the Rutter. Children who score below a certain cut-off score on the rating scale would continue in the school's mainstream and only those above the cut-off would be looked at more intensively. Or the question may be asked, does the child in fact have a reading problem? Screening would involve ascertaining if there is a discrepancy between the child's cognitive level of performance and his actual reading achievement. If the discrepancy is sufficiently great, the child would be involved in further assessment and remediation procedures.

Level II

At the second level of inference the school psychologist would study in more detail the factors which might be involved in the presented problem. For example, the school psychologist might ascertain that the child talks only when alone with the teacher, becomes nervous when questioned, mumbles shyly when greeted, never offers to help, but is pleased if asked to do something, etc. The psychologist might then attempt to put all these separate statements together and come up with the generalization that the child shows a lack of confidence and is somewhat inhibited.

Level III

As we go to Level III an attempt would be made to provide an integrated theory of the child's functioning within his environment. Finding out that the child's inhibited behaviour occurs mostly in his classroom when he attempts a reading assignment, but he is more open and relaxed on the playground and at home, may lead to the conclusion that 'lack of competence' in learning how to read may be the primary factor with which we have to deal (that is fear, tension in possibly making mistakes). Our plans for action (remediation) must therefore incorporate a programme to help reduce this tension as well as address the specific mechanics of his reading errors. A Level II approach might have involved administering a test of visual memory span with the result that a distinct deficit in this area was found. Before hypothesizing that visual memory was a factor that might have some bearing on the child's reading problem, we might teach the child some sight words and within a short time length check again on the extent of retention of such words. At this level of inference we would also administer a standardized diagnostic reading test which would give us in-depth information as to the child's competencies in the various facets of the reading process. We would also want to compare the child's performance with his age mates. However, we would not be content with one kind of reading test. We might also give an informal reading inventory (IRI) and note carefully the kinds of errors the child makes. This inventory would be chosen carefully since the standards used to define instructional level vary widely from one IRI to another. For example, one IRI defines 'instructional' level as no more than 10 errors in 100 words, while another IRI defines instructional levels as 4 to 8 errors per 100 words.

Inferential thinking at a sophisticated level would require the school psychologist to offer an integrated theory of the child's functioning and his/her difficulty in reading. Inferences at this level would not be of the order: 'the child is having difficulty in learning to read because of a visual memory deficit. Such a deficit was ascertained from the child's low score on the *X* visual motor test'. Unfortunately such inferences are common within education and psychology today. Level III inferences also would not be based on simply performing a task analysis of what skills the student has and determining the various subskills which should be considered.

Providing an *integrated* theory of the child and his learning problem along with an appropriate intervention programme must be the main objective in the diagnostic/remediation analogue.

Many remediation programmes appear to offer only a screening function or a narrow view of the child's learning difficulties. The school psychologist who attempts to offer an overall theory of the child's functioning from a circumscribed battery of tests consisting of the WISC-R, the Bender, the HTP, and WRAT-R is operating at just as low an inferential level as the teacher or educational specialist who uses only an IRI or brief criterion-referenced tests to make diagnostic judgements and remedial suggestions.

An integrated plan of action would include consideration of the behavioural characteristics of the child, coping strategies that the child is utilizing, the quality of the teacher–child interaction, and competencies of teaching personnel in addition to reviewing appropriate educational variables.

Problems in remediation research

Several problems in the research literature on remediation may be identified. One major problem is the selection method used in the identification of children for remediation. Often the group of children is so heterogeneous that a given remedial approach may fail to indicate significant results. For example, children may be chosen mainly on the basis of a large discrepancy between their ability test scores and current achievement test performance. Such a group will include both the 'true' learning disabled children as well as those whose deficient reading performance may result from emotional problems or other variables. Such problems are likely not to be addressed by the particular remediation technique under study.

This problem typically arises when American researchers accept the school system's label of a child as learning disabled. Most commonly, schools use a 'discrepancy' formula. Children whose current achievement level is one to two standard deviations below their ability level are likely to be classified as 'learning disabled'. Any study of such children which purports to identify appropriate remediation methods is automatically suspect because the use of a discrepancy formula *alone* cannot determine 'true' learning disabled students.

A second major problem in remediation studies that is almost completely neglected is that of the Hawthorne effect (Roethlisberger and Dickson 1939). The Hawthorne effect is so named from the demonstration carried out in the assembly room of the Hawthorne plant of the Western Electric company. A number of different changes were made in work conditions at this plant. As the study continued it became evident that it was not the experimental changes that produced improved output but the greater interest in the plant workers which increased their motivation to do well.

In the school environment, students participate in a study that investigates a 'new' method, procedure, or technique, and is therefore novel and different. These students receive additional attention from teachers or other school personnel. These variables, which are not a part of the particular 'treatment', may themselves be responsible for post-test changes in student performance, that is the Hawthorne effect.

Educational or psychological personnel who become involved in research on new or different teaching methods are likely to be highly interested and involved in their work with the children. The students react positively to the new approaches and an improvement in academic performance can be expected because a different approach and extra attention are provided. Because the Hawthorne phenomenon should be considered in such research projects, the editor of one medical journal has stated that improvement in academic performance must be maintained over a three-year period before the particular teaching technique can be truly considered to be an advance. Research studies which do not meet this criterion are not published (Lennox 1983). Few educational interventions with school-children would qualify for any conference presentation or publication if such requirements were invoked for educational and psychological journals!

Well-known specialists in the remediation of 'dyslexia' or 'severe reading disability' have also emphasized that there is no one method which will automatically ensure success and that any method which is used must be utilized in a flexible manner. Orton, Fernald, Delacato, Miles, Gillingham, and Woolman, all of whom utilized quite different approaches in working with children with severe reading problems, did agree there is no *one* method which is a guarantee of success. Emphasis is placed by these authorities on a structured approach and the centrality of the child's motivational status. Particularly emphasized is the primacy of the child in planning a remediation programme rather than just looking at specific methods (Sampson 1976).

While almost every aspect of the child's condition has been investigated and found to be at times a factor of importance in learning difficulties such as cognitive abilities, perceptual abilities, social and emotional conditions, coping style, and so on, it is noteworthy that so many prominent authorities have formed a consensus on the value of looking at the motivational state of the child and providing a remedial programme which takes into account the emotional status of the child, his feelings, and attempts to lessen the child's anxiety.

Studies of various remediation approaches have also been plagued by emphasis on investigating single factors (Level II types). While the importance of visual perceptual retardation has been amply demonstrated in a number of investigations of reading disabled children (Gredler 1978), the results of studies of children with reading problems have never shown that a single factor, whether it be visual perception, auditory memory, or mental ability can be assumed to be the primary cause of all reading disabilities.

The 1960s and 1970s were replete with studies purporting to demonstrate the primacy of visual perceptual remediation. In the 1970s and 1980s other approaches came to the fore — such as behavioural methods claiming to produce startling improvement in almost all cases.

Currently there are educators who reject 'processing' approaches and state that all remediation must follow a 'task analysis' model in order to be successful.

The confusion in ascertaining which remedial approach may be of value is compounded by statements claiming that all intervention methods used to date have failed to demonstrate their value (Hicks 1986).

The interpretation of remediation research is further complicated by 'fads' in treatment methods and doctrinaire approaches. A recent review of American textbooks in special education observed that a number of authors will eloquently defend a particular remediation technique yet fail to offer empirical evidence of its real superiority over other techniques (Gredler, forthcoming). The field of special education and school psychology is ill served by the presence of what can be described as the 'doctrinaires' — educators and psychologists who so emphasize one approach or remediation method that they neglect to discuss data which indicate that some children may fail to progress with the use of their preferred technique.

Professional personnel frequently underestimate the degree to which the remediation field is subject to fads. An approach used by many educators for a number of years falls out of favour; an educator emphasizes the value of a different method and if such a method receives monetary support from a private foundation, government support, or media emphasis, then these different methods come into favour and so the cycle of acceptance and rejection continues.

One example of a doctrinaire approach is the unabashed championing of the use of the criterion-referenced methodology for teaching and the measurement of educational objectives: '[Special needs] children could literally work their way out of special attention by meeting identified criteria' (Duffey and Fedner 1978: 249). While close monitoring of children as they acquire skills is to be applauded, substitution of this assessment/intervention process for one where ability and perceptual variables are emphasized is really only a substitution of one set of limited variables for another such set. For the diagnostic/intervention process to be a meaningful one, superficial inferential interventions will need to be discarded.

In attempting to get into the mainstream as many children with special needs as possible, children with severe learning difficulties have tended to be ignored by the school. Such children are those who demonstrate *continued* learning problems after exposure to developmental reading and corrective reading. Developmental reading is defined as a system of teaching reading which incorporates a sequential development of reading skills within a group programme. Corrective reading consists of methods used to correct poor habits in reading or to fill in gaps in knowledge acquired during the developmental reading programme (Kirk and Chalfant 1984).

In one school a behavioural programme was devised for a group of inner city children who demonstrated distinct gaps of knowledge in learning the sounds of different symbols. Material reinforcers were introduced wherein tokens were given to the child if the child learned a specified number of words and they were identified correctly at subsequent teaching sessions (Hamblin *et al.* 1971).

The programme did pay off in increased learning of the symbols presented and is one behavioural method which certainly could be utilized when children need a corrective reading programme. However, it would be most doubtful if such reinforcement exercises in themselves would be found to be sufficient for the remediation of children with severe reading disabilities or that such a programme could suffice as the only intervention method which should be used.

Remediation approaches of importance

Despite the various factors which may affect the validity of remediation research, a number of investigations have been carefully formulated and implemented. Some of these research projects are now described.

Diagnostic prescriptive teaching as a remediation method

One intervention approach that has received substantial attention over the past several years is the relationship of modality functioning to the child's progress in reading. According to this concept, the child shows a preference in the use of one sensory channel over another when learning to read.

To ascertain modality preference a variety of measures has been used. One such measure is the Mills learning methods test (Mills 1956). A child's modality strength is determined by asking him/her to read a number of new words over a period of four days. A modality preference is based on a score reflecting the child's score on a test of immediate recall and retention.

Cooper (1969), using a revision of the Mills learning methods test, studied the differences in the learning modalities of good and poor first-grade readers of normal intelligence under four different learning methods: visual, auditory, kinaesthetic, and a combination approach. The visual modality involved stressing the word length and configuration; the auditory modality stressed the sounding out and blending of syllables — basically a phonic approach; the kinaesthetic approach emphasized tracing and copying the syllable; and the combination approach utilized parts of all the above approaches.

Cooper noted the number of trials required for a child to learn five syllables under each teaching condition (the acquisition score). Twenty-four hours later the child's retention of the syllables was measured for each condition (the retention score). Cooper demonstrated that good readers were able to learn new syllables in fewer trials than poor readers, regardless of the modality approach selected. The results also indicated that no modality approach was significantly better for good readers *as a group* or poor readers *as a group*.

However, significant differences were found in a number of individual cases as to the importance of modality preference. For example, one 'poor' reader was able to learn to read the words to criterion in only two trials when using an auditory approach while ten trials were required for the kinaesthetic approach. Another 'poor' reader was unable to learn any of the new words presented regardless of the modality method used even after ten trial attempts had been made with each modality approach.

The results of this study raise several points of educational significance. Many teachers are convinced of the value of the kinaesthetic method for helping all poor readers. However, the data from Cooper's study do not support the unrestricted use of that method as an aid for poor readers. While Cooper found no mean score differences among the groups of poor readers as to modality preference, this finding cannot be used to deny that modality preference is of no consequence or importance in individual cases. The reporting only of mean scores for a group studied may obscure the fact that in some individual cases modality preference is definitely a factor of importance. This fact is illustrated by the example given above of the one poor reader who was able to learn the five new words presented to him more easily when taught to him via the auditory modality than with the kinaesthetic approach.

The value of such a study is that the school psychologist and other educational personnel must carefully tease out important variables during the assessment intervention process. This type of investigation follows the conceptual model of the assessment process wherein there is a thoroughgoing review of the child's learning environment (a Level III approach). Utilizing a sophisticated diagnostic/intervention model requires evaluation of a number of hypotheses and deductions before being able to arrive at a valid intervention programme for the child's difficulties. Some specialists believe that there are important underlying psycholinguistic correlates of learning disabilities and that if such correlates are ascertained and strengthened improvement in reading will result.

The effectiveness of diagnostic prescriptive teaching has long been a topic of discussion. Arter and Jenkins (1979) vehemently argue against the continued use of the processing approach 'until a more adequate research base' is established. In fact, they call for a moratorium on advocacy of diagnostic/prescriptive teaching and on the classification and placement of children utilizing differential processing ability tests. It would appear that this more adequate research base has been partially provided by the recent investigations of Naylor and Pumfrey (1983). Their work raises significant questions as to whether such a wholesale indictment against prescriptive and/or processing approaches should be accepted.

Naylor and Pumfrey worked with sixty poor readers aged 7 to 8 years. A deficit in psycho-educational functions as measured by the ITPA was found in auditory closure and visual sequential memory. Three intervention programmes were utilized. One group received a language programme based on ITPA-type activities; another group utilized materials from the Peabody language development; and a third group, the control, worked with a number programme. Intervention time totalled two sessions of forty-five minutes each of remedial teaching for twelve weeks. Children were tested for achievement level at the conclusion of the treatment programme and again ten months later.

The results indicated that both language subgroups improved in psycholinguistic development as measured by the ITPA. But more importantly the two language groups made significant gains in word comprehension and word recognition on a standardized achievement test as compared to the controls, both at the end of the treatment programme and ten months later.

Such research demonstrates the value of the use of a language programme in improving psycholinguistic functioning *and* achievement in reading. Naylor and Pumfrey (1983) offer some thoughtful points as to the reasons why this specific programme paid off in improved reading performance. Their curricula followed the recommendations offered by the Kirks for remediation. However, they comment that many of the ITPA activities suggested do not necessarily follow from the ITPA model. They mention that the Kirk programme is multi-modal (visual, auditory, kinaesthetic), as well as multi-level and multi-process. They see it as similar to other remedial programmes but with a particular emphasis on conceptual and sequential activities.

Naylor and Pumfrey (1983) further postulate that the effectiveness of their remediation was due to the use of some reading and writing activities in the treatment approach. They suggest that the Kirk treatment approach reflects more of a general language orientation where a number of subskills are worked on during the course of treatment. The carefully conceptualized study of Naylor and Pumfrey has shown the efficacy of a process approach to the remediation of reading problems in one group of 7–8 year olds.

Further support for Naylor and Pumfrey's research comes from two prior studies with other groups of poor readers (Pumfrey and Naylor 1978) and from the work of Burkholder in the 1960s. Burkholder (1968) worked with second-grade children who were retarded in reading in Tucson, Arizona, schools. She states that her instructional exercises were mainly at the integrative language level. However, analysis of her programme indicates that her treatment programme taught many more language skills than those just at the automatic integrational level. As mentioned earlier (Gredler 1978), the whole programme was made to be a very attractive option to regular school activities with a positive reinforcing environment. Psycholinguistic processing deficits as measured by the ITPA were noted. A careful programme based on the subtests of this battery was then used in the remediation programme, which was conducted for three months. Gains in such reading skills as oral reading, study skills, and word meaning were noted after the treatment programme and most importantly, the gains were maintained in oral reading and study skills for several months.

According to Burkholder the most important variables operating in this remediation programme were the following

1 the use of special materials, carefully prepared,
2 the programming of the presentation of such materials in small graduated steps,
3 the introduction of a different teaching personality, one from outside the school environment,
4 a positively reinforcing environment which as probably aided by the small group structure (i.e. groups were made up of four or five children) and a relaxing atmosphere, where errors could be made without fear of punishment.

(Burkholder 1968: 92)

The gains in reading most likely resulted from a complex interplay of a number of these factors operating over the treatment period.

Burkholder's study is one of the best illustrations of the importance of considering a number of different variables when analysing the improved performance of children who participated in a remedial programme. It is refreshing to note that Burkholder freely acknowledges the influence of a 'new teaching environment', the use of different materials, and a warm supportive atmosphere for learning without threat of punishment. At the same time it is important to recognize that significant gains were made in the children's reading performance utilizing an approach which stressed the underlying processes which are purported to affect reading development. And at no time was reading *per se* taught during the intervention process. The improvement in performance continued over a period of six months without further intervention.

The work of Pumfrey, Naylor, and Burkholder justifies the importance of assessing the developmental learning disabilities of the child, and emphasizing the fact that we must adequately assess these prerequisite skills in order to make sure that the child will progress satisfactorily in academic subjects. Such a procedure is needed for successful remediation of young children who demonstrate severe reading problems (Kirk and Chalfant 1984).

Remediation of verbal memory

A number of research studies have indicated that deficiencies in verbal memory are found in seriously retarded readers. Since successful reading reflects competence in verbal memory, deficits in this area should be further investigated.

The importance of verbal memory deficits and the utilization of approaches to compensate for these deficits have been discussed for some years (see Gillingham and Stillman 1960). Hulme (1981) also postulates that the presence of a verbal memory problem will contribute to problems in a child who is beginning to learn to read. Since a large number of words must be learned by rote through an arbitrary association between a word and its written form, children with verbal memory problems will experience difficulties at the beginning stages of the reading process. In studies of verbal memory difficulties in severely retarded readers, Hulme found the use of tracing letters to be an important teaching aid to improvement in performance. According to Hulme, improvement is the result of the retarded reader's ability to profit from the use of a visual memory strategy. Tracing letters and words also improved the child's performance on visual-verbal paired associate learning.

It is important to note experimental evidence of the utility of such remediation strategies for children severely deficient in verbal memory. Hulme's research indicates that assessment and remediation of this perceptual factor remains important.

Remedial approaches which emphasize the instructional environment

In another investigation of retarded readers Gredler (1978) worked with a group of children aged 7.2 to 9.8 with a Hemmon-Nelson IQ average of 81. These children had attended school for two to three years but had not yet learned the basic sight words for those grades.

The subjects were selected from twenty-five children identified by the teachers as those with definite reading problems. Although the children attending this urban school were predominantly middle class, the majority of the twelve referred children were of lower socio-economic status. The children chosen for the study performed poorly on a standardized reading test, with scores which averaged at the sixth percentile for this grade level. The study was implemented for a period of two months with the child averaging three lessons a week.

The programme presents fifty-nine words in twenty-five programmed units. Each lesson is contained in a cartridge which holds a film strip loop and a continuous audiotape. The film strip pictures appear on a video display unit (called a 'teledesk') in front of the child and the teacher's words are heard through a speaker or headphones. The child responds to the audio questions both by placing plastic word plaques on the video screen and by verbally responding to taped questions.

The theoretical assumption behind this study was that inadequate teaching methodology is a major contributor to children's difficulties in learning to read. Emphasis on just micro-analysis of phonemes, use of routine sound exercises with de-emphasis on meaning, frequently contribute to some children's failure. Therefore well-designed instruction with emphasis on the sentence as the true unit of language rather than word or letter should improve learning (Higgins 1971).

Higgins (1971) also states that a child will be able to read a word automatically, without iconic or pictorial clues when the input-output frequency exceeds 100. For example, the child will see the word 'same' 116 times, hear the word 137 times from the tapes, speak the word 77 times (modelled from the tape or read in context), and then place the plaque on the interface 12 times. The total input-output for 'same' is 342. It is anticipated that after a child uses a word in a meaningful context, the child will then rely on the orthography of the word.

The pre-test/post-test design of the study (Hardyck and Petrinovich 1969; Gourevitch 1965), with each student providing his own control score, indicates that substantial progress was made by the children. Since the study was conducted with low achievers, some pre-test and post-test gain was expected due to regression toward the mean. However, the gains which were significant at the 0.001 level cannot be explained away by this phenomenon.

Use of an instructional programmed system which provided an interesting format, along with a rich matrix of visual, verbal, and motor input-output, contributed to substantial gains in word recognition. The children enjoyed and looked forward to the interaction with the assistant, who stayed with them while they completed the lesson. This gave the children an opportunity to interact with an adult in an essentially non-authoritarian atmosphere.

All the teachers had previously commented on the children's poor learning strategies. Despite this observation the increase in number of words learned was indeed significant both statistically and educationally. The progress made suggests that a similar instructional approach should be considered and incorporated in remedial strategies for some children seriously retarded in reading.

It is also possible to devise a similar curriculum without utilizing the equipment made use of in this programme. The important factor was the immersion of the child in a rich instructional environment. The children enjoyed their new environment and their motivational level was enhanced. It should be understood that curriculum planning for these children within the regular classroom was minimal; without further attention from the regular class-teacher, the progress of these children in the class would probably remain minimal.

While these children had not been labelled as 'learning disabled' their performance on oral recognition skills tests was similar to many children referred as learning disabled. The importance of this study is that the results provide further evidence of the need for the school psychologist and educational specialist to be cognizant of a number of various instructional approaches which may be recommended for use with a minimum of time and expense.

'Time-to-learn' classroom material

That a child's difficulty may stem in part from the organization and instructional methodology of the classroom has been mentioned frequently by various educators (Gredler 1978). Further planning on the ways that the teacher may individualize instruction for children with learning problems should be undertaken.

In a study of such variables, Gettinger (1978) developed measures of time-to-learn for academic tasks which included vocabulary, math concepts, reading comprehension, reading for facts, math computation, and dictation for spelling. She then compared this learning rate measure with a measure of intelligence and with school achievement. Learning rate was defined as the number of trials to mastery on a specific task.

Results demonstrated that some students learned the academic material to the same achievement criterion level from six to nine times as fast as the slowest regular class students. Correlations of time-to-learn measures with achievement were higher than with IQ/achievement measures (e.g. 0.84 to 0.89 in comparison to 0.58 to 0.74 for IQ/achievement).

Gettinger suggests that stating that a child needs three times as many trials to learn twelve spelling words or two times as long to learn twelve vocabulary words may give more helpful diagnostic remedial information about the child's learning performance than describing the pupil's IQ score as being at *X* percentile.

This suggestion has obvious implications in working with children who have reading disabilities. Administering appropriately developed 'time-to-learn' tests may be a helpful first approach to identify rate of learning of the retarded reader and then appropriate curriculum programming for the student could be prescribed.

Another implication of attending to this time variable is that the teacher may determine relatively early in the school year which children require more instructional time. Resources could then be brought to bear on attempting to provide such intervention before the whole apparatus of the special education complex is brought into play.

The research studies by Gettinger and Gredler as described have value not only for use with the severely retarded reader but also for those children who have been previously described as in need of corrective reading.

An educational therapy approach for retarded readers

The affective component of the instructional environment is seldom emphasized in the remedial process by educators. Often a child's emotional needs are either inadequately understood or neglected unless grossly disturbed behaviour is shown. Much of today's remediation of children with learning disabilities takes the form of merely a direct attack on the mechanics of the reading process (Salvia and Ysseldyke 1981).

In an action research project undertaken by Gredler (1978) the establishment of a positive relationship with the child was of prime importance. School-teachers referred children from the first, second, and third grades who had failed in reading, were repeating with little current progress, or were in danger of being retained in grade. Emphasis was placed on two areas: a positive relationship between a graduate student who served as tutor, and use of sophisticated instructional methods. Instructional methods used included the Programmed Reading Kit (Stott 1962); *System 80* Material (1977) and various reinforcement programmes. Major emphasis was placed on the use of the Stott materials.

Some referred children were so sensitive to their lack of progress in school tasks that they refused at first to become involved in the testing of their academic skills. Many children showed an initial distrust and other negative behaviour towards adults who were working with them in the remediation centre. Also some children were fearful of responding and making mistakes.

Fear of the teaching adult, concern about possible failure, and anticipation of punitive reaction from the tutor were important behaviours that had to be dealt with during the remediation sessions. These reactions are common in children who are having continued difficulties in learning (Rie 1974).

At the completion of the remediation sessions 65 per cent of the children were able to read at the instructional level material which when presented twelve weeks earlier had been classified at the frustration level. Moreover 65 per cent of the children were also able to read at least one book level above their entering reading level (e.g. originally they may have been at the primer level; now they were at the first-grade level). Further, 23 per cent of this group of children were now able to read material a minimum of two book levels above their original assessment.

Once again a combination of factors was instrumental in the improvement in performance: emphasis on a therapeutic environment, motivated personnel, and sophisticated remediation programming. It was also important to remember that this reading improvement resulted from a time increment of only twenty hours spread over a period of thirteen weeks.

Lawrence (1971; 1972) in a series of pioneering studies emphasized the value of counselling by volunteer adults in leading to a higher level of performance in reading. Reduction of the child's level of anxiety was the main objective and *no* specific reading intervention was provided. The solid gain produced by these intervention studies once again demonstrates the importance of a therapeutic environment when organizing any remedial intervention.

Use of computer-assisted instruction (CAI) as a remediation method

The use of computer technology is increasingly touted as a means of improving the child's reading performance. Some version of computer technology has been used in the American classroom for the last twenty years (McDermott and Watkins 1983).

A CAI study completed several years ago has provided a detailed analysis of the utility of the computer with 6-year-old children. Fletcher and Atkinson (1972) compared the reading grade of pairs of children. One child of each pair received CAI in reading in addition to regular class instruction and the other child received only the regular classroom instruction. Computer-assisted instruction was provided for a five-month period during the first grade but the children received no such instruction while in their second year of school. The computer-assisted instructional sequence was limited to twelve minutes a day during first grade. During the remainder of the school day, classroom activities were the same as those for the control group. Standardized test results administered at the end of the first year indicated an average increase of five months over that of the control group. Test results at the end of the second grade reflected a difference of 4.9 months in favour of the CAI group who had no intervening CAI treatment during that academic year.

Also noteworthy is the fact that while the reading performance of both boys and girls improved when exposed to CAI, the relative rate of improvement was greater for the boys. This is an important result since in many American schools boys typically lag behind girls at the end of the first and second grades.

This study also indicated that supplementary instruction was definitely needed to reinforce the regular instructional programme offered. Atkinson (1974) states that CAI should not necessarily be utilized in all phases of reading instruction. He considers that CAI provides individualized instruction which cannot be matched by the teacher even when working with a group composed of only four or five children. Atkinson attributes the higher performance of girls to the predominance of female teachers in the school. Also he considered that girls were better at memorization, which in turn helped them to cope with a curriculum that emphasized sight word procedures.

The result of this CAI study is similar to the findings with several other investigations. Specifically regular instruction, when supplemented by CAI, is found to be more effective than normal classroom instruction alone (Edwards *et al.* 1975).

Writing-to-Read project

A more recent approach to initial reading instruction is that of the Writing-to-Read project (Martin 1973). Designed to aid young children to learn to read more effectively, the programme has been field-tested on 10,000 children in the USA. In this programme children learn to write words by combining the forty-two phonemes into words. Students learn to spell the words phonemically. The computer provides a high degree of individual attention as well as multi-sensory experience in word construction. Words are typed into the computer, the children see the word constructed on the monitor, and then they repeat the phonemes along with the computer voice (Rotenberg 1984). The programme is composed of three parts: a computer program in which the child is led through a sequenced, self-paced cycle of interacting learning; work journals which reinforce their activities and are similar to the computer program; and a language development programme which provides the child with a number of different activities to apply the language arts skills.

Preliminary results of this approach to initial reading are found in standardized test data from the Winston-Salem, North Carolina school system. Mean reading scores of the CAI children at the end of first grade were at the eighty-ninth percentile in comparison to the control group's mean score at the sixty-ninth percentile.

Further evidence of the value of this programmed approach as a remedial intervention method is found in the results of a study of third- and fourth-grade retarded readers. After twelve weeks of utilizing the Writing-to-Read programme, fifty-five minutes a day, significant improvement in reading performance resulted (Thompson 1985).

CAI with learning disabled children

There have been very few studies of the use of CAI with children designated as having severe learning problems. However, a detailed study conducted recently in some Phoenix, Arizona, schools made use of the entire population of 205 'learning disabled' children from grades 1–6 (McDermott and Watkins 1983).

Computer-assisted instruction was provided through a micro-computer program which covered fundamental to advanced elementary maths and word spelling skills. Instruction continued for one entire school year from September to May. In the experimental group CAI was substituted for the same amount of time devoted to spelling/maths instruction in the conventional group. Results indicated 'no clear advantage over traditional remedial instruction for elementary and junior high level children who are learning impaired' (McDermott and Watkins 1983: 86). The authors suggest that various combinations of computerized and conventional remedial instruction will be needed and that the success rate will also vary partially as a function of the severity of the learning problems and the different learning styles encountered.

The rationale for use of CAI

A number of different reasons have been proposed as to why CAI might be more effective than conventional instructional approaches with children who are identified as needing remediation. These include

1. the fact that CAI is better able to adapt to the pace of the student (Martin 1973);
2. information is provided to the student as to the correctness of his response after he has made a response, and providing immediate knowledge of results or feedback is important (Annelli 1977);
3. machine instructional programs appear to clarify the problem more easily and provide the 'required frequency and subtlety of reinforcement' which is needed (Skinner 1972);
4. CAI makes more effective provision for active and passive feedback during learning sequences than does conventional instruction (Annelli 1977).

Other studies of importance for remediation of learning disabled children

In a study undertaken by Erskine (1972) children who were at risk for reading were identified. These children then received a diagnostic prescriptive programme of reading readiness activities for two 45-minute sessions per week for a total of sixteen weeks. Erskine concentrated on activities which would be considered to strengthen underlying 'ability clusters' of these children. The resultant improved readiness test scores led Erskine to state that this was a worthwhile approach in preparing children for reading activities.

Recent analysis of the effects of mastery learning on children's learning evidence suggests that immediate improvement in academic performance may be accounted for just by the frequent testing and feedback offered to children. Advocates of mastery learning instead, would emphasize that the entire teaching — feedback — corrective process used in the diagnostic prescriptive cycle would be needed (Slavin 1987: 51–2). Therefore any 'new' remediation approach may produce performance gains merely by providing more opportunities for such testing. Closer monitoring in a positive way of a child's learning progress is an action which is to be applauded. Although such a monitoring process is in place certain children may continue to perform below grade level after several weeks of school and will require a more involved assessment/intervention.

Task analysts often fail to offer sufficient help when a child does not achieve a learning outcome. Their explanations of the child's inadequate learning performance tend to centre around the fact that the child lacks essential prerequisite skills. The rationale given for this deficiency is that the child has had no opportunity to practise the skills (Smead 1977). Important mediating variables such as motivation and attitudes, however, are not considered. The school or educational psychologist must remember to always gauge such factors when faced with a child referred for learning problems.

Structuring the passage of time

Sociologists have long pointed out that individuals try to reduce the uncertainty of events that occur in their lives. This is done by establishing 'time-tables' or reference points that can be readily observed as indicators of progress toward a particular objective (Roth 1963). Such time-tables are constructed by hospital patients, for students within the school system, and by business executives with a corporation.

The American school is one example of an institution which has a highly organized and standardized time-table. After children begin kindergarten they are expected to march forward one grade a year in a 'lock step' until they graduate together from high school (Roth 1963). In recent years the public's concern over the 'deviant' student has led to the introduction of 'mainstreaming' for many EMR students [American classification of mental retardation in children] and increasing resistance to retention in a grade as a solution to a child's learning problems.

The introduction of classes for the 'ld' child in the USA has been in effect an attempt to provide a more effective method of handling children's lack of academic progress without necessarily keeping the child back for a whole year.

While adequate progress can be assured over the course of a year for a large number of children through the effective use of quality teaching, mastery learning, and positive teacher–child relationships, there is no way that individual differences in academic performance can be completely eliminated in the course of a one-year period. It is therefore to be expected that children, as well as teachers, will feel some degree of stress if a child's academic progress is not meeting the particular reference 'markers' which have been established. One of the important side results in implementing a well-organized programme of remediation is that such a programme often times brings about a suspension of excessive 'time-table' pressures to which the failing child has been subjected. All the effective intervention programmes which have been described in this chapter (e.g. Lawrence 1972; Burkholder 1968; Rie 1974; Gredler 1978) provide a more benign atmosphere where unwarranted pressures have been removed from the child's instructional environment in so far as possible. Under such conditions most children respond in a more positive manner.

Style of teaching: a forgotten variable

An important element in fostering intrinsically motivated learning focuses on the attitudinal structure of the teacher. It is hypothesized that a teacher who establishes a trusting relationship with the child and who reflects a positive empathic approach in her contacts with the student will be more successful in promoting effective learning and more positive self-concepts (Deci and Ryan 1985).

Effective classroom learning is composed of several factors: stimulating learning material, constructive feedback to the child, as well as the establishment of a trusting and supportive interpersonal environment. An effective interpersonal environment is defined by Deci and Ryan as an 'informational' one — a classroom setting which emphasizes autonomy, enhances the child's learning strategies, and which acknowledges ambivalent feelings that may arise out of the learning setting.

For Deci and Ryan the important factor is that the class climate should reflect an 'informational' tone rather than one which is 'controlling'. A controlling environment would be a classroom where the child is under pressure to feel and behave in certain specified ways. Excessive evaluation of children's performance, overemphasis on grades, the too frequent use of rewards as a means of motivating the child to learn, all are factors that may be interpreted by children as a controlling influence and lead to a detriment in learning.

Recent trends in American education have emphasized competency testing which in turn increases the use of standardized testing as a measure of the child's performance in the classroom and leads to a more standardized curriculum. Such developments make for a more rigid atmosphere and leave fewer options for the teacher and student to establish a freer and more autonomous educational climate (Deci and Ryan 1985).

One response to such pressure has been the passage of legislation in North Carolina abolishing mandatory standardized testing in grades 1 and 2 of the public schools. This is a positive development in helping to provide a more positive climate for learning in the early grades.

Remediation of learning difficulties: a final summary

From this discussion it is seen how many factors must be considered in order for an effective remedial intervention programme to be implemented. The school psychologist is one support person who should provide a leadership role within the school by adequately conceptualizing the problem learning situation, undertaking an extended assessment process, and then utilizing some of the intervention methods described in previous pages.

A more careful approach to the assessment/remediation process would lead to a better selection of an appropriate remedial programme for the child. The school psychologist should be acquainted with a number of effective techniques varying from judicious use of reinforcement methods to a sophisticated games approach as found in Stott's Programmed Reading Kit (Stott 1962).

Children with serious learning problems that have continued over an extended period of time might well need more in-depth intervention programmes such as have been outlined by Pumfrey and Naylor (1983), Burkholder (1973) and Hulme (1982).

The Hawthorne effect, the bane of all research projects, can be definitely minimized as a factor in influencing the academic gains of the child if adequate control groups are provided and if the performance gains of the student are maintained at a consistent rate over an extended time period. It should be remembered that unless the remedial intervention is very poorly planned and carried out the academic performance of the students at the end of a short-term project will *always* be better. If, as in Naylor and Pumfrey's study of retarded readers, an adequate control group is planned that calls for increased participation of the control students then we can have more confidence in whatever significant results do occur. This is because steps have been taken to contract the influential effects of the participation factor.

Because the motivational status of the child is so important for successful intervention, the school psychologist should be able to assess the child's attitudes adequately in this area. Then an attempt should be made to work with the teacher to help provide a true 'informational' climate of learning so as to reduce the child's level of anxiety and concern about his learning problems.

Providing leadership in all of these areas is obviously no easy matter. However, added attention to appropriate assessment/intervention procedures and programmes will ultimately pay off in an improved learning situation for the child with learning problems.

References

Annelli, C. M. (1977) 'Computer assisted instruction and reading achievement of urban third and fourth grades', unpublished doctoral dissertation, Rutgers University, New Brunswick, NJ, USA.

Arter, J. A. and Jenkins, J. R. (1979) 'Differential diagnosis-prescriptive teaching: A critical appraisal', *Review of Educational Research* 49: 517–55.

Atkinson, R. C. (1974) 'Teaching children to read using a computer', *American Psychologist* 29: 169–78.

Burkholder, R. B. (1968) 'The improvement of reading ability through the development of specific underlying or associated mental abilities', unpublished doctoral dissertation, University of Arizona, USA.

Cooper, J. D. (1969) 'A study of the learning modalities of good and poor first grade readers', unpublished doctoral dissertation, Indiana University, USA.

Deci, E. L. and Ryan, R. M. (1985) *Intrinsic Motivation and Self-Determination in Human Behavior*, New York: Plenum Press.

Duffey, J. B. and Fedner, M. L. (1978) 'Educational diagnosis with instructional use', *Exceptional Children* 44: 246–51.

Edwards, J., Norton, S., Taylor, S., Weiss, M. and Dusseldorf, R. (1975) 'How effective is CAI? A review of the research', *Educational Leadership* 33: 147–53.

Erskine, R. G. (1972) 'Developing reading potential: identification and instruction of disadvantaged high risk readers in kindergarten', unpublished doctoral dissertation, Purdue University, Hammond, Indiana, USA.

Fletcher, J. D. and Atkinson, R. C. (1972) 'Evaluation of the Stanford CAI program in initial reading', *Journal of Educational Psychology* 63: 597–602.

Gettinger, M. (1978) 'Is time-to-learn or measured intelligence a stronger correlate of school learning?', unpublished doctoral dissertation, Columbia University, New York, USA.

Gillingham, A. and Stillman, B. W. (1960) *Remedial Training for Children with Specific Disability in Reading, Spelling and Penmanship*, Boston, Mass: Educators Publishing Service.

Gourevitch, V. (1965) *Statistical Methods: A Problem-Solving Approach*, Boston, Mass: Allyn & Bacon.

Gredler, G. R. (1978) 'Learning disabilities and reading disorders: A current assessment', *Psychology in the Schools* 15: 226–38.

——— (forthcoming) 'Special education in the 80's: A critical analysis', *Psychology in the Schools*.

Hamblin, R. L., Buckholdt, D., Feritor, D., Kozloff, M., and Blackwell, L. (1971) *The Humanization Processes: A Social, Behavioral Analysis of Children's Problems*, New York: Wiley-Interscience.

Hardyck, C. D. and Petrinovitch, L. S. (1969) *Introduction to Statistics for the Behavioral Sciences*, Philadelphia, Penn: Saunders.

Hicks, C. (1986) 'Remediating specific reading disabilities: A review of approaches', *Journal of Research in Reading* 9: 39–55.

Higgins, C. F. (1971) *Trimodal Programmed Instruction in Reading: Background and Rationale*, Albany, New York: Learning Research Center, Board of Education.

Hulme, C. (1981) *Reading Retardation and Multi-Sensory Teaching*, London: Routledge & Kegan Paul.

Kirk, S. A. and Chalfant, J. C. (1984) *Academic and Developmental Learning Disabilities*, Denver, Col: Love.

Lawrence, D. (1971) 'The effects of counselling on retarded readers', *Educational Research* 13: 119–24.

——— (1972) 'Counseling of retarded readers by nonprofessionals', *Educational Research* 51: 48–51.

Lennox, B. (1983) 'The editor regrets and the Hawthorne effect', *Medical Education* 17: 347–8.

Martin, J. (1973) *Design of Man-Computed Dialogues*, Englewood Cliffs, NJ: Prentice-Hall.

McDermott, P. and Watkins, M. W. (1983) 'Computerized vs. conventional remedial instruction for learning disabled pupils', *Journal of Special Education* 17: 81–8.

Mills, R. E. (1956) 'An evaluation of techniques for teaching word recognition', *Elementary School Journal* 56: 221–5.

Naylor, J. G. and Pumfrey, P. D. (1983) 'The alleviation of psycholinguistic deficits and some effects on the reading attainments of poor readers: A sequel', *Journal of Research in Reading* 6, 2: 129–53.

O'Donnell, L. E. (1972) 'Theoretical framework of reading retardation: After data gathering and before remedial action', unpublished doctoral dissertation, University of Illinois, USA.

Poteet, J. A. (1973) *Behavior Modification: A Practical Guide for Teachers*, Minneapolis, Minn: Burgess.

Pumfrey, P. D. and Naylor, J. G. (1978) 'The alleviation of psycholinguistic deficits and some effects on the reading attainments of poor readers', *Journal of Research in Reading* 1: 87–107.

Rie, H. E. (1974) 'Therapeutic tutoring for underachieving children', *Professional Psychology* 5: 70–5.

Roethlisberger, F. J. and Dickson, W. J. (1939) *Management and the Worker*, Boston, Mass: Harvard University Press.

Rotenberg, L. (1984) 'Booting up for reading', *Teaching and Computers* 1: 16–19.

Roth, J. A. (1963) *Timetables*, Indianapolis, Ind: Bobbs-Merrill.

Salvia, J. and Ysseldyke, J. (1981) *Assessment in Special and Remedial Education*, Boston, Mass: Houghton Mifflin.

Sampson, O. C. (1976) 'Fifty years of dyslexia: A review of the literature, 1925–75 II Practice', *Research in Education* 15: 30–53.

Skinner, B. F. (1972) *Cumulative Record: A Selection of Papers*, New York: Appleton-Century-Crofts-Meredith.

Slavin, R. E. (1987) *Mastery Learning Reconsidered*, Baltimore, Md: Center for Research on Elementary and Middle Schools, Johns Hopkins University.

Smead, V. S. (1977) 'Ability training and task analysis in diagnostic/prescriptive teaching', *Journal of Special Education* 11: 113–25.

Stott, D. H. (1962) *Programmed Reading Kit*, Toronto: Gage.

Sundberg, N. D., Tyler, L. E., and Taplin, J. R. (1973) *Clinical Psychology* 2nd edn, New York: Appleton-Century-Crofts.

System 80 (1977) Arlington, Ill: Borg Warner Educational Systems.

Thompson, E. (1985) 'The effect of the writing to read program on low reading ability students', unpublished doctoral dissertation, University of Denver, Col., USA.

Chapter ten

Specific difficulties in reading and spelling

Elaine Miles and T. R. Miles

How intervention differs from initial teaching

It is useful to distinguish the kind of teaching which children are given after they have been found to be experiencing difficulty from the teaching which they receive when they are initially learning to read and write. The two are different for a number of reasons.

The first is that in the case of intervention a fresh start is needed. Whether a wrong method has previously been used, whether methods unobjectionable in themselves have been ineffective as a result of poor teaching, or whether, indeed, there is no obvious reason for children's difficulties, the position is the same. An approach is needed which is not associated with failure, which will engage the children's interest, and which, above all, will bolster their self-esteem.

Second, the initial approach will of necessity have been one devised for children of a younger age level, whose interests were at this level and who had their own particular needs as regards the curriculum. For example, turning letters of the alphabet into personalities which suggest the letter may have considerable appeal for a child at infant school but could well be despised by older children. This can be true even when the children do not know all the letter-sounds. Moreover even if they themselves do not object to such a method there is still the risk of ridicule from their peers.

Third, one has to consider the question of urgency. In most circumstances the objective of intervention is to equip the pupils to function again in the class situation, since at present their skills lag behind those of their classmates. It is necessary, therefore, not just that they should make 'average' progress but that they should move faster than average in order to catch up. To achieve this it may be necessary to take some short cuts, for example by using the same techniques for teaching both reading and spelling. Such compression of subject matter is more feasible with an older child than a younger one and in 'special lesson' conditions as opposed to the conditions of the classroom.

Fourth, it is possible that current practice at the early stages of teaching may have been lacking in some ingredient which needs emphasis for a minority of children but not for the majority. It is this minority with which the present chapter is concerned.

The dyslexic child's difficulties

Over two decades ago, Chall (1967: 200–57) called attention to the dominant influence exerted on infant school teachers by basic readers and their manuals. She claimed that their detailed guidance encouraged teachers to spend such a disproportionate amount of time on comprehension and subject matter that the phonic elements in these readers tended to be neglected; as a result children could be found who had 'missed out' on this crucial aspect of reading and spelling. In support (Chall 1967: 160–73) she cites evidence, based on six research reports dated between 1922 and 1946, which points to the conclusion that in the great majority of cases of poor readers there was extreme difficulty with word recognition and analysis. She also suggests that children who lack a knowledge of phonics find it difficult to make progress later.

Now the English alphabet can be thought of as a way of 'coding' the sounds of speech; and if there are, indeed, children who fail to master this code, it is clearly desirable to try a particular intervention strategy, not indeed as a substitute for the strategies mentioned earlier (giving the child a fresh start, making the material interesting, etc.) but as an essential addition to them. This is particularly urgent in the case of dyslexic children.

If one adheres to the strict definition of the term 'dyslexia' (Critchley 1970; Critchley and Critchley 1978), what is implied is some kind of anomaly of development which is of constitutional origin. If a child is failing at reading and spelling and is also dyslexic the implication is that his difficulties are to an extent the result of such an anomaly and are, indeed, one manifestation of it. Some educationalists, for example Tansley and Panckhurst (1981), recommend use of the term 'specific learning difficulties' in preference to 'dyslexia'. In our opinion, however, the two terms can be treated as synonymous, since no one, to our knowledge, has specified what a child would be like who has specific learning difficulties but is not dyslexic.

Some of the typical characteristics of these children have been described by T. R. Miles (1983). For instance a large number of the children whom he tested had experienced difficulty in learning arithmetical tables, while some of them had at least residual confusions over left and right and many were weak at recall of auditorily or visually presented digits. The Bangor Dyslexia Test (T. R. Miles 1982) comprises a series of such items, with a method of scoring which takes into account hesitations, special strategies, and the like as well as the correctness of the responses. The authors' claim is that such difficulties are to be found from time to time in any child; if, however, one comes on a child who has adequate intelligence and who has had relevant learning opportunities, and if such a child, in addition to under-achievement at reading or spelling, displays a sufficient number of the above difficulties, then it becomes plain that one is encountering a distinctive pattern which 'makes sense' rather than a random collection of disconnected responses. If one also finds that similar difficulties have occurred in other members of the child's family the 'coherence' of the pattern becomes even more striking.

Since this chapter is concerned primarily with intervention no attempt will be made to review the evidence on dyslexia comprehensively. In brief, however, the view that a constitutionally caused limitation is involved is supported by evidence both from biology and from experimental psychology.

Relevant biological research has been summarized by Vellutino (1987) (for fuller details see also Stevenson *et al.* 1987; DeFries *et al.* 1987; Smith *et al.* 1983; Duffy 1985; Galaburda 1985; Galaburda *et al.* 1987). The main conclusions appear to be as follows

1 in twin studies reading disability has a higher concordance rate in monozygotic than in dizygotic twins;
2 there is evidence that chromosome 15 may be involved;
3 some poor readers show differences on electrophysiological measures;

4 'mapping' techniques suggest that left hemisphere functioning is different in some poor readers in comparison with controls,
5 post-mortem examinations so far suggest that in the case of the genuine dyslexic there is symmetry between the two hemispheres of the brain — something which is found in only about 20 per cent of normal brains.

All this evidence is compatible with the idea of a constitutionally caused limitation which affects certain features of language; and if these findings are taken in conjunction with the behavioural evidence the simplistic thesis that 'we do not need the concept of dyslexia' becomes extremely difficult to maintain.

On the psychological side the quantity of research is too great to be summarized in a short space, and we shall therefore limit ourselves to a few examples.

Aaron (1987) gave tests to seven poor reader college students with adequate comprehension skills (as judged by an IQ on the Wechsler Adult Intelligence Scale of over 95), to seven other poor reader students with weaker comprehension skills (WAIS score less than 85) and to seven normal readers. Some of the tests were designed to measure the subjects' decoding skills and some to test their understanding of what was being read. In six out of the seven tests a clear picture emerged, that is that the first group were weak at the decoding tasks and the second group at the comprehension tasks. Since the first group corresponds to those commonly called 'dyslexic', Aaron concludes that there are 'qualitative differences . . . between dyslexia and other forms of reading disability (1987: 124).

That among under-achievers in general there are more boys than girls has been confirmed on many occasions (see e.g. Rutter and Yule 1975). If dyslexics are not a distinct group, however, there would be no reason to expect a different boy:girl ratio among allegedly dyslexic under-achievers from that found with other under-achievers. Yet in the National Cohort Study (all children born in Britain between 6 April and 11 April 1970), Miles and Haslum (1986) and Miles and Haslum (forthcoming), using as criteria for dyslexia specified responses to items taken from the Bangor Dyslexia Test (T. R. Miles 1982), showed that the ratio of boys to girls was considerably higher in the one group than in the other. This finding is difficult to square with the claim that dyslexic under-achievers are not a separate group.

In addition, if there is no such distinguishable group, then alleged dyslexics would not be expected to perform any differently in the relevant cognitive tasks from normal achievers who are at the same reading or spelling level. It has been shown, however, that there are at least some respects in which dyslexics perform differently not just from children matched for chronological age but from children matched for reading or spelling age. Thus when Baddeley *et al.* (1982) compared fifteen dyslexic boys (mean age 12 years 10 months) with fifteen chronological-age-matched controls and fifteen reading-age-matched controls (mean age 9 years 11 months) by asking them to read lists of words and non-words aloud, they found that the dyslexic boys needed longer time to read the lists even when compared with the reading-age-matched controls (68.00 sec. per list of thirty-four items as against 31.96 sec.). Similarly Ellis and Miles (1977) report that when fifteen dyslexic boys (mean age 12 years 0 months) and fifteen spelling-age-matched non-dyslexic boys (mean age 8 years 5 months) were required to identify arrays of five, six, or seven tachistoscopically presented digits the dyslexic boys were appreciably slower. These findings are hard to square with any hypothesis other than that of a specific limitation.

In addition there is striking agreement from many studies that among dyslexics there are deficits on the phonological side. Vellutino (1987: 20) has summarized the position as follows: 'Along with other researchers we have been finding that dyslexia is a subtle language deficiency'. He characterizes the phonological deficits by speaking of 'the inability to represent and access the sound of a word in order to help remember the word'. He goes on to speak of 'deficient phonemic segmentation', which he describes as the 'inability to break words into component sounds'. Confirmatory evidence for a similar view will be found in Liberman *et al.* (1982), and in Brady *et al.* (1983), while a very useful summary of relevant research findings will be found in Brady (1986). (For a comprehensive critique of earlier work in the area see Vellutino 1979.)

The commonly reported limitations of dyslexics in the area of short-term memory may in fact be a consequence of their lack of phonological skills. It is well established that they are weak at recall of auditorily presented digits (Rugel 1974; Thomson 1982) and at recall of visually presented letters or digits (Stanley and Hall 1973; Ellis and Miles 1977). It is also of interest that Steeves (1983) found that a group of gifted dyslexics scored higher than some of their non-dyslexic peers on the Raven Standard Progressive Matrices (Raven 1958), scored on a level with them on a test of mathematics part of which involved computation, and scored below them on the Wechsler (1945) memory test. There appears to be no difference between dyslexics and non-dyslexics in iconic memory (Vellutino 1979; Ellis and Miles 1981), nor in some aspects of long-term memory (Nelson and Warrington 1980). Although the claim that 'dyslexics have a poor short-term memory' lacks something in specificity, it nevertheless seems to us to be true as far as it goes and to be something which teachers need to take into account.

Implications for teaching

It was pointed out in the previous section that poor readers and spellers have often been found to be weak at word recognition and analysis (Chall 1967), and that some of them, for constitutional reasons, experience difficulty in acquiring phonological skills (Vellutino 1987). It was also suggested that the commonly reported weakness in short-term memory could be the result of this phonological deficiency. There is therefore good reason to devise intervention strategies which will address these problems; in particular there is a case for using methods which are basically phonic in character.

To have established this point is crucial. Resistance to a phonic approach has tended to come largely from those who stubbornly refuse to believe that there is anything specific about the nature of these children's difficulties.

A particularly significant research project, and one which has practical implications for remediation, is that of Bradley and Bryant (1978; 1983; 1985; see also Bryant and Bradley 1985). When they studied 368 4- and 5-year-olds who had not started to read, they found a high correlation between the children's ability to discriminate and categorize sounds in spoken words at this pre-reading stage and their progress in reading and spelling three years later (*r*-values being between 0.44 and 0.57), differences in intelligence having been allowed for. They then carried out a training study using sixty-five of the children who had performed poorly on the sound categorization test and who had still not started to read by ages 5 and 6. These children were presented with pictures and trained to pick out the sounds in the word represented by the picture, and it was found that even after quite a small number of training sessions in sound categorization — 40 over a two-year period — there were improvements in reading and spelling which were greater than those of control children who either received no extra training at all or were taught to categorize the same pictures conceptually (e.g. 'pig' and 'cat' as animals). It should be noted that what was discovered was a weakness in oral language, which showed itself before either reading or spelling were introduced.

Those who have made a special study of teaching children with these specific difficulties regularly attribute their successes to the distinctive method which they have adopted. This is basically the kind of phonic approach which involves strengthening the links between the appearance of the written letters, their sound, and the writing of them. Thus the programmes devised by Gillingham and Stillman (1969), Hickey (1977), and Hornsby and Shear (1977), along with the Edith Norrie Letter Case, originally devised in Copenhagen, and the syllabus used at our own Unit in Bangor, are all variants of this approach. Its effectiveness has been demonstrated in a study by Hornsby and Miles (1980). The children in this study had been taught at centres which used one or other of the above programmes; each child was used as his/her own control, and comparisons were made between reading/spelling progress before the start of the teaching and reading/spelling progress during it. The differences were striking: in a sample of over 100 severely retarded readers and spellers only 10–15 per cent failed to make satisfactory progress.

These specialist teachers apart, however, there has not been a general acceptance of this kind of approach. In the first place, some critics argue that one should always teach to strengths rather than to weaknesses in order to give the pupil confidence. However, this argument assumes that for any child the acquisition of phonological skills is something optional; there is good evidence that such a view is mistaken. In particular it has been argued by Frith (1986) that there is a definite stage in learning to read, for which mastery of the alphabetic code is essential, and that the acquisition of more sophisticated approaches to written material is impossible unless the child has passed through this preliminary stage successfully. If

Frith's model is correct, then it seems most unlikely that a non-phonological approach could ever repair the omission. If, in addition, the child is dyslexic or, in other words, has a constitutionally caused weakness which makes the acquisition of phonological skills difficult, the likelihood of success by some other method seems very remote indeed. A pupil's strengths can in fact be turned to advantage in other ways; for instance artistic skills can be used in drawing a picture which encapsulates the theme of basic words in *ea* ('a meal on a beach by the sea'). Moreover it is entirely possible to give pupils a taste of success even when one is teaching in an area where they are weak; this can be achieved by adjusting the pace so that they can succeed at each stage before moving on.

There is a second way in which undertaking phonological teaching would seem to go against current practice. There is a widely held assumption that poor readers can be divided into two groups: those with visual weaknesses and those with auditory weaknesses. The theoretical basis for this dichotomy, however, is unsound (compare Liberman 1983). In particular it appears to arise from a too literal and restricted interpretation of the brief labels attached to psychological tests. What is labelled a 'visual discrimination test' is often very different from what is labelled an 'auditory discrimination test' in many ways other than the difference in modality even though these factors cannot all be mentioned in the label. Just because a child scores higher on a visual discrimination test than he did on an auditory discrimination test it does not therefore follow that he has 'an auditory weakness'. To cite an example which one of the authors has used earlier (E. Miles 1981), a test may be given in which there is a letter on the left of the page and a row of letters along a line to the right from which the matching letter must be chosen. Such a test is usually called a 'visual discrimination test'; and, indeed, it *is* visual, *does* involve discrimination, and *is* a test. But it has other features as well. In particular it calls for retention of the look of the letter, or possibly its name, while the person searches along the line for a similar letter, and it calls for good co-ordination in that he must record the answer manually by ringing a particular letter without deviating to a different line. By contrast, in an 'auditory discrimination test', for example that of Wepman (1973), there is nothing comparable to searching along a line: the person has to listen to two words and compare them, giving the task his undivided attention since he cannot 'go back over'. It is, of course, still possible that different individuals, whether dyslexic or not, have different modality preferences (Spache 1976); but even though it is true in our experience that some dyslexics find it hard to work in sounds, we have never found the teaching of phonological skills impossible, and it is what they need. It is a mistake to assume that, like their non-dyslexic peers, they will pick up these skills automatically regardless of what method is used.

Third, it is sometimes argued that the possession of such skills is not the sign of a good reader since good readers cannot necessarily tell you what is the sound in the middle of a word; for example, if asked, they can correctly read the word *meet* or the word *light* without being able to say what the middle sound is. Now we fully agree that conscious use of phonic skills is not all that necessary when reading has reached a sophisticated level; and this may be particularly true in the case of a word such as *light* which is somewhat irregular and whose orthographic features may therefore be more obvious than the exact phoneme-grapheme correspondence. In general it can be said that good spellers are able to proceed by analogy (Frith 1980: 501). Dyslexics, however, have to proceed much more deliberately: because of their memory limitation they may fail to notice particular orthographic features and they may therefore have no choice but to think consciously of the spelling principles which they are applying.

Finally, there is the argument which we mentioned at the start of this chapter, that an intervention strategy should be different in kind from the method used initially. In the case of some children this might seem to debar one from the use of a phonic approach. As was indicated above, however, phonic skills are *not* optional; and in fact the intensive structured programme which is suitable for dyslexics is in many ways quite different from the 'phonics' often taught at infant school: it is geared more to the intervention situation than to initial teaching and is more suitable for children of an older age than for those in the infant class.

From what has been said it follows that one should not regard the phonic approach as one of several alternative methods of 'teaching reading'. This implies that different methods are, as it were, rival candidates for our allegiance or rival competitors in a horse race! The phonic approach addresses *one particular aspect* of reading. We do not, of course, dispute that a dyslexic child, like any other child, should be encouraged to think of the meaning of the words in front of him, not just their phonic structure, and should consider their function within the sentence. In our Unit, however, we have never found that appreciation of meaning suffers as a result of adopting a phonic approach. Indeed, many parents of children taught by members of our team have described to us how eventually, one day, they found their children in their bedroom reading — having at last discovered the magic of books.

'Teaching reading' is in any case too limited an objective. The great advantage of an approach that is structured, phonic, and multi-sensory is that it is economical: reading and spelling can help each other along. This is because the phonological aspect of reading is closely related to spelling. In the case of dyslexics, if one tries to emphasize other aspects of reading and thus diverts them from a close examination of the structure of individual words, one may be losing the last chance of establishing accuracy in reading, while, as regards their written work, unless they develop the habit of scrutinizing words in detail they will be unable to acquire that 'spelling sense' which will enable them to spell words that they have not specifically learnt. If a pupil is weak at both reading and spelling, it is surely good sense, initially at least, to teach reading in a way which benefits spelling, not in a way which hampers it.

The teaching situation

Let us now shift the scene to the teaching situation. Those who teach dyslexic children can immediately identify cases where weakness in using phonic cues handicaps reading progress and even more, of course, spelling progress. An 11-year-old boy of well above average ability once came to the Unit, bringing with him, as requested, a book to read. It turned out to be an Enid Blyton, much too difficult for him to read properly, although clearly the book of his choice. Being remarkably adept at using context to make up for his deficiencies, he proceeded to read the gist of it with great aplomb, with no more hesitation than if he had been able to read every word. Here are some of the substitutions that he made:

Words in the book	*Words read by Richard*
Mrs Jones	his mother
Saturday	Sunday
replied	said
asked	said
aches and pains in his legs	pins and needles

In all the examples given on the left, there is some phonological problem for the reader to solve. How does 'Mrs' relate to what we say? How does one account for that extra syllable in the middle of Saturday? (Everyday pronunciation tends to omit it and say 'Sat/day'.) The stress in 'replied' is most unexpectedly on the suffix, rather than on the main part of the word, and the suffix in 'asked' is absorbed, reducing the word to one syllable. It was no doubt safer to say 'said' for both than attempt the transcription. The word 'aches' is very odd in that it has consonants in the middle and vowels on the outside, contrary to the normal structure, and also has the less common sound <k> for 'ch'. The substitute phrase that Richard produced in bypassing this word was brilliantly invented. He must have recognized and understood the word 'aches' to produce it, but clearly he could not manage the word itself. Similarly he understood the *function* of the other words that he avoided, but his final version was inaccurate: the old man in the story did not have pins and needles, which any way do not 'ache' (more probably he had gout or rheumatism!), and 'Sunday' gives us a wrong picture of the background as against 'Saturday'.

Sometimes pupils referred to our Unit at a lower level of reading, e.g. a 7-year level, have reached stalemate, because up to that point they have relied on 'sight words', which they have identified on a partial decoding basis. Now their memories can hold no more, and not having learnt to decode properly they have no fall-back procedure. Once they have been trained in phonic skills, however, they can begin to move again. One 10-year-old boy, David, virtually a non-reader, although he knew a few 'sight' words, had moved to a new school and was a puzzle to his head-teacher, who was trying to help him with his reading. 'I tell him the words, and he seems to know them,' he exclaimed, 'but next day he has forgotten them again!' In this case testing showed that the boy had fundamental weaknesses in the phonic aspect of reading, being unsure, for example, which sounds were made by 'sh' and 'ch' respectively. His phonic skills were too unreliable to support his identification of words, and his memory simply could not hold them without that backing.

Dyslexics always have memorization problems, and it is for this reason that the early writers of programmes for them always insisted on two points: first, teaching had to be systematic, structured, and cumulative; second, it had to be multi-sensory.

A structured, systematic, cumulative approach gives a cohesion that makes it easier to memorize the material than would teaching isolated word-families. It starts with correspondence of single letters to single sounds and moves on to blends such as 'sp' and 'cr', to digraphs such as 'th' and 'ai', and then to syllables. At our Unit we also supply the pupil with a record book, for which he himself provides an index; in it he sets out each group of letters that he learns, so that he can himself use it for reference and not have to rely all the time on rote learning.

The multi-sensory approach, derived from the ideas of Fernald and Montessori, is portrayed in the Gillingham and Stillman manual by a model, which they call a 'language triangle', expressing the close association of visual, auditory, and kinaesthetic elements on which their technique is based (Gillingham and Stillman 1969: 40). However much ideas may change as to the exact neurological basis for this procedure, it cannot be disputed that reading, writing, and spelling are multi-sensory activities; experience has shown that dyslexics thrive when they have this sort of support. After all, even in the learning process of ordinary children there is much interaction between the information given them by their eyes and ears. It is often only when small children see the *t*'s in 'little' that they realize that the pronunciation 'lickle' is not quite what they have been hearing! To give dyslexic children separate visual material to practise, which has no phonological relevance, or sounds to discriminate, without reference to the written letter, is depriving them of aids to their learning.

The inclusion of the kinaesthetic sense as well as visual and auditory — a Fernald technique — has its limitations, because it is much the weakest sense, and sometimes in the Gillingham tradition its use has seemed exaggerated and artificial. However it has been demonstrated by Bradley (see Bryant and Bradley 1985: 132–3) that the Gillingham and Stillman technique of Simultaneous Oral Spelling, which involves saying the letters, writing them, and looking at them all at once, is in fact a more effective way of learning to spell a word than any combination of two of these. The drawback is that it does not extend beyond the one word, unlike the study of word families.

In adaptations of the Gillingham and Stillman approach not enough importance has always been attached to the link with oral language. Thus Hickey in her Language Training Course states, 'The importance of the alphabet in education is that it is the basis of the English language' (1977: 14). In so saying she makes the written language her starting-point, not acknowledging oral language as the basis on which the written language is built. Yet Bradley and Bryant's research with 4- and 5-year-olds, already mentioned (pp. 204–5), has made very clear the importance of the ability to discriminate spoken sounds in words as the basis for reading and spelling. Teachers who observe dyslexic children closely will readily observe that they do not use oral language *in their learning*, however much they may use it to communicate; even language which is used to communicate is not always clearly expressed (Stirling and Miles 1986).

Here is an example of a pupil from our Unit who showed particular reluctance to verbalize:

Peter was doing an exercise in which he had to draw a line linking a pair of initial consonants in a left-hand column with the appropriate vowel + consonant in a right-hand column, to form a word, e.g.

sh	ap
cl	ut

He was not being very successful in fitting the letters together. The teacher therefore told him to sound the word out, and demonstrated, saying, ' "Shap", is that a word? "Shut", is that a word?' He was quite happy to shake his head or nod when she did this, but when she asked him to try for himself he was very reluctant, and managed no more than a few grunts and mutterings. Indeed, dyslexic pupils often seem to have an aversion to spelling aloud. However such verbal self-regulation is very important. Vygotsky has claimed that

> Our findings indicate that egocentric speech does not long remain a mere accompaniment to the child's activity. Besides

> being a means of expression and of release of tension, it soon becomes an instrument of thought in the proper sense — in seeking and planning the solution of a problem.
>
> (Vygotsky 1986: 31)

If our dyslexics are to monitor themselves with their thoughts, they must not be allowed to leave all the talking to the teacher. In addition, exercises in workbooks or in computer programs should never be done merely visually but should involve the pupils' saying the word to themselves. Similarly reading aloud, though not the ultimate objective, has its place in initial teaching.

Another aspect of teaching that has not always featured prominently in programmes is 'understanding'. The early pioneers concentrated on getting an 'automatic' linkage of the visual, auditory, and kinaesthetic elements. One does, of course, want the child to reach a point where phonic cues, if used at all, are used without any conscious decision; but this is a long-term objective. From the beginning, however, the child needs to make linguistic judgements, for example to appreciate the distinctive functions of consonants and vowels.

Teaching children with specific learning difficulties is not easy; and since fast progress has to be made one cannot use just *any* approach, the most recent fad, or the last series to be launched by its publishers with an expensive flourish. One has to study carefully the children's needs and their weaknesses and adopt an approach which is specifically addressed to these weaknesses. Otherwise they will miss out on skills which non-dyslexic children acquire effortlessly.

References

Aaron, P. G. (1987) 'Developmental dyslexia: is it different from other forms of reading disability?', *Annals of Dyslexia* XXXVII: 109–25.

Baddeley, A. D., Ellis, N. C., Miles, T. R., and Lewis, V. (1982) 'Developmental and acquired dyslexia: a comparison', *Cognition* 11: 185–99.

Bradley, L. and Bryant, P. E. (1978) 'Difficulties in auditory organisation as a possible cause of reading backwardness', *Nature* 271: 746–7.

——— (1983) 'Categorising sounds and learning to read: a causal connection', *Nature* 301: 419–21.

——— (1985) *Rhyme and Reason in Reading and Spelling*, Ann Arbor, Mich: University of Michigan Press.

Brady, S. (1986) 'Short-term memory, phonological processing, and reading ability', *Annals of Dyslexia* XXXVI: 138–53.
Brady, S., Shankweiler, D., and Mann, V. A. (1983) 'Speech perception and memory coding in relation to reading ability', *Journal of Experimental Child Psychology* 35: 345–67.
Bryant, P. E. and Bradley, L. (1985) *Children's Reading Problems*, Oxford: Basil Blackwell.
Chall, J. S. (1967) *Learning to Read: The Great Debate*, New York: McGraw Hill.
Critchley, M. (1970) *The Dyslexic Child*, London: Heinemann.
Critchley, M. and Critchley, E. A. (1978) *Dyslexia Defined*, London: Heinemann.
DeFries, J. C., Fulker, D. W., and La Buda, M. (1987) 'Evidence for a genetic aetiology in reading disability twins', *Nature* 329: 537–9.
Duffy, F. H. (1985) 'The BEAM method for neurophysiological diagnosis', *Annals New York Academy of Sciences* 457: 19–34.
Ellis, N. C. and Miles, T. R. (1977) 'Dyslexia as a limitation in the ability to process information', *Bull. Orton Society* (now *Annals of Dyslexia*) XXVII: 72–81.
——— (1981) 'A lexical encoding deficiency I', in G.Th. Pavlidis and T. R. Miles (eds) *Dyslexia Research and its Applications to Education*, Chichester: Wiley.
Frith, U. (1980) 'Unexpected spelling problems', in U. Frith (ed.) *Cognitive Processes in Spelling*, London: Academic Press.
——— (1986) 'A developmental framework for developmental dyslexia', *Annals of Dyslexia* XXXVI: 69–81.
Galaburda, A. M. (1985) 'Developmental dyslexia: A review of biological interactions', *Annals of Dyslexia* XXXV: 21–33.
Galaburda, A. M., Corsiglia, J., Rosen, G. D., and Sherman, G. F. (1987) 'Planum temporale asymmetry: reappraisal since Geschwind and Levitsky', *Neuropsychologia* 25, 6: 853–68.
Gillingham, A. and Stillman, B. W. (1960) *Remedial Training for Children with Specific Difficulty in Reading, Spelling and Penmanship*, Cambridge, Mass: Educators Publishing Service.
Hickey, K. (1977) *A Language Training Course for Teachers and Learners*, London: privately published.
Hornsby, B. and Miles, T. R. (1980) 'The effects of a dyslexia-centred teaching programme', *British Journal of Educational Psychology* 50: 236–42.
Hornsby, B. and Shear, F. (1977) *Alpha to Omega*, London: Heinemann.
Liberman, I. Y. (1983) 'Should so-called modality preferences determine the nature of instruction for children with reading disabilities?', Paper read at 2nd World Congress on Dyslexia, Halkidiki, Greece.
Liberman, I .Y., Mann, V. A., Shankweiler, D., and Werfelman, M. (1982) 'Children's memory for recurring linguistic and non-linguistic material', *Cortex* 18: 367–75.
Miles, E. (1981) 'A study of dyslexic weaknesses and the consequences for teaching', in G.Th. Pavlidis and T. R. Miles (eds) *Dyslexia Research and*

Its Applications to Education, Chichester: Wiley.
Miles, T. R. (1982) *The Bangor Dyslexia Test*, Wisbech, Cambs: Learning Development Aids.
——— (1983) *Dyslexia: The Pattern of Difficulties*, Oxford: Basil Blackwell.
Miles, T. R. and Haslum, M. N. (1986) 'Dyslexia: anomaly or normal variation?', *Annals of Dyslexia* XXXVI: 103–17.
——— (forthcoming) 'Towards a prevalence figure for dyslexia'.
Nelson, H. E. and Warrington, E. K. (1980) 'An investigation of memory functions in dyslexic children', *British Journal of Educational Psychology* 71: 487–503.
Raven, J. C. (1958) *Standard Progressive Matrices*, London: H. K. Lewis.
Rugel, R. P. (1974) 'WISC sub-test scores of disabled readers', *Journal of Learning Disabilities* 7: 48–55.
Rutter, M. and Yule, W. (1975) 'The concept of specific reading retardation', *Journal of Child Psychology and Psychiatry* 16: 181–97.
Smith, S. D., Kimberling, W. J., Pennington, B. F., and Lubs, H. A. (1983) 'Specific reading disability: identification of an inherited form through linkage analysis', *Science* 219: 1,345–7.
Spache, G. D. (1976) *Investigating the Issues of Reading Disabilities*, Boston, Mass: Allyn & Bacon.
Stanley, G. V. and Hall, R. (1973) 'A comparison of dyslexics and normals in recalling letter arrays after brief representation', *British Journal of Educational Psychology* 43: 301–4.
Steeves, J. (1983) 'Memory as a factor in the computational efficiency of dyslexic children with high reasoning ability', *Annals of Dyslexia* XXXIII: 141–52.
Stevenson, J., Graham, P., Fredman, G., and McLoughlin, V. (1987) 'A twin study of genetic influences on reading and spelling ability and disability', *Journal of Child Psychology and Psychiatry* 28: 229–47.
Stirling, E. G. and Miles, T. R. (1986) 'Oral language of dyslexic adolescents', *Child Language Teaching and Therapy* 2, 2: 143–53.
Tansley, P. and Panckhurst, J. (1981) *Children with Specific Learning Difficulties*, Windsor: Nelson/NFER.
Thomson, M. E. (1982) 'The assessment of children with specific reading difficulties (dyslexia) using the British Ability Scales', *British Journal of Educational Psychology* 73: 461–78.
Vellutino, F. R. (1969) *Dyslexia: Theory and Research*, Cambridge, Mass: MIT Press.
——— (1987) Dyslexia, *Scientific American* 256, 3: 20–7.
Vygotsky, L. (1986) *Thought and Language*, translation newly revised and edited by A. Kozulin, Cambridge, Mass: MIT Press.
Wechsler, D. (1945) A standard memory scale for clinical use, *Journal of Psychology* 19: 87–95.
Wepman, J. M. (1973) *Auditory Discrimination Test*, Los Angeles, Calif: Western Psychological Services.

Chapter eleven

Approaches that work with remedial readers

Lee Mountain

'Let's leave no stone unturned' is a good slogan for remedial reading teachers since they are constantly trying to turn up new instructional approaches to use with their students. Many remedial reading programmes are heavy on structure and repetition but light on motivation and variety. So it is often up to the teacher to inject motivation, variety, and fun into these programmes. Remedial reading teachers are succeeding in adding these extras by using the following educationally sound approaches with their classes:

1 inventiveness games for stimulating creativity,
2 branched fiction for choices in plot direction,
3 pantomime and creative dramatics for involvement in stories,
4 vocabulary scavenger hunts for word study,
5 mnemonics for spelling,
6 rhyming riddles for teaching synonyms,
7 opinion polls for participation in story discussions,
8 language experience for reading students' writings,
9 tape recordings for book reports.

Not only do these approaches help remedial readers learn, but also they enable these students to have fun while learning. Let's consider them, one by one, for classroom use.

Inventiveness games for stimulating creativity

Any approach that bolsters the self-image is a good intervention to try with remedial readers, since their self-images are often poor. Success in a creative endeavour does a lot to bolster the self-image, so creative successes are good for remedial readers (Deeds 1981).

They can experience creative success through inventiveness games. One such game is a Robinson Crusoe simulation, in which they are stranded on a desert island with only a few items salvaged from a shipwreck. They have to think of creative new uses for these items to help with survival. Suppose, for example, that a mirror was one of the items washed up on shore after the shipwreck. A mirror is usually used for looking at oneself, but a creative new use for survival purposes might be to focus the sun's rays and start a fire or to signal for help.

This Robinson Crusoe simulation is an easy one to do on the spur of the minute, or repeatedly since a new set of items can be generated at will simply by asking your students for something from each pocket or purse. They can put these items on a table and form a circle around the table. It is advisable to give them a minute or two to look at the items on the table and think about how they could make good use of at least one of them. Then they can take turns walking up to the table, picking up one item, and explaining a new use for it.

You can extend their thinking and their creativity by changing the location of the shipwreck from a desert island to an arctic peninsula to a jungle. This simulation is a good pre-writing activity for survival stories.

Inventiveness can be applied to many areas. To give your students some physical activity via inventiveness games, you might have them stand in a large circle and demonstrate as many different ways as possible of moving across the room (no repetitions allowed). After the obvious ways of walking, running, skipping, hopping, and crawling, they may get more creative with somersaulting, cartwheeling, rolling, or leap-frogging. For another active variation, you might put four objects on the floor near the four corners of a desk. Then tell your students, 'Clasp your hands behind you. Your task is to get these objects from the floor up on to the desk.' This challenge usually elicits some highly creative gymnastic feats in which toes and teeth are sometimes put into operation.

For a scientific application of inventiveness, you might try an egg-packing project with your class. Each student should hardboil some eggs at home and should invent a method of packing an egg that will keep it from cracking even when the packing is dropped from the height of a table. Your pupils' packings may range from a box of confetti to a jelly mould. Some will experience the great satisfaction of inventing packings that work.

You can stimulate creative thinking and inventiveness, directly related to reading and writing, by saying, 'Suppose you need to leave an urgent message for someone to read, but you have no paper and pencil, pen, or crayon for writing. How will you manage?' Remedial readers have been known to come up with such creative solutions as burning the message into leather, scratching it on a rock, using a knife to carve the letters on wood, forming letters with string, pebbles, and beads, and cutting out newspaper letters to spell the message. This kind of inventiveness game can help remedial readers discover and feel good about their creativity, develop better self-images, and extend their confidence in situations that involve reading and writing (Mountain 1986).

Branched fiction for choices in plot direction

The term 'branched fiction' brings to mind microcomputer stories in which the students press a key to interact with the print on the monitor to make the program 'branch' to a new screen. Branching, however, started with books. Many programmed books of the 1960s used branching to enable students to skip material they already knew or to turn back to material they needed to review.

Branching has a different purpose in fictional books — a somewhat recreational purpose — quite similar to the purpose in microcomputer programs. Branched books allow readers to determine the direction of the plot. At the bottom of each page of the book, the readers make a choice, and are then eager to get to the next page and find out where their choice has led.

Consider this example from the branched book, *Journey Under the Sea*

> But no sooner do you get out of the kelp, than you are caught in the vortex of a giant whirlpool!
>
> If you try to swim out of the whirlpool, turn to page 69.
>
> If you dive into the vortex of the whirlpool, hoping to reach the bottom and get out, turn to page 70.
>
> (Montgomery 1979: 53)

The preceding example is typical of the format of all the stories in the Choose Your Own Adventure Series of branched books.

In the Attention Span Series of branched stories, the format involves three choices at the bottom of each page, as shown in the following excerpt from *Time Trip* when the hero comes out of a time machine:

> Clouds of cold gray fog rose around Joe. For a few moments he felt as light as a leaf, floating through the fog. Then suddenly he knew there was something solid beneath his feet again. A second later everything came into focus and Joe saw a . . .
>
> | | | |
> |---|---|---|
> | Flying lizard (continued on page 11) | Streak of lightning (continued on page 13) | Pyramid (continued on page 15) |
>
> (Mountain 1978: 9)

Readers keep choosing from among the three cliff-hangers on each page, and they thereby direct the plot into their areas of interest.

Both of these branched series have an additional area of appeal for remedial readers: they are written at low readability levels. According to the Fry Readability Graph (Fry 1977), the Attention Span Books have second- to third-grade readability. The span of grade levels is wider for the Choose Your Own Adventure Series, but they are designed as high-interest low-readability stories. So your remedial readers can choose the direction of the plot within readability levels that they can handle.

Branched books have a measurably positive effect on the interest attentiveness, and comprehension of remedial readers (Crawley 1978; McDaniel 1979), and branched books are much more reasonably priced than the branched microcomputer programs of interactive fiction. Both the books and the computer disks, however, share 'repeat' appeal. Readers go back again and again to their favourite branched books and disks to try new choices and take different routes through the story.

Pantomime and creative dramatics for involvement in stories

Acting out the movements and conflicts of fictional characters is fun for your remedial readers; it is also an effective instructional approach since it promotes reader involvement (Cazden 1972). Pantomime and creative dramatics give your students opportunities to act out parts of the stories they read and thereby to become more involved in those stories.

At the simplest level, pantomime can be used for vocabulary development. You might say to your remedial readers, 'There are many words that have meanings akin to the meaning of the word *walk*, and you met some of those words in yesterday's story. These words are called synonyms of the word *walk*. I'll pantomime a synonym of the word *walk*, and I want you to guess what it is.' After you demonstrate *strut* or *mince* or *slink* to show the variations of walking, you might want your students to take over pantomiming.

They can work up to pantomiming pairs of words for the class to guess. Such antonyms as *fast* and *slow*, *attract* and *repel*, and *ascend* and *descend* are easy pairs that can be demonstrated well with physical movement. Some sets of homonyms can also be reinforced with pantomime, for examples, *rain* and *reign*, and *pair*, *pear*, and *pare*.

At a more advanced level, remedial readers can move from pantomime to creative dramatics. They can create short dramatic scenes that focus on the conflicts of fictional characters. Suppose your remedial readers have started on a story in which the main character wants to convince her cousin to stop studying and go to a party with her. But the cousin has a very important test the next day and wants to spend the evening studying. Obviously the two characters have opposing objectives. Pairs of your students might take the parts of the two characters, act out what they predict will happen in the story, and thereby become much more involved and interested in the rest of the plot.

To help your remedial readers use creative dramatics well and produce lively, entertaining scenes, you need to assist them with structure. They need supervised planning time and a bit of rehearsal (Baron and Byrne 1983). You might say to a pair of dramatists from your remedial reading class

> Now that the two of you have a plan for the beginning, middle and end of your scene, you both need to put your ideas into words. Try a minute or two of conversation. Is it interesting? Does it lag in the middle? Do you need more spirit in the conflict? Are both of you really pushing for your objectives? Or is one person giving in too soon or too easily? Are you using movement and body language as well as speech? Don't memorize your lines. It's too easy to sound stilted and unnatural if you've over-

> rehearsed. But you'll do a better job in your presentation if you have walked through your scene a few times, both in terms of physical activity and conversation.

Then let the show go on, hopefully to the applause of the rest of the class.

Your readers will return to the story, eager to find out how the author resolved the conflict. But they may like their resolutions better than the author's. Either way, they will have been involved in predicting while reading, which is the essence of the reading process (Savage and Mooney 1979). When they predict, and then act out the prediction via creative dramatics, they stay mentally 'on task' regarding their reading material.

Vocabulary scavenger hunts for word study

Some of your remedial readers have been on scavenger hunts for lists of items at picnics and parties. So a scavenger hunt as a vocabulary lesson will be a real treat. Your class will be eager to read the list of items, meet in teams, and plan who will bring in each item. Some of the 'items', of course, are the new words that you want to add to their reading vocabularies.

Students remember words better when they can get their hands on objects or pictures that match the words (Reynolds and Flagg 1977; Bower 1972). They also feel more confident with their new vocabulary after hearing, saying, and writing the words during team meetings. Listing the words in categories helps students with retention. Vocabulary scavenger hunts are designed to involve all these activities with words — categorizing, listing, hearing, saying, writing, finding associated pictures, and bringing in objects that match the words.

Before you start on this type of lesson, be sure that all of your students understand how scavenger hunts work. Some of them will already know, but for others your Vocabulary Scavenger Hunt may be a first. One remedial reader, when asked about her previous scavenger hunt experience, told the class,

> It was on a picnic. The leader gave everybody the same list of things to find, acorns and leaves and stuff. I read my list and decided which things would be easy to find and which things

would be hard to find. Then the leader divided us into teams. My team captain asked me which things I could find, and he put my name down for those things. The other people said what they could find and away we went. My team brought in everything on the list, so we won the scavenger hunt.

As a classroom activity, a Vocabulary Scavenger Hunt usually takes two days. On the first day each pupil receives a list of items to read and categorize. Also on the first day the class is divided into teams. Each team meets and plans which person will try to find which items. At home that evening each student does the actual hunting. If team members can't find the objects or pictures they promised to bring, they should phone other members of their team to see if those students can help.

The next day each team meets in class and checks off the items or pictures they brought. Most scoring systems allow more points for a real item than for a picture, drawing, or tracing. Each team then shows its findings to the class and gets its score. The team with the most points wins.

In short, the following four-step procedure sums up the lesson plan for each Vocabulary Scavenger Hunt:

1 Each student works alone, categorizing as many as possible of the items on the Vocabulary Scavenger Hunt word list. The student rewrites the list in categories.
2 The students meet in teams to discuss the words on their lists so that they can reach agreement on the categories. Then they relist the words, correcting each other's errors.
3 They decide who will try to find the item or picture for each word.
4 They bring in items and pictures for points at scoring time.

The worksheet that follows shows the format of a typical Vocabulary Scavenger Hunt. This format is standard, but the word lists can be changed to include any main category that has subcategories. You might design Vocabulary Scavenger hunts for foods (vegetables, fruits, nuts), holidays (Halloween, Christmas, Easter), clothes (hats, jackets, pants, shoes), etc. (Vaughan *et al.* 1979).

Vocabulary scavenger hunt for containers

1 On this hunt, your team should find the items listed below or pictures of those items. Before you meet with your team, divide this list into categories. Write each word under one of the headings below.

cup	tumbler	goblet	saucepan
trunk	suitcase	casserole	bottle
mug	skillet	backpack	double boiler
kettle	dufflebag	briefcase	hatbox

For packing For drinking For heating

2 Meet with your team. Discuss the words until your whole team can agree about which items belong under each heading. Write lists below that show the group's best thinking.

For packing For drinking For heating

3 Decide who will bring in each item or its picture, drawing, or tracing. Write that person's name by the item. Now go find your items, and bring them to class tomorrow.

4 After finding your items, meet with your team again. Go over the list, item by item. Let each member show what he brought. Use a point system to figure your score. The team with the most points wins.

These lesson are also useful for developing the schema or background knowledge that enables readers to comprehend material in their content area textbooks (Cunningham *et al*. 1987). Students who have categorized, talked about, listed, sketched, handled, and used a thermometer and a barometer are truly 'ready' to read about these instruments in a chapter about weather. So Vocabulary Scavenger Hunts can help remedial readers with both word recognition and comprehension.

Mnemonics for spelling

Mnemonics, or memory aids, are tricky associations that can help a remedial reader with those personal spelling demons that cause repeated mistakes.

Here is an example of mnemonics at the primary level. Johnny just couldn't seem to remember the differences in spelling and meaning between *here* and *hear*. He would write, 'Did you here my dog bark?' For a simple mnemonic, his teacher underlined the *ear* in *hear*.

Another familiar mnemonic says that the princi*pal* is your *pal* and a principle is a ru*le*. Many people mentally mispronounce *Wednesday* to help themselves spell the word. The best and most helpful mnemonics are the ones that students make up for themselves. A pupil named Celeste remembered how to spell *license* by associating the order of the *c* and *s* with the order of those letters in her own name.

After you have taught, tested, retaught, and retested a set of spelling words, you might use mnemonics to encourage your students to try again to remember the spelling of the words they are still missing. A student who can think of a good mnemonic feels creative, and usually wants to tell the rest of the class about the good association she has come up with. Explaining the mnemonics aloud is a further memory reinforcement. Some teachers even have a mnemonics bulletin board to feature the creative thinking of their students. So mnemonics may help some of your remedial readers finally manage to master a few of spelling words that have tripped them repeatedly (Tyson and Mountain 1982).

Rhyming riddles for teaching synonyms

It is fun to compose rhyming riddles, and remedial readers can do it — and can learn synonyms thereby. Many of your students may already know some rhyming riddles, such as 'What do you call a joyful father? A glad dad'. Another answer for that same riddle would be 'A happy pappy'. The rule is that the adjective and noun in the answer must rhyme, and they must be synonymous of the adjective and noun in the question.

Remedial readers can compose such riddles if you use the following three-column strategy. Draw three columns on the chalkboard, and label them A, B, and C. In column A, list three synonyms for an adjective, for example, for the adjective *wonderful*.

A	B	C
Synonyms for *wonderful*		
1 fine		
2 super		
3 terrific		

Your remedial readers could probably think of many more synonyms for *wonderful*, but just to show how this technique works, three will do.

In column B you need three nouns that rhyme with the three adjectives in column A. For the adjective *fine*, students might suggest *sign*, *line*, and *wine*. Any one of these rhyming words would suffice, but for this example we will use *wine*. So you write *wine* in column B beside *fine*. In the same way, you elicit rhyming nouns to follow the adjectives *super* and *terrific*, so your board now looks like this:

A	B	C
Synonyms for *wonderful*	Nouns that rhyme with adjectives	
1 fine	wine	
2 super	trooper	
3 terrific	Pacific	

You now need the words for column C. These words must be synonyms of the nouns in Column B. For example, a synonym for *wine* would be *liquid*; a synonym for *trooper* would be *policeman*; a synonym for *Pacific* would be *ocean*. When you fill in these three words in column C, your columns are complete, and your students have all the words they need for composing rhyming riddles.

A	B	C
Synonyms for *wonderful*	Nouns that rhyme with adjectives	Synonyms for nouns
1 fine	wine	liquid
2 super	trooper	policeman
3 terrific	Pacific	ocean

Here is the formula for composing the riddles:

Question: What do you call a wonderful C?
Answer: A B.

Let's fill in the letters with the words in columns A, B, and C.

What do you call a wonderful liquid? Fine wine.
What do you call a wonderful policeman? A super trooper.
What do you call a wonderful ocean? Terrific Pacific.

By using this simple strategy you can enable your remedial readers to compose riddles and learn synonyms at the same time. While they are increasing their vocabularies, they are also reinforcing their knowledge of rhyme, adjectives, and nouns. You can even get learning about syllables from these lessons if you choose to ask for ynonyms of one, two, and three syllables.

To vary the challenge, you might have your students start with the answer for a rhyming riddle and compose a suitable question to go with it. For example, take the answer *Fat cat*. One student might come up with the question, 'What do you call an overweight Siamese?' Another might head for the thesaurus to create, 'What do you call an obese feline?' Still another might say, 'What do you call a plump tabby?' All of these rhyming-riddle questions demonstrate that their composers know synonyms for the words *fat* and *cat*.

After a few teacher-guided lessons on synonyms via rhyming riddles, many students can operate on their own to compose these riddles. Dedicated riddlers quickly realize the value of both the thesaurus and the rhyming dictionary. These reference books have practical applications for writers of rhyming riddles.

According to Herzberg (1987), recognition by peers is one of the best motivators, and boys and girls give each other lots of recognition and positive feedback for composing funny riddles. Students say that the best part of this type of lesson is the time when they get to ask each other the rhyming riddles they have composed independently.

Opinion polls for participation in story discussions

Discussions of stories often involve only a few students, and much of the talking during the discussion is done by the teacher. The opinion poll technique promotes more student involvement and less talking by the teacher. It also offers remedial readers a good chance to participate.

This is how it works. First, push the desks back far enough to clear some floor space near the blackboard. Label four sections of the blackboard (1) Right, (2) More Right Than Wrong, (3) More Wrong Than Right, and (4) Wrong. Second, have the students stand near the side walls to listen to the 'cases' from their stories. Read a case aloud. Then give the class fifteen seconds during which the students must walk to the section of the blackboard that best represents their position and line up in front of Right, Wrong, or one of the middle positions. In other words, each student physically takes his or her stand. Here is a sample case.

> In the story we started yesterday, the class was being noisy during study time. Lots of pupils were talking when they were supposed to be reading silently. So the teacher changed everybody's seat. Do you think the teacher was right? More right than wrong? More wrong than right? Wrong? You have fifteen seconds to take your stand in front of one of the four blackboard sections.

As soon as all the class members have taken their stands by lining up in front of the blackboard sections, let them start defending their positions. There is no need for the teacher to lead this discussion. It is bound to be student-centred, and it may be heated. With the opinion poll technique, most teachers can stimulate class discussion without saying a word.

The only time that an opinion poll can fail to stimulate discussion is when the great majority of class members are in close agreement about the case. When the line-ups are quite one-sided, just accept agreement and go on to a different case.

The following cases were taken from primary materials (Crawley and Mountain 1981):

1 Billy was playing on the swings with his friend Larry. Cheryl yelled to Billy and told him to come over and eat chocolate cookies with her. Billy left Larry. Was Billy right? More right than wrong? More wrong than right? Wrong?

2 Jane's mother told her to go straight home after school. Mary wanted Jane to go to the playground after school. Jane decided to go to the playground for a little while. Was Jane . . . ?

3 Ron and Dick earned two dollars raking leaves. Ron wanted to spend the money on candy, so he bought two dollars worth of candy. Was Ron . . . ?

These cases were taken from materials for middle-grade students (Crawley and Mountain 1981):

1 Judi wanted to go out with her friends on Wednesday night. She had a lot of homework to do so she talked her brother Scott into doing it for her. Was Scott . . . ?
2 Mother prepared a new asparagus casserole dish. Dick hates asparagus and refused to try even a small helping of the dish. Was Dick . . . ?
3 Carla let Jim hide his cigarettes in her school locker. When the teacher found them, Carla said, 'They're Jim's, not mine.' Was Carla . . . ?

Opinion polls can be developed from all levels of reading material. They can stimulate the thinking of remedial readers, and provide these students with opportunities to participate in class dicussions of stories.

Language experience for reading students' writings

The assumptions of the language experience approach are (1) what students can think, they can say; (2) what they can say, they can write or dictate; (3) what they can write they can read. The approach works especially well with remedial readers. They can read their own compositions much more easily than they can read the writings of textbook authors.

Before you can use the language experience approach with remedial readers, however, you need to get them to put some words on paper, and remedial readers are notoriously reluctant writers. To overcome this reluctance, you can use a three-step procedure in which the reward of immediate readership is ensured.

Step one is to be sure each participant has paper, a crayon or felt-tip pen, and a pin. Say, 'You are going to write one word on your paper. Write it in big letters that can be seen all the way across the room. Your word will be the word you would use at the end of this sentence: I feel _____' You might explain that more than one word is permissible if the writers want to expand on their feelings.

Step two is to have all the writers pin their word on their clothing. All the writers now stand and circulate in silence, reading one another's words. Some words will stimulate curiosity, so each student will probably want to get back to at least one fellow-writer to converse about feelings.

Step three is to have those conversations. Tell your students, 'Go back to the person whose word interested you most. Ask him why he feels that way.'

To expand on this experience, all your remedial readers write a complete sentence and pin it on themselves. They choose one of the following openers to copy, and they complete the sentence: 'If I had one wish . . .' 'When someone yells at me . . .' 'I'd like to buy . . .' 'My children won't have to . . . because . . .' Again the participants read and talk about each other's sentences.

To expand still further, each writer can generate a sentence from scratch. Say, 'Write a sentence describing the personality of one person in this group that you like. Don't describe the person's looks or clothing; write about the way he or she talks and acts. On the other side of your paper, write the person's name.' After all the students have pinned their papers on themselves so that only the descriptive sentence shows, say, 'You can whisper one guess after each description that you read. If your guess is correct, you and the writer should go and give the description to the person whose name you guessed. If your guess is incorrect, just move on and try again after reading someone else's description.'

You can gradually work your students up to complete paragraphs. Remedial readers seem more willing to put their ideas on paper when immediate readership is ensured. With the procedure given in this experience, you can guarantee that each of your writers will be read immediately by an interested audience. Even your weakest readers are usually able to read the writings of their peers.

When you want your remedial readers to compose longer pieces of writing, you might try group-composition procedures such as story building. For this procedure, your students sit in groups. All the group members start a story at the top of their paper. After a few minutes, you say, 'Pass', and the students pass their story to the person on their right. The students also receive the beginning of a story from the person on the left. After reading what the preceding writer has composed, they add material of their own, before the next time you tell your students to pass along their papers. When the papers have gone full circle, the group members can work together to revise the draft they like best so that they can read it aloud to the class. The reading practice, of course, is just as important as the writing practice, but your remedial readers don't even realize how much reading they are doing with the language experience approach.

This approach also lends itself to story writing when you get each student in your class to create a character. The paragraph(s) about this character should reveal his or her name, age, appearance, activities, background, goals, likes, and dislikes. The class then forms into groups of three members each. They read their character descriptions to each other. Together they work out a plot and setting for a story in which their three characters interact, and they read it aloud to the class.

Another popular group-composition activity involves letter writing. Again you have groups of your remedial readers sit in circles. You give each of them an envelope. Then all the students write and sign a short 'I have a problem' letter on the front of the envelope. They pass their envelopes around their circle to collect replies. All the respondents must write their own replies and sign it before reading any of the other replies that are already in the envelope.

When the envelope gets back to the original writers, they read all the replies and choose the one they like best to read aloud to the class. That reply is posted beside the letter on the bulletin-board display of these letters and answers.

All of these language experience strategies involve speaking and listening as well as writing and reading. Treating reading as part of the whole-language process seems to make it easier for remedial readers.

Tape recordings for book reports

Remedial readers are familiar with the idea of using visual aids in their oral book reports, but they seldom think of using audio aids, such as tapes. Cassette tape recorders are simple to operate, both for playing tapes and for making new tapes. Here are some samples of easy ways that remedial readers in the upper grades can use tapes in book talks.

They can compare taped interview data with book data

> *Student speaking:* My cousin just moved here from New York, and I read a book about New York. So, I decided to tape-record an interview with my cousin and see if she'd say the same things about New York that the book said. The book said that New York had a fine transportation system. But just listen to what my cousin said on this tape.

This student's book report included three other contrasts between what the book said and what the cousin said, as well as some points of agreement. The speaker went back and forth between his own oral remarks and the taped interview.

Another student used this approach in a report on a book about drug abuse. He formulated a question about each chapter and tape-recorded a paramedic's answers. Then he reported in his own words what the book said. The two sources of data were in close agreement.

They can tape background music to reflect a character's mood

> *Student speaking:* In one chapter the hero is snowed under with homework and a part-time job besides. He's as busy as a bee and it's getting to him. He feels like he's just buzzing from one thing to another as fast as he can go, but still not keeping up. I'm going to read you these paragraphs about the thoughts that run through his mind while he's so busy, and at the same time I'm going to play background music that ties in with his mood. It was hard to find background music that was just right for this mood, but I was lucky. My sister has a big collection of tapes, and after a lot of listening I found 'The Flight of the Bumblebee' and it sounded just right for his mood.

A group of readers can tape a conversational passage

Sometimes a group of remedial readers will enjoy the same book or story and will want to do a report together. They will enjoy even more the experience of making a tape together.

Student speaking: Hemingway's story, 'The Killers', starts out with a very sparse conversation. We had to tape this conversation and erase it five times before we got everything right. But from this little bit of tape you can get an idea of Hemingway's style of writing.

The group who prepared this report got audience participation after the tape. They asked questions of the audience about the conversation. Then they had to replay the tape to support some points about Hemingway's style.

Other groups of remedial readers who used this approach presented their taped passages as radio skits. Any material with good conversational passages can be adapted for dramatic presentation on tape.

The preceding descriptions show how short segments of tape can pep up book reports. The excerpts demonstrate some of the benefits students gain by using these approaches — such benefits as preparation, motivation, and organization. Therefore, it is worth your time to convince your remedial readers that their book talks need tapes (Mountain 1976).

Conclusion

The nine preceding approaches work well with remedial readers. They are the extras that can help you motivate as well as teach. Every instructor needs a bag of tricks, an unending supply of something new and different. But the remedial reading teacher needs these extra motivators even more, since her students are often negative about their regular lessons.

Each of the approaches has the added benefit of being a strategy that can and should be used repeatedly. None of them are 'one-time wonders'. All are suitable for use throughout the school year. You might use a different *inventiveness game* every month to stimulate creativity. If your remedial readers get hooked on *branched books*, they have long lists of titles to peruse. Your frequent use of *pantomime and creative dramatics* will keep your students actively involved in their reading material. Word study is constant and continuing in remedial reading classes, so *vocabulary scavenger hunts* could be scheduled every couple of weeks. Some teachers use *mnemonics* after every spelling test. After you introduce *rhyming riddles*, your students will request this approach every time you bring up synonyms. *Opinion polls* are an equally popular activity for discussion time. You probably use some variation of the *language experience* approach every time you connect speaking and writing with reading. And book reports are always with us, so pepping them up with *tapes* is a good extra for your students to have in mind all year.

The remedial reading teacher who is constantly trying new approaches is truly leaving no stone unturned in her effort to help her students.

References

Baron, R. and Byrne, D. (1983) *Social Psychology: Understanding Human Interaction*, Boston, Mass: Allyn & Bacon.

Bower, G. H. (1972) 'Mental imagery and associative learning', in L. W. Gregg (ed.) *Cognition in Learning and Memory*, New York: Wiley.

Cazden, C. B. (1972) *Child Language and Education*, New York: Holt, Rinehart, & Winston.

Crawley, S. (1978) 'The effect of branched, unbranched, and basal stories on pupils interest as evidenced in attention and attitudes', unpublished doctoral dissertation, University of Houston, Texas.

Crawley, S. and Mountain, L. (1981) 'Opinion polls and values clarification', *Social Studies* 71, 6: 271–2.

Cunningham, P., Crawley, S., and Mountain, L. (1987) 'Vocabulary scavenger hunts, a scheme for teaching schema', in K. Vandermeulen (ed.) *Reading Horizons, Selected Readings*, Kalamazoo, Mich: Western Michigan University Press.

Deeds, B. (1981) 'Motivating children to read through improved self concept', in A. J. Ciani (ed.) *Motivating Reluctant Readers*, Newark, Del: International Reading Association.

Fry, E. (1977) 'Fry's readability graph: clarification, validity, and extensions to level 17', *Journal of Reading* 21, 2: 242–52.

Herzberg, H. (1987) 'One more time: how do you motivate?', *Harvard Business Review* 87, 5: 109–17.

McDaniel, N. (1979) 'The effects of two types of reading material on the reading attentiveness, attitudes and comprehension of Black junior-high low-achievers', unpublished doctoral dissertation, University of Houston, Texas.

Montgomery, R. A. (1979) *Journey under the Sea*, New York: Bantam.

Mountain, L. (1976) 'The book reporter's TNT: talks need tapes', *Journal of Reading* 17, 6: 442–6.

——— (1978) *Time Trip*, Providence, Rhode Island: Jamestown Publishers.

——— (1986) 'Releasing the remedial reader's creative power', *Journal of*

Learning Disabilities 19, 1: 5–7.
Reynolds, A. G. and Flagg, P. W. (1977) *Cognitive Psychology*, Cambridge, Mass: Winthrop Publishing.
Savage, J. and Mooney, J. (1979) *Teaching Reading to Children with Special Needs*, Boston, Mass: Allyn & Bacon.
Tyson, E. and Mountain, L. (1982) 'A riddle or pun makes learning words fun', *Reading Teacher* 36, 2: 170–3.
Vaughan, S., Crawley, S., and Mountain, L. (1979) 'A multiple-modality approach to word study: vocabulary scavenger hunts', *Reading Teacher* 32, 4: 434–7.

Name index

Subject index